Successful Time Manag For Dummies®

Cheat Sheet

Quick Decision-Making Considerations for Work

One of the challenges of working in a busy environment is determining what considerations to evaluate, and in what order, in making business decisions. This conundrum is especially true for employees who fill the "worker bee" roles and aren't yet at the executive level. On what should you base critical time-investment decisions when you haven't been given clear direction? I recommend assessing your options in the following order:

1. **Which task creates the most financial benefit for the company?**

2. **Which task serves the customers best?**

3. **Which task best supports the company's business vision, core values, core purpose, and goals?**

4. **Which task best supports my boss's goals and objectives?**

5. **Which task best aligns with my personal goals and objectives?**

6. **Which task affects other areas the most?**

   - How many departments will this affect?
   - How many people will this involve?

   - What effect will this task have on my time or my boss's time?
   - What will this task cost?

Effective Meeting-Preparation Questions

You aren't always in control of the meetings you're required to attend, but you can help take back your time by asking questions that can guide the meeting to a successful and quick conclusion — or help ascertain whether you need to be part of the discussion:

- **What is our agenda for this meeting?**
- **What are we hoping to accomplish by the end of the meeting?**

- **What action point do you want me to record?**
- **Who do I assign this to?**
- **What time frame should we attach to this?**

Travel Itinerary Checklist

Whenever you travel, carry a comprehensive itinerary, which I call a travel map, with the contents in the exact order you'll need them. Some of the details captured in your travel map may include the following:

- ❏ **Airline information**
  - ❏ Flight numbers
  - ❏ Departure and arrival times
  - ❏ Record locators
  - ❏ Seat assignments
  - ❏ Phone number for the reservation line
- ❏ **Terminal information for connecting flights**
- ❏ **Ground transportation details (for each leg of your trip)**
  - ❏ Car rental reservation numbers or car service information
  - ❏ Costs quoted when making reservations

- ❏ **Hotel information**
  - ❏ Reservation number
  - ❏ Address and contact details
  - ❏ Map (if you're driving to the hotel)
  - ❏ Shuttle details (if applicable)
  - ❏ Room information (type or preferences) requested and rate quoted
- ❏ **Meeting details**
  - ❏ Location, description, and address
  - ❏ Contact information
  - ❏ Driving directions
  - ❏ Start and stop times

Successful Time Management For Dummies®

Cheat Sheet

Seven Steps for Starting Tomorrow Right

Organization is simply a system that you can replicate day after day: a system that leads to consistency of work performance and mastery of your time. If you complete these seven steps each night before you leave the office, every day following will start off right:

1. **Clear your desk.**

   Put everything back into a file drawer, even if you plan to take those items right back out in the morning. Eliminate items to be filed or thrown away.

2. **Make tomorrow's to-do list.**

   List all the projects, tasks, telephone calls, meetings, and objectives you want to accomplish the following day.

3. **Prioritize the tasks on your to-do list.**

   Be sure to complete the prioritizing completely from A-list activities (those with heavy penalties if they're not completed) to lower-level tasks that can be delegated (D-list) or eliminated (E-list). (See Chapter 4 for more on prioritizing.)

4. **Delegate all tasks, projects, and calls that someone else can do.**

   If you can't completely delegate the tasks because of their complexity or because a staff member is gone the next day, at least send a quick memo or e-mail letting the person know that the assignment is coming.

5. **Determine what you need to accomplish to make tomorrow a great day.**

   By determining a goal, you increase your intensity, focus, and urgency from the time you walk through the door.

6. **Prepare your workspace for tomorrow's A-1 priority task.**

   Assemble all the materials you'll need and neatly stack and organize them on your credenza or desk.

7. **Rate your day.**

   To get better use of your time tomorrow, set aside time to reflect on today. Ask yourself the following questions:

   - What went well today? What didn't go well?
   - Did you complete everything on your to-do list?
   - What did you learn today?
   - What would you have done differently?

For Dummies: Bestselling Book Series for Beginners

Successful Time Management

FOR DUMMIES®

by Dirk Zeller

Wiley Publishing, Inc.

Successful Time Management For Dummies®

Published by
Wiley Publishing, Inc.
111 River St.
Hoboken, NJ 07030-5774
www.wiley.com

Copyright © 2009 by Dirk Zeller

Published by Wiley Publishing, Inc., Indianapolis, Indiana

Published simultaneously in Canada

For general information on our other products and services, please contact our Customer Care Department within the U.S. at 800-762-2974, outside the U.S. at 317-572-3993, or fax 317-572-4002.

For technical support, please visit www.wiley.com/techsupport.

Wiley also publishes its books in a variety of electronic formats. Some content that appears in print may not be available in electronic books.

Library of Congress Control Number: 2008938869

ISBN: 978-0-470-29034-7

Manufactured in the United States of America

10 9 8 7 6 5 4 3 2 1

About the Author

Dirk Zeller started his entrepreneurial business career almost 40 years ago through lemonade stands. He has been recognized as an efficient time manager and top sales performer in every field he's entered, from professional racquetball to business sales of advertising, marketing, and event sponsorship to consumer-direct sales fields such as real estate. His time management skills were legendary in the real estate field, where he sold over 150 homes a year while working Monday through Thursday, taking Friday, Saturday, and Sunday off.

Dirk has been teaching, coaching, and training success, sales, and time management strategies to executives, managers, and salespeople since 1998, when he founded Sales Champions and Real Estate Champions. He is one of the most sought-after speakers in time management, peak performance, and sales. He has spoken on five different continents to hundreds of thousands of people.

Dirk is one of the world's most published authors on success, time management, productivity, sales, and life balance. He is the author of five top-selling books, including *Telephone Sales For Dummies* and *Success as a Real Estate Agent For Dummies*. He has more than 400 published articles to his credit, and over 350,000 people read his weekly newsletter.

The time that's most valuable to Dirk is the time enjoyed with his wife of 19 years, Joan, his 6-year-old son, Wesley, and his 3-year-old daughter, Annabelle. He and his family reside in Bend, Oregon. You can reach Dirk at

Sales Champions
5 NW Hawthorne Ave., Suite 100
Bend, OR 97701
Phone 541-383-0505
E-mail info@saleschampions.com
E-mail info@dirkzeller.com
Web site www.saleschampions.com

Dedication

Nothing reflects the passing of time more than growth and changes in our children. It seems like just yesterday that Joan and I received the call that changed our lives as we exited my 96-year-old grandmother's funeral. The call was from our pastor's wife, Linda Johnson. She said a baby boy had been born that morning in Hood River, Oregon, and asked if we wanted him. The next day, Joan and I walked out of the Hood River Memorial Hospital with our son, Wesley.

In the last six years since that moment, the time has passed like a blink of an eye. We have added another blessing in Annabelle, who also has a divine and miraculous story. In those years, which seem like mere moments in time, it seems like seconds ago we got our first smile, giggle, crawl, and walk out of each of them. We had joyous celebrating recently when we realized we had changed our last diaper for probably the next 20 years!

I dedicate this book to my two precious time clocks of life, Annabelle and Wesley. The time with you two moves too quickly. I, as all parents, fight to stay in the moment, enjoy every moment, and relive those moments before they are gone. You two have taught me more about time's value, joy, and its ever-marching-on characteristics than anyone else in my years on Earth. I love you both deeply and praise God for the honor he bestowed on me to be your dad.

Author's Acknowledgments

I always have to thank my team at Sales Champions and Real Estate Champions. It is truly an honor to be surrounded by so many talented people. I must especially thank my Senior Management Team; Don Cunningham, the President of both companies; and Julie Porfirio, Senior Vice President of Operations. You both have worked hard to insulate me so I could take on another *For Dummies* book.

To Jody McBride, my Assistant, who labored over my handwritten words to type, organize, revise, and edit the whole manuscript — thanks. This book would not have existed without your fine work.

To Tracy Boggier, my Acquisitions Editor at Wiley; Kristin DeMint, Project Editor; and Erin Calligan Mooney, Editorial Program Coordinator, who stepped in to help lend a hand.

To Betsy Sheldon, who did another masterful job of taking my writing and morphing it into the wonderful *For Dummies* format.

To my wife, Joan, my son, Wesley, and my daughter, Annabelle. Thank you for your patience and grace. There is a sacrifice of time that we all make when I am writing a book!

Publisher's Acknowledgments

We're proud of this book; please send us your comments through our Dummies online registration form located at www.dummies.com/register/.

Some of the people who helped bring this book to market include the following:

Acquisitions, Editorial, and Media Development

Ghostwriter: Betsy Sheldon

Project Editor: Kristin DeMint

Acquisitions Editor: Tracy Boggier

Senior Copy Editor: Danielle Voirol

Assistant Editor: Erin Calligan Mooney

Technical Editor: Adam Hayes

Editorial Manager: Michelle Hacker

Editorial Assistants: Jennette ElNaggar, Joe Niesen

Cover Photo: ©Graphistock

Cartoons: Rich Tennant (www.the5thwave.com)

Composition Services

Project Coordinator: Katherine Key

Layout and Graphics: Reuben W. Davis, Nikki Gately, Sarah E. Philippart, Christine Williams

Proofreaders: ConText Editorial Services, Inc., Amanda Steiner

Indexer: Broccoli Information Management

Publishing and Editorial for Consumer Dummies

    Diane Graves Steele, Vice President and Publisher, Consumer Dummies

    Kristin Ferguson-Wagstaffe, Product Development Director, Consumer Dummies

    Ensley Eikenburg, Associate Publisher, Travel

    Kelly Regan, Editorial Director, Travel

Publishing for Technology Dummies

    Andy Cummings, Vice President and Publisher, Dummies Technology/General User

Composition Services

    Gerry Fahey, Vice President of Production Services

    Debbie Stailey, Director of Composition Services

Contents at a Glance

Table of Contents

Part III: Confronting Challenges to Time Management   121

Part V: Advanced Time Management for Specific Folks

Introduction

Time is the only resource that people can't borrow, buy, or barter. And time refuses to follow one of the main tenets of the law of supply and demand: the idea that when the demand goes up to a high level, the supply will increase to meet the demand. People may use different amounts of time to accomplish results, but everyone is endowed with the same amount of time each day: 86,400 seconds.

Your ability to manage that time is really one of the top two causes of success or failure in your life. Investing greater amounts of time into a need, goal, objective, or even weakness can tip the balance of success in your favor. At numerous crossroads in life, I had to be willing to apply more time than my competitors to achieve a competitive advantage over them in the marketplace. I certainly didn't take for granted that my mental power was far superior to that of my competitors. Rather, my willingness to invest more time in certain tasks or use my time more effectively equalized the playing field.

Of course, if you invest too much time at work, you can be a success at the office but a failure at home. A true champion always has his or her pulse on home life and invests the right amount to keep vital relationships in life growing and thriving. The good news is that this book has both arenas covered. Congratulations on investing in yourself, your success, and your life!

About This Book

Successful Time Management For Dummies is about using your time more effectively to create greater results at the office and at home. It helps you with your organizational habits, discipline, systemization, goals, values, management style, persuasion, and even travel. This isn't just a book of theory; rather, it's one of real techniques, strategies, and tools that I've personally used, taught, coached, and spoke about. I've seen them bring forth a bounty of results in my life as well as in the lives of countless others.

Here, I help you mentally wrap your brain around the problems of time management. Then I explain how to establish a solid system that you can replicate over time. I introduce you to prioritization systems, time-categorization systems, time-blocking strategies, and appointment-setting strategies.

Note that in the spirit of saving you time, this is also a reference book. In other words, you don't have to read it from cover to cover. Just look up what you need and put those ideas in action.

Conventions Used in This Book

To make this book as easy to use as possible, I use the following conventions throughout:

- All Web addresses appear in monofont.
- Some Web addresses may break across two lines of text. In such cases, I didn't insert any hyphens to indicate the break, so if you type exactly what you see — pretending the line break doesn't exist — you'll get to your Web destination.
- New terms appear in *italics* and are closely followed by an easy-to-understand definition.
- **Bold** is used to highlight keywords in bulleted lists or to identify the action parts of numbered lists.
- I indent and italicize dialogues throughout the book. You can use them verbatim or with minor tweaks to increase your success in time management.

What You're Not to Read

Personally, I think you should read every word of this book. I wrote it, after all! However, if you're the bare-bones-info type, you can skip the sidebars that appear throughout the book. Those gray boxes contain interesting, often anecdotal information that's related to the topic but not essential to understanding it.

Foolish Assumptions

When I wrote the book, I assumed a few things about you, my dear reader:

- You want to use your time better. You expect to gain more time with your loved ones, you want to ramp up your success at work, or you're looking for a little of both.
- You know that effective time management isn't a one-stop fix; it's a comprehensive effort that requires looking at all time-draining culprits. You're willing to invest the effort needed to develop your time-management skills (or create them if they don't currently exist!).
- You're willing to be patient with yourself throughout the difficult process of self-betterment, knowing that in the end, all your efforts will be worth your while.

How This Book Is Organized

I divided this book into six major parts to help you find what you need as quickly as possible. The content is organized so you can choose to read only the topics that interest you or the entire part. Here's what you can find.

Part 1: Beginning the Revolution: Simple Steps to Start With

Part I presents an overview of the most important matters to master in order to succeed in managing your time effectively. I begin by helping you grab back control in Chapter 1 and then help you establish and align your goals with your time in Chapter 2. In Chapter 3, I help you understand the value of your time down to the minute.

Part II: Establishing a Good System

Anyone who is effective in time management has created a personalized time-management system. Even though the system is customized, it needs to follow many of the strategies and principles I present in this part. Chapter 4 delves into prioritization strategies and tools, taking you deep into the most important characteristics of a great time manager. It also tells you how to time-block your way to greater success. In Chapter 5, I show you how to overcome the organizational challenges in your workspace and desktop while also taking the confusion out of technological organization in Chapter 6. I close out this part with Chapter 7, which presents ways to save your time and lower your frustration about being on the road — all from an expert traveler's perspective.

Part III: Confronting Challenges to Time Management

No matter your time-management skill or strategy, challenges will always appear regularly, trying to throw you off track. I anticipate these challenges and share how to convey your message with power, precision, clarity, and brevity in Chapter 8. In Chapter 9, I attack the elephant in the room for most people: the interruptions during the course of the day. I gently coach you on lowering your level of procrastination in Chapter 10 so you can be positive about yourself, your skills, and your results. In Chapter 11, I guide you in how to make wiser, better, and faster decisions so you move yourself off the fence of indecision.

Part IV: Maintaining Efficiency When Working with Others

No one works in a vacuum; everyone relies on others to help, administrate, serve, sell, manage, guide, and lead. In Chapter 12, I help you deal with a most frustrating woe: managing your time when you work for a supervisor who makes doing so difficult. Most people have experienced numerous times of death-by-meeting in their business careers, so in Chapter 13, I help you craft rules and a process to avoid that dead end. I close out this part with Chapter 14, which provides the skills to qualify prospects, prepare appointments, and compel your customers to act without delay.

Part V: Advanced Time Management for Specific Folks

This part contains the tips for you to take your business and career to the highest level no matter your job title. I kick off this section with Chapter 15, on increasing the performance of support staff through time management. I next work with my favorite group of people — salespeople — to increase their sales through time-management techniques designed for them in Chapter 16. In Chapter 17, I coach owners and executives to squeeze more time out of their already overcommitted days. Finally, I close out this part with management strategies, tactics, and coaching and teaching systems and tools so you can pass on your new knowledge to others.

Part IV: The Part of Tens

Every *For Dummies* book ends with the famous Part of Tens. In this one, you get five tip-packed chapters on time-wasting behaviors, time-efficiency habits, time-savers for your personal life, fine-tuning your focus, and my personal favorite: time-saving technologies.

Icons Used in This Book

To help you navigate this book a bit better, you can rely on the icons in the book's margins. The icons act as little signposts pointing out the important info.

This bull's-eye icon points out little-advertised nuggets of knowledge that are certain to give you an edge in increasing your time-management skills.

This icon denotes critical information that you really need to take away with you. Remember these points, if nothing else. They address the issues that you come across repeatedly with time management.

 Consider this the flashing red light on the road to making a sale. When you see the Warning icon, you know to steer clear of whatever practice, behavior, or response I indicate.

 These icons tell you that I've cracked open the archives of my life experiences or my successful clients' life experiences to help illustrate a point.

Where to Go From Here

In this book, I use the classic *For Dummies* fashion: You have easy access to the precise information you need when you need it. You can start at page one and read through or hop around, targeting the areas you need the most help with first. Keep this book close by to help you wring the most you can out of life in the scant 24 hours you have each day.

Part I is a good place to start because it helps you deal with the mental barriers to time management that can seem to form an unscalable wall. After that, you may want to pick topics that cause you the most challenge or frustration. For instance, you can check out Chapter 11 for ways to beat procrastination or see Chapter 13 so you can get a handle on upcoming meetings. On the other hand, if you feel you have your time strategy pretty much under control but are looking for a tune up, you may go right to Part V first. There, I address how to take time management to the highest level through customized plans for your job or job title.

The truth is that no matter where you take your first plunge, the water's fine. You can find plenty of valuable information that you can use to increase your performance without increasing your hours at work.

Part I

Beginning the Revolution: Simple Steps to Start With

The 5th Wave   By Rich Tennant

"Right now I'm working on my time management through reprioritization, meditation, and limiting visits from my pain-in-the-butt neighbor."

In this part . . .

Seems like everyone's had some version of the dream in which you're trying to move toward something, yet each step is a monumental effort. You feel as if you're running in water, your legs weighted like lead. It doesn't take a Freudian analyst to figure that one out: You feel that you're not achieving your ambitions, not because of some external barrier, but because you're tripping yourself up.

You can look to yourself for the reasons behind your time management successes as well. And that's great news. In Chapter 1, you assess where you stand in terms of time management, discover the importance of setting up a system, and get started with some basic guidelines. Chapter 2 walks you through the process of pinpointing your goals and connecting them to your time management efforts. And in Chapter 3, I support a fundamental truth — time is money — and explain how you can calculate the value of your time.

Chapter 1

Setting Yourself Up for Success

- -

In This Chapter

▶ Tapping into your time-management strengths

▶ Building a solid system of time management

▶ Facing up to time management's biggest challenges

▶ Addressing issues with others

▶ Applying time-management skills to all facets of your life

- -

*T*ime is the great equalizer — everyone has the same amount in a day. No matter who you are, where you live, and what you do, you clock the same 24-hour cycle as the next person. One person may be wealthier than another, but that doesn't earn him a minute more than the poorest people on the planet.

If that simple fact seems a bit discouraging, think of it this way: You may not have the power to get yourself more time, but you *do* have the power to make the most of it. You can take your 365 days a year, seven days a week, and 1,440 minutes in a day and invest them in such a way that you reap a return that fulfills your life and attracts the success you dream of.

That's what this book is about: taking control of how you spend your time to make sure you're using it how you really want to. You really are in control of your time, even though you don't always feel like it — even if you have a job that demands overtime; even if you have kids who keep you in the carpool loop; even if you have dreams and goals that involve developing new skills or furthering your education.

All in all, discovering how to manage your time well is part mental restructuring and part creating a system. Effective time management requires a little introspection, some good habits and organizational skills, and more than a few logistical and tactical tools. But all are achievable, and all are covered in this book. So if you have the time — and I assure you that you do — get ready for a journey that's certain to, if not buy you more time, show you how to make the absolute most of the 24 hours in your day.

Getting to Know Yourself

Although everyone gets the same number of hours to work with each day, what people don't have in equal amounts are other valuable assets: skill, intelligence, money, ambition, energy, passion, attitude, even looks. All these unique reserves play into your best use of time. So the better you understand yourself — your strengths, weaknesses, goals, values, and motivations — the easier it is to manage your time effectively. In this section, you look at your strengths and goals, think about how much your time is worth, and observe personal energy and behavior patterns that affect your focus throughout the day.

Assessing your strengths and weaknesses

As a young man, I thought I was good — okay, I admit it; I thought I was *great* — at a much larger group of skills, tasks, and jobs than I do today. In fact, the older I get, the more I realize the list of what I'm *not* good at dwarfs the lists of things I *am* good at. Being consciously competent at those few, however, gets me a lot further than being unconsciously incompetent, as I once was. Despite my poor academic record in high school, as a young adult, I was a quick study at what I needed to do to be as successful in life as I wanted to be. At some point, I saw the light and realized I needed to face up to what I had to do to get where I wanted to go.

First, I took stock of my assets: I tallied up my strengths, skills, and even my weaknesses. And I identified things I needed to work on and things I needed to leverage. That's when I realized that although some people were smarter, were more educated, had more money, and knew more influential people than I did, I had the same amount of time as anyone else. And if I wanted to get ahead, it was up to me to harness my time and invest it in such a way to get a greater return. My willingness to invest more time to gain the edge helped equalize the playing field for me and help me achieve the success I enjoy today.

Chances are that by this point in your life, you've discovered some skills that you come to naturally or perhaps have worked hard to acquire. Maybe you're a master negotiator. Or a whiz with numbers. You may be a good writer. Or you may have a silver tongue. Whatever your strengths, developing the handful that brings you the most return on your efforts, propelling you forward to attain your goals, is a more productive course of action than trying to be the best at everything. For most people, these strengths typically number no more than a half-dozen.

In addition to pinpointing your strengths, you need to identify the areas where your skills are lackluster. Then figure out which tasks are essential for meeting the goals you want to accomplish, and build those skills. Invest time in honing and maintaining your strengths, and improve the weaknesses that you need to overcome to reach your goals. **Remember:** To be successful, you need to be selective.

Throwing money away

I once saw a woman in a parking lot throw pennies on the ground. When I asked her what she was doing, she told me she'd just read about a multimillionaire who had calculated his worth, and based on the value of an hour of his time, he determined that it wasn't worth the few seconds it'd take for him to pick up a dollar bill from the sidewalk. She, however, had decided that although it was worth her time to pick up a dollar, she could afford to part with a few pennies.

I think she missed the point, but there's a lesson in this experience: You're always on the clock. Time *is* money, and yours has a value. Giving away your precious time without a sense of its value is like throwing money on the sidewalk. By knowing what your time is worth, you can prioritize those tasks that yield the greatest return, delegating or eliminating those tasks that provide little to no return on your time investment.

Naming goals to give you direction

You know how it is: When you're working toward something, keeping your focus is much easier. A woman may want to lose weight, for example, but perhaps she struggles to stick to a diet or exercise plan. But if her son's wedding is looming three months away on her calendar, she may be more inspired to stay on track, cutting back on second helpings and getting in workouts.

Your goals can serve as inspiration in adopting good time-management skills. After all, managing your time isn't really a benefit in and of itself, but managing your time so you can spend more of it doing what's important to you *is* — whether you're saving for a retirement of travel and adventure or buying the house in the perfect neighborhood.

Using your aspirations to fire up your time management success means you have to identify your goals and keep them in the front of your mind. Pinning down what's most important to you may require some soul searching. Write down your goals — all of them — and follow these guidelines:

- ✔ **Cast a wide net.** Go for the big goals, such as joining the Peace Corps, as well as the not-so-big ones, such as getting an energy-efficient car next year.

- ✔ **Think big.** Don't rein in your dreams because they seem unrealistic.

- ✔ **Be as descriptive as possible.** Instead of "build my dream house," flesh it out: Where is this house? How big? What features does it have? What does it look like? When do you want to move in?

- ✔ **Don't limit goals to a single category.** Think about goals for your career, your personal life, your social situation, your financial status, and any other facet of life that's important to you.

The process of goal-seeking can be a fun and energizing experience, and it's one you can explore at length in Chapter 2. You also see how your current time use can affect the forecast for your future.

Assigning your time a monetary worth to guide your priorities

Most people think about the value of their time as it relates to on-the-job activity. The fast-food worker knows he earns a minimum wage per hour. The freelance artist advertises a per-hour rate. The massage therapist charges for her services in half-hour and hour increments. But to be truly aware of the value of your time, you need to carry this concept into your personal life as well. The value of time in your personal life is at least as valuable as your work life time. In some cases, personal time is priceless.

One of the most important points to remember as you work through this book is that it's okay not to get everything done. What's critical is making sure that the *important* things are getting done. By assigning value to your time and using the skills you acquire from this book, you can clearly identify what's important and make conscious, wise choices. For example, if you need to save another $200 per month because you want to start an account for your children's college education, you may determine that putting in an extra shift at work may not be worth the loss of time with your family, even at time-and-a-half pay. Or if you really detest yard work, then paying someone else $50 to cut your grass may be a fair trade for the extra two hours of time watching the game.

Breakout! Sharpening your focus with time off

About ten years ago, as I was evaluating my sales results, I puzzled over a drop in my numbers at the ninth week when I'd been working without a break. It didn't take me long to realize that my lower results reflected my drop in focus. And it's a pattern I could see in previous months. I realized the best course of action, rather than gutting it out, was to get out. I needed a vacation.

I also found that I didn't need a full week's vacation to return to work revitalized and refreshed.

I simply needed a mini-break, about four days over the course of a long weekend to step away from the work routine and see the world through another lens, whether holing up with my family or making an escape to the beach.

To this day, I lay out my whole year in advance, based on this rhythm. As I've aged, I see the need for a break every eight weeks, and as I approach the next decade of my career, I anticipate it shrinking to seven weeks. The recharge number is still four days.

In Chapter 3, I help you calculate what an hour of your time is worth —
regardless of whether you're on the clock at work — so you can figure out
where to invest the most time. And in Chapter 4, I introduce you to the universal
truth that 20 percent of your efforts produce 80 percent of the results. So after
you uncover which efforts produce that return, you can crank up those efforts
to increase your results. Most success comes from prioritizing activities that
produce results and giving them the focus they warrant, so anything you can
do to increase your powers of concentration serves you well.

Identifying your rhythm to get in the zone

Athletes talk about being *in the zone,* a place where positive results seem to
stick like a magnet. Well, I'm here to tell you that the zone isn't some magical
place where wishes come true. Anybody can get there, without a lucky token
or fairy dust. What it takes is focus, singular focus.

As an ex-professional athlete in racquetball in the 1980s, I can say I've been
in the zone a number of times. And I've experienced that same distillation of
focus and electric energy on work projects as well — times when my volume
and quality of work was bordering on unbelievable. If you can get your focus
under control, you can visit the zone every day and make great things happen.

If you know your rhythms — when you're most on, what times of day you're
best equipped to undertake certain tasks — you can perform your most
important activities when you're in the zone. Everyone works to a unique
pace, and recognizing that rhythm is one of the most valuable personal
discoveries you can make. Some of the aspects you need to explore include
the following:

- ✔ How many hours can you work at a high level each day?
- ✔ What's your most productive time of the day?
- ✔ How many weeks can you work at high intensity without a break?
- ✔ How long of a break do you need so you can come back focused
  and intense?

Chapter 25 offers advice on attaining focus, including ten easy-to-adopt
habits that nurture success.

Following a System

Effective time management requires more than good intent and self-
knowledge. To keep your time under careful control, you need a framework. In your arsenal of time-management ammunition, you want to stock

organizational skills, technology that helps keep you on track, and planning tools that help you keep the reins on your time, hour by hour, day by day, week by week, and so forth.

Establishing a solid system you can replicate is a key to succeeding in managing your time. Systems, standards, strategies, and rules protect your time and allow you to use it to your best advantage. These skills are applicable whether you're the company CEO, a salesperson, a midlevel manager, an executive, or an administrative assistant. No matter your work or your work environment, time management is of universal value. (Visit Part V for chapters that spell out particulars for your job situation.)

Scheduling your time and creating a routine

Sticking to a time-scheduling system can't guarantee the return of your long-lost vacation days, but by regularly tracking your meetings, appointments, and obligations, you reduce your odds of double-booking and scheduling appointments too close. And by planning ahead, you make sure to make time for all the important things first.

For years, I've followed the time-blocking system, which I detail in Chapter 4. The system ensures that you put your priorities first (starting with routines and then moving to individual tasks/activities) before scheduling in commitments and activities of lesser importance.

Such time-management techniques are just as applicable to the other spheres of your life. There's a reason why I advise you to plug in your personal commitments first when filling in your time-blocking schedule: Your personal time is worthy of protection, and you can further enhance that time by applying time-management principles.

Organizing your surroundings

A good system of time management requires order and organization. Creating order in your world saves time wasted searching for stuff, from important phone numbers to your shoes. But even more, physical order creates mental order and helps you perform more efficiently.

Yes, your workspace should be clean and orderly, with papers and folders arranged in some sort of sequence that makes items easy and quick to find. Your desk should be cleared off, providing space to work. Your important tools — phone, computer, calculator — ought to be within reach. And your day planner, of course, should be at your fingertips. Your briefcase, your meeting planner, even your closet has an impact on your time management success. (For more on keeping your office in order, read Chapter 5.)

Using time-saving technology

Organization extends beyond your work area: Not only should your computer be nearby, but the files, documents, and contact information on that computer should be ordered for quick access. The computer stores your address list, tracks your correspondence, and contains your calendar and upcoming appointments.

But that's just the beginning. Today's teleconferencing and videoconferencing equipment means you can hold weekly meetings with your colleagues who live on the other side of the globe without anyone having to turn in a travel expense report. Cellphones and PDAs mean you can conduct business on the road without having to pull off to find a phone booth.

The schedule will set you free

Too many people feel that all this structure is too restrictive. They think the freedom they seek with their schedules and their lives is contained in a more flexible environment. They're afraid establishing a routine will keep them wrapped in the chains of time.

However, most people waste too much time figuring out each individual day on the fly. They react to the day rather than respond. *Reacting* is a reflex action that turns over your agenda to others, and that can't possibly lead to freedom. *Responding* is a disciplined act of planning that determines where and how you'll invest your time.

For example, suppose you have a set place in your schedule to respond to phone calls and problems. You've established the routine of dealing with these issues in predetermined time slots. You can hold off on your response until later — when you're calmer, more focused, and in a problem-solving mentality — instead of reacting because you're dealing with the issue now.

Planning how to spend your time, which at first glance seems opposed to freedom, is the only pathway to the true mastery of time. With the right routine come simplicity, productivity, and freedom. The "what am I going to work on today?" or "what's my schedule today?" never happens. And when you get the important work out of the way, you free yourself to do what you really enjoy.

If you're a free spirit and what I'm suggesting just fried your circuits, start with a small amount of routine. Ask yourself, "Can I establish a daily routine to try it out? What can I do without having it send me into withdrawal?" Then implement a new routine every week. You'll add more than 50 new pieces of structure to your schedule in a normal work year and see a significant improvement in your freedom.

In fact, technology is advancing at such a rapid pace that it's a struggle to keep up with all the advances. In Chapter 6, I present an overview of the many technologies at your disposal to help you make the best use of your time. And Chapter 24 names some of my favorite time-saving devices.

Overcoming Time-Management Obstacles

Anyone can conquer time management, but it's not always easy. If your experience is anything like mine, sometimes your days feel like a video game, where you're in constant threat of being gobbled up on your course to the finish line. But instead of cartoon threats, your obstacles are your own short-comings (poor communication skills, procrastination, and the inability to make wise and quick decisions), time-wasting co-workers and bosses, phone and people interruptions, and unproductive meetings.

Communicating effectively

Communicating effectively is one of the best ways to maximize your time. One of the biggest time-wasters on company time is, no surprise, talking with co-workers. But what may be a surprise is that the abuse *isn't* a function of weekend catch-up discussions that take place at the water cooler or the gossip circle at the copy machine. Rather, it's the banter at the weekly staff status reports, the drawn-out updates of projects that never seem to conclude, the sales presentations that get off-track. It's all the meetings that could be as brief as 10 minutes but somehow take an hour or more.

At your disposal, however, is an amazing weapon for taming these misbehaving encounters: your words. With a few deft remarks, you have the power to bring these meetings to a productive close.

In Chapter 10, I provide specific insight on which types of situations are most appropriate for each of the primary communication methods — face-to-face, verbal only, and written — and I present plenty of ideas for communicating your message and posing questions strategically, succinctly, and successfully so your communication ends in results, action, and decisions — whether you're leading a meeting or simply attending it.

Circumventing interruptions

Interruptions creep into your workday in all sorts of insidious manners. Besides the pesky co-worker stepping into your office with "Got a sec?" interruptions come in the form of unproductive meetings, phone calls, hall conversations that drift into your office and distract you, even the "you've got mail" icon that creeps onto the lower corner of your computer monitor.

Additionally, most poor time managers interrupt themselves by trying to do too much at once. Study after study supports that multitasking isn't the most effective work style. The constant stops and starts disrupt a project, requiring startup time each time you turn back to the task.

I explore a number of these interruptions in Chapter 11, and I offer plenty of advice on preempting such disruptions, as well as cutting them short so you can get your train of thought back on the track.

Getting procrastination under control

Sometimes, it's tempting to use interruptions as an excuse to postpone a project or a task. How nice to have someone else to blame for not getting started! And before you know it, you've found so many good reasons not to do something that you've backed yourself into a really tight eleventh-hour corner, and the pressure's on.

Say you're writing a 400-page book and you have 10 months to complete the project. You have almost a year to put this thing together. Looking forward, your task requires you to complete 40 pages per month — little more than a page a day. That's too easy! You can afford to put it off for a while. Wait for a couple of months, and then you'll need to produce 50 pages a month. Still doable. But at some point, *doable* starts to morph into *impossible*. But when? When you're down to four months and pressured to crank out 100 pages per month? Or do you wait until the last minute and find yourself struggling to complete nearly 15 pages per day?

Procrastination has a lot of causes, but most of the reasons to procrastinate leave you headed for trouble. Chapter 12 addresses the perils of putting things off and offers secrets to overcoming that all-too-human tendency to postpone until tomorrow what you could've done today.

Making decisions: Just do it

One of the easiest things to put off is making a decision. Even sidestepping the smallest decisions can lead to giant time-consumption. Think about it: You scroll through your e-mail and save one to ponder and respond to later. You revisit a few times and still can't bring yourself to a commitment. So you get more e-mail from the sender. To stave off making a decision, you ask a couple of questions, which requires more time and attention. By the time the issue is resolved and put to bed, you may have invested five times more attention than if you'd handled it at once.

Many factors create the confusion and uncertainty that prevents you from making sound but quick decisions. Often, part of the struggle is having too many options. Most people have a tough enough time choosing between pumpkin and apple pie at the Thanksgiving table. But every day, you're forced to make decisions from choices as abundant as a home-style cafeteria line. Having options is usually a good thing, but too much choice is overwhelming, even paralyzing.

In Chapter 13, I offer some advice to help you narrow your options for a quicker, right-on decision. I also reveal a little-known technique for successful decision-making: using and blending your natural behavioral style with your decision-making system.

Garnering Support While Establishing Your Boundaries

Sometimes your family, friends, and co-workers are your biggest challenge to managing your time successfully. Whose phone calls interrupt your train of thought when you're on a roll? Who expects you home for dinner, despite a pressing proposal deadline? For whose meetings do you have to take a break from your critical research?

Yet despite all the challenges they throw your way, these same folks can also serve as your allies as you pursue the quest of better time use. Getting them on board and perceiving them as comrades in shared goals is a great way to offset the interruptions that they also inevitably bring to the table.

Balancing work and time with family and friends

All work and no play, as they say, means something is askew with your life balance. Recognize that although your job and career are critical components of who you are, they're also a means to support aspects of your life that, I suspect, are more important to you: your personal life, which includes your family, your friends, your community, and your leisure and social activities.

If you find yourself constantly putting in long hours at work for months on end, something's off-kilter: Either you're not managing your time effectively, or something's wrong with your job. No one — not even Wall Street lawyers — should be putting in 70-hour weeks on a regular basis. A 70-hour work week leaves little time for sleep, recreation, family, or relationships.

Still, getting the support of family members is critical for success. There's no doubt that my family comes before my job, but that doesn't mean I can drop work whenever I want. So my wife, Joan, and even my two children, six-year-old Wesley and two-year-old Annabelle, are my supporters, and we all work together to manage our time so we have more of it together.

See Chapter 5 for tips on managing your time when working in a home office and Chapter 3 for info on putting a value on personal time.

Streamlining interactions with co-workers and customers

Most people find themselves in a work environment in which they regularly interact with others, whether co-workers, business associations, or customers. The workday is rife with opportunities for interruption, distraction, and time-wasting. In addition to the phone calls and cubicle pop-ins, you have business appointments, associates who keep you waiting, or meetings that are unfocused and poorly run.

Maintaining control of your time at work requires you to develop some ways to manage meetings, appointments, and other work interactions so they're as efficient and productive as possible. In Chapters 15 and 16, I explore tactics for planning, setting, leading, or just plain attending such gatherings. Whether you initiate the interaction or you're merely a participant, you can have some control over the meeting.

Ah, but what if you're in sales or a customer service capacity? In such positions, taking control of your time is a little more challenging. To make the sale, you want to take as much time as your prospect wants. And when addressing a service issue, your most important objective is to make the customer happy. But you can be successful in sales and serve your clients well and still keep control of your time. In fact, in Chapter 16, I show you how to speed up the decision-making process during sales so you get a positive answer sooner.

Keeping your boss on track

Trying to keep co-workers from impinging on your productive time is ticklish enough; things get even more sensitive when you have to tell your boss that you don't have time to waste. But your supervisor is often the one who throws the most curveballs your way when it comes to using your time in the most productive way. How do you deal with the boss who waits to the last minute to drop a big project on your desk that needs to be done yesterday?

When trying to keep a rein on a time-wasting boss, you need to be prepared to summon up all your powers of diplomacy. You also need to be more direct from the outset. You may even have to suggest some of the time-management tips and tools from this chapter and others. I show you how to help your boss stay on track in Chapter 14.

Keeping Motivation High

According to Earl Nightingale, the dean of the personal development industry, "Success is the progressive realization of a worthy goal or worthy ideal." His definition doesn't confine achievement to a fixed point but instead presents success as a journey. Like most goals, mastering your time-management skills isn't something that happens overnight.

Throughout the process of working to improve the way you manage your time, you'll occasionally encounter points where you start feeling disappointed, wondering whether your efforts are paying off. Whenever you hit those lows — and you will — remember to give yourself credit for every step you make in the right direction. One great way to stay motivated is to link incentive to inducement: In other words, reward yourself. For example, if you complete certain actions that tie to your goals, give yourself Friday afternoon off. Or savor an evening on the couch with a good movie or dinner at a favorite restaurant. Do whatever serves as an enticing reward.

Take motivation to the next level by involving others in the reward. Let your spouse know that an evening out awaits if you fulfill your week's goals before deadline. Tell the kids that if you spend the next couple of evenings at the office, you can all head for the amusement park on Saturday. I guarantee this strategy is a sure-fire way to supercharge your motivation.

As you work through this difficult but worthy bout of self-improvement, keep your mind on the positive side and remember two simple truths:

- You're human.
- Work always expands to fill the time you allow for it.

No matter how productive I am, whether I have just a couple things to accomplish or a sky-high pile on my desk, and whether I leave work on time or stay late, there's always something that doesn't get done. So I don't get hung up on those things I don't accomplish — I just keep my eyes on the goal, prioritize accordingly, delegate what I can, and protect my boundaries carefully so I take on only as much as I know I can handle while still remaining satisfied with all parts of my life. When you start to get frustrated about the never-ending flow of work that comes your way, remind yourself that you're blessed with more opportunities than time — and that's not a bad place to be.

Chapter 2

Linking Time Management to Life Goals

*T*oday, more than at any time in history, you have limitless opportunities, especially if you're living in the United States. However, having so many choices can lead to confusion, distraction, and wasted time. Achievement in anything in life takes focus, diligence, and patience. So the question arises: Can getting a handle on your most precious lifelong dreams and desires help you get more done on a day-to-day basis? Absolutely! Say, for example, you and your spouse have always dreamed of taking six months to travel the world while you're still young enough to hoist a backpack. Such a focus may motivate you to put in extra hours or accelerate your sales quotas at work to build up the necessary funds and time for that adventure.

Even long-range goals can shape the way you use your time in the here and now. Suppose your goal is to retire to a modest cabin in the Smoky Mountains and spend the rest of your life writing the Great American Novel. Even if that goal is 30 years away, your priority *now* is more likely to be on investing your income and perhaps taking some writing courses rather than on building a 4,200-square-foot home and learning to ski — or it should be, anyway, because the preparations you need to make first and foremost are the ones that'll enable you to build that cabin and have the money and time to write.

Everyone has dreams and goals for the future. But in order to accomplish more in less time, to create a sense of urgency and command efficiency, having a clear sense of goals and purpose is critical. In this chapter, I guide you in the process of committing your goals to paper; categorizing, balancing, and breaking them down into manageable chunks; and allowing that powerful action to spur your productivity.

Understanding Why You Need to Put Your Goals on Paper

Some studies calculate that only about 3 percent of goal-setters document their aspirations. And I can assure you that these folks are the ones who have the most money, influence, power, prestige, freedom, and time to work toward their dreams. Why? Because, as numerous studies suggest, people who clearly define and write down their goals are more likely to accomplish them — and in a shorter time frame and more direct fashion. People who don't clarify and write out their goals invest more time and accomplish less.

When you take the time to write down your goals, you clarify them and sharpen your vision for attaining them, which allows you to do the following:

- ✔ **Take control of your life.** By identifying what's most important to you and putting it on paper, you tell your brain that this isn't a dream to be ignored as a hope-to, wish-to, or would-like-to. It's really something for which you're willing to invest time, effort, energy, and emotion.

- ✔ **Map out the most direct route to achievement.** When you put your goals in writing, you're setting your sights on the destination before you begin. Your life goals become the framework for how you prioritize and manage your time. You begin the process of planning and strategizing about the steps you can take to achieve that goal. Your brain starts to look for the best, most direct route and the route with the lowest time investment.

- ✔ **Limit detours.** Ever hear the saying "If you don't know where you're going, any road will take you there"? Problem is, if you head off on just *any* road, you're likely to end up in a place you don't want to be. By documenting your goals, you can more easily gauge whether an effort is likely to bring you closer to or further away from them. With your goals in front of you, you make fewer wrong turns and invest less time in trial-and-error dead ends. If you know that "be an outstanding father" is at the top of your written list, then overtime, extra assignments, travel, and other actions that take you away from your kids won't distract you as easily; you know you're more likely to achieve this goal by spending time with your kids, going to their games, taking walks, throwing a ball, playing dress-up, going to the park, or writing a note.

- ✔ **Stay motivated.** Written goals fuel motivation, inducing you to perform at a higher level and at a faster rate in order to achieve.

Establishing Your Fabulous 50

As you put together your list of goals, you need to consider the five core aspects of wants that I cover in this section. My mentor Jim Rohn taught them to me when I was in my 20s. These five questions dramatically reduced the amount of time I needed to achieve many of the goals that are now crossed off my goal sheets, and these same questions can help you expand your thinking so you can have more, be more, and achieve more.

As soon as you finish reading this section, read no further until you get your goals on paper. Your task after reading this section is to come up with at least 50 goals that you want to accomplish within the next 10 years. As you brainstorm your list of goals, keep a few points in mind to make your goal-setting effective:

- **Make sure your goals line up with your *wants*.** Don't evaluate goals based on what you think you need, deserve, or can realistically achieve; attack it by what you want. Your success is determined by how you invest your time each day.

- **Think big.** "Go big or go home" is a philosophy I encourage my clients and workshop participants to embrace. Many shy away from setting big goals for a range of reasons, from fear of disappointment to concern that they may not have the drive to pursue them.

  If you approach your dreams conservatively — going after what you think is reasonable or realistic — your odds of getting beyond that are slim to none. But if you let your imagination go and pursue the big dream, the odds of reaching that level of joy and fulfillment are in your favor. Big goals and big dreams cause you to stretch, strain, and go for what you really want in life. They connect with the best use of your time and energy.

- **Pick a time somewhere in the future and work backward from there.** For any goal that stretches further than ten years, break it down into smaller goals with shorter time frames to increase your focus, intensity, and commitment. See the later section "Assigning a time frame to each goal" for details.

- **Make your goals measurable.** When you establish a measurable, quantifiable goal, you know you can't fudge on whether you achieved it or not. You either hit the target or you don't. You also know where you stand at any given time. Goal measurement naturally falls into two categories:

  - **Number-based goals:** Measuring your progress toward a goal is pretty easy when the goal is number-based. You know when you've acquired a million dollars or lost 30 pounds, for example. The bank statement or scale is pretty simple to read. As you craft financial and other goals that are associated with numbers, be specific. Do you want to earn a certain annual salary? To put away a certain amount of money each year? To run a certain number of miles by September?

- **Non-number-based goals:** To measure a non-number-based goal, focus on how you'll know when you've accomplished it. For example, will some organization's seal of approval establish you as a world-renowned archeologist? Will being elected president of the chamber of commerce constitute being a business leader in the community? Will having your children expressing greater thanks for your efforts as a parent equate to being a better dad or mom?

As you identify and record 50 goals you'd like to achieve in the next 10 years, contemplate the following 5 core questions to guide your goal setting.

What do you want to have?

The question of what you want to have focuses on material acquisitions. What possessions do you yearn for? A swimming pool? A sailboat? Do you fantasize about owning a sports car? Do you dream of a formal rose garden landscaped into your backyard? Someone to cook and clean for you? Your own private jet? Winter vacations in the Caribbean? If your home environment is a priority, imagine the place you want to live. An expansive ranch overlooking the Pacific Ocean? A Fifth Avenue penthouse? An off-the-grid abode that runs on solar and wind power? A villa in Tuscany?

Although possessions are important to consider, they're typically a means to an end: They enable you to create the lifestyle that you want to have.

One of the best goals I set and achieved was to own two houses, one as my primary residence and one to which I could retreat. Achieving that goal also motivated me to better invest time during work hours so I could enjoy spending long weekends at my second home.

What do you want to see?

When you ask yourself what you want to see, think experiential acquisition. Travel is likely to be a key focus. I'm certain you can easily come up with at least ten places you want to see. Have some world wonders fascinated you? The Pyramids of Egypt? The Great Wall of China? I travel internationally a few times a year on business, and it only fuels my desire to see more parts of the world and expand my awareness of how other people live.

Your desire for new sights may lean toward unfamiliar geography — the desert lands of the Southwest if you're a New England native or the Rocky Mountains in winter if you hail from a lowland home. Perhaps your *see* goals are more personal. You may have always wanted to visit the country your ancestors came from or even visit the small town in the Midwest where your great-grandparents met and raised a family.

Using what works for you

Individualism is key when crafting your goals, and it applies to both *what* you record and *how* you record it. Perhaps typing your goals or entering them in an electronic spreadsheet is easiest for you. Or maybe you find that your thoughts flow best when you write them down by hand. The important thing to remember is that whatever method best enables your mind to flow freely and inspires you to craft your goals is the one you should use. Don't let others sway you in how to craft and define your goals or what your goals should be.

Consider this little-known fact about yours truly: This is my third *For Dummies* book, and I've written all three books by hand. This archaic approach may seem ridiculous in today's high-tech publishing environment; dictating my thoughts into a recorder for transcription would certainly be easier and less time-consuming than writing everything by hand. But not for me. For whatever reason, the direct connection among my hand, pen, eyes, and brain enables me to create a better book. Inspiration comes to me frequently while writing thoughts down, so I stick to my routine and get someone with more time to type my writing into an electronic file.

What do you want to do?

Most likely, many of your goals are connected with the question of what you want to do at some point in your life. Whereas the possessions you want to acquire help create your lifestyle, the action-oriented question you consider here focuses more on bigger events and feats outside the daily realm. Because this category is vast, I have my clients consider three main aspects of this question:

- **Activities:** You may want to include some once-in-a-lifetime experiences, such as snorkeling with sea turtles or hiking Mt. Kilimanjaro. What about a goal of regular exercise four times a week? Or maybe you want to see Celine Dion in concert.

- **Skills:** For example, have you always wanted to speak Spanish or Mandarin Chinese? Do you wish you could play the piano or electric guitar? Have you put off a new experience — snow-skiing, surfing, fly fishing — because you thought it was too late to learn? Whether these skills can enhance your career or financial state or are simply actions that bring personal pleasure, cast a wide net and list the ones that intrigue you most.

- **Career:** How do you want to seek fulfillment through your career? Be honest with yourself and sort out how you'd like to measure that success. Do you yearn to be recognized as the top authority in your field? To win an international award? To write an influential book?

ANECDOTE

Appreciating personal growth

Consider this true-life story: I made my first million by the time I was in my early 30s, but I can wholeheartedly say the value I gained from attaining that goal wasn't the money (which, unfortunately, I lost a pretty good chunk of through some poor investments I made). Of deeper and lasting value are the personal characteristics and skills that I gained through the process of strategizing, acting, and investing my time on my way toward the goal. Because I'd changed as a person as a result of the process, the steps toward reaching that goal again weren't nearly so challenging, and the characteristics I developed through the process enabled me to meet other goals as well.

I grew with each new goal I worked toward. To reach my goals in real estate sales, I had to increase my focus and discipline. When I decided to go into coaching and speaking, I had to develop better behavioral analysis and leadership to get others to follow my coaching and teaching. And to reach my goal of writing books that would help readers achieve success, I had to gather new skills in organization, critical thinking, and patience due to all these editors in the publishing business.

What do you want to give?

Andrew Carnegie, the great steel entrepreneur, met his goal to amass a fortune in the first half of his life. His goal for the second half was to give it all away. Many of the public libraries in the United States, Canada, and the United Kingdom exist today because of his philanthropy.

An important way to balance all the *want, see,* and *do* items on your Fabulous 50 list is to include *give* goals as well. What are you willing or interested in giving back? How do you want to share your good fortune with others? Which causes are near and dear to you?

TIP

Your *give* list may include specific monetary goals — "give 10 percent of my income to charity" — but you may find more fulfillment by tying in your giving goals to your other interests. For example, if your career aspirations involve writing a bestseller, supporting a charity that champions literacy or volunteering to teach adults to read may be goals that touch a chord with you. If you dream of traveling to exotic destinations, you may participate in a humanitarian mission, bringing medicine and other important supplies to people in a developing country. If you care deeply about environmental initiatives, maybe you want to look into ecotourism or green volunteering opportunities.

Who do you want to become?

To a degree, what you want to have, see, do, and give determine the person you want to become. But you should still envision and write down how you see yourself developing *while* you achieve these goals. The real value of goals isn't what you achieve — it's in the accumulation of knowledge, skills, discipline, and experience you gain through learning, changing, improving, and investing yourself as you work toward your goals. Often, those newly discovered or carefully developed traits are the only lasting acquisition that stands the test of time.

Don't get me wrong — I'm not suggesting that you become someone other than who you are; rather, I'm encouraging you to earnestly and honestly evaluate the characteristics and disciplines best suited for your ambitions. To identify the areas you should focus on, take a look at all the goals you've written down so far (if you haven't yet read the preceding sections, complete them before moving on here). Then ask yourself the following questions when considering your goals as a whole:

✔ **What personal characteristics do you need to change or improve?** Do you need assertiveness training to deal more effectively with your boss or co-workers? Do you need to work on interpersonal skills? Does your anger get in the way of your success because you get frustrated so easily?

✔ **What disciplines do you need to work harder at practicing consistently?** Are you able to delay gratification and do what you need to when it needs to be done? Are you able to save regular amounts from your current paycheck, or are you waiting to make more money before you start the savings process? What if that extra money never shows up?

 If you're struggling to identify areas where you need to work on personal development, take at look at people who have achieved what you want; then evaluate your characteristics and disciplines as compared to theirs.

Labeling and Balancing Your Fabulous 50

After you draft a list of the 50 goals you want to achieve in the next 10 years, your next task is to assign a category and time frame to each of them. Creating categories for your goals and establishing time frames to achieve them sharpens your focus and increases your intensity, which can reduce the time required to achieve your goals. It also allows you to quickly and easily see whether your time investment to the various areas of your life as well as the size and difficulty of your goals are appropriately balanced.

 The objective isn't to spread an equal number and depth of goals among the six categories; the aim is to identify whether one or two of the categories is light compared to the others and to determine whether you need to pay more attention to those areas of your life to develop them. In the end, the purpose is to create a well-rounded system of goals that addresses your whole person and that you'll have the motivation to actually work toward.

Assigning a time frame to each goal

I firmly believe you can have anything you want; you just can't have it all at once and all right now. Just because you establish a goal to lose 20 pounds doesn't mean you'll wake up tomorrow with 20 pounds missing from your body. Realizing your goal involves a process that requires specific activity and time.

There are no unrealistic goals, but there may be unrealistic time frames. The world is full of people who have accomplished great things with the application of extensive time. Edison, for example, was said to have failed in excess of 10,000 times in his search for the right filament for the incandescent light bulb. Imagine the time frame necessary to fail 10,000 times!

Remember that your Fabulous 50 list names goals that you want to accomplish within the next 10 years. That said, you may want to see some of them come to fruition much earlier. Some may be immediate — just a year away. Others may require you to first achieve some intermediate goals. For instance, say your goal is to double your income within three years. You know you're unlikely to receive anywhere *close* to a 100-percent raise at your current job, so you start exploring other options: a new job that pays more and has a fast-track career path, a second job, freelance or contract projects that you can do on your off-hours, or a real-estate investment that brings in rental income.

Before you head to the next section, go back through your list of 50 goals (which you create earlier in "Establishing Your Fabulous 50") and write a 1, 3, 5, or 10 next to each goal to indicate whether you want to achieve that goal within 1, 3, 5, or 10 years.

When you start thinking about the time you need to attain your goals, make sure you're being reasonable. Whether or not the time frame for your goals is reasonable depends entirely on your situation. To help you stay on track, follow these steps:

1. **Consider the time frame you'd *ideally* like to accomplish this goal.**

   Would you be happy if you accomplished it one year or even three years later than your ideal, or are you intent on accomplishing it by a certain time?

2. **Assess the complexity of the goal.**

3. **Determine what new knowledge or other resources you may need to accomplish the goal.**

   See the "Pinpointing Resource Needs" section, later in this chapter, for guidance.

4. **Consider what time frame someone else needed to accomplish a similar goal.**

After you label each goal with a time frame, tally up the number of goals you have for each time slot and record those totals in Figure 2-1. Then assess the spread of your goals across those time frames to see whether they're well balanced.

Timeframe	Number of Goals in This Timeframe
1 year	
3 years	
5 years	
10 years	

Figure 2-1: Balance your goals across time frames with this chart.

Especially when finances are involved, keep in mind that you should enjoy the *process* of working toward your goals. Although planning for the future is important, you're guaranteed only the present. You don't want to rob yourself of all enjoyment now — better to live a balanced life while you implement your plan and adjust it as needed when circumstances throw you for a loop.

Categorizing your goals

After you assign a time frame to each of your 50 goals, your next step is to assign a category to each one. Typically, your goals fall into one of six categories:

C = Career

F = Family

H = Health

M = Money/financial

P = Personal

S = Spiritual

When determining which category each goal falls under, you'll find that some goals fall naturally in one specific category. A goal to get be promoted to supervisor at work, for example, is an easy C. Other goals, however, aren't so easy to peg. Going back to school to earn an MBA may be a C for career, but it also may be a P for personal. Place the goal in whichever category you most closely associate with it or feel free to place some goals in multiple categories.

Now go back through your list of 50 goals and write the appropriate category letter next to each one. After you label each goal with a category, count the total number of goals you have for each category and record those numbers in Figure 2-2. Then assess the spread of your goals across those categories to see whether they're well balanced. Are you light on health goals? Should you pay more attention to your spiritual life?

Category	Number of Goals in This Category
Career (C)	
Family (F)	
Health (H)	
Money/financial (M)	
Personal (P)	
Spiritual (S)	

Figure 2-2: Balance your goals across categories with this chart.

Targeting 12 Goals to Start With

At this point, you should have a list of 50 goals you want to accomplish over the next 10 years, all labeled according to the time frame you want to achieve them in and the aspect of your life that they fall under (see the preceding section). A large list ensures you have new goals to move to when you accomplish your first goals. However, concentrating on all your goals at once leads to frustration, distraction, and ultimately, failure.

The next step is to break down your list of 50 into some manageable chunks, which helps you focus your energy where you need it most. You won't allow others to interrupt you as frequently, and you'll work with a greater sense of urgency because you have things to do, places to go, people to meet, things to see, time frames in which to accomplish them, and goals to cross off.

Narrowing down your list

To whittle your long list of goals down to a manageable size, choose the three most important goals within each time frame: three that you want to achieve within one year, three before the three-year point, three within five years, and the last trio within ten years.

As you accomplish goals on your top-12 list, revisit your Fabulous 50 and recalibrate your top 12, adding new goals and crossing off the ones you've completed. Keep reviewing your goals on at least a monthly basis. You want to see the progress you're making. With your increasing confidence, you're likely to feel more comfortable with more daring, bolder, and challenging goals. And by resetting your goals, you continue to stoke that momentum.

Noting why your top-12 goals are important to you

Too frequently, people fixate on how they'll accomplish or achieve something. However, the real magic to achieving goals is contained in the *why*. If the *why* is large enough, the *how* becomes easy.

It's been nearly 20 years since I first read Napoleon Hill's landmark book, *Think and Grow Rich!* He guided me to delve deep within myself to explore the *whys* of my aspirations and motivations — and so much more. I'm now known worldwide for my success in real estate sales and my ability to sell 150-plus homes a year on a four-day work week. That was no accident — it was a goal of mine from the start, and I'm certain I've succeeded because I had a clear understanding of the *why* behind it.

Here's my story: My dad worked a four-day week when I was growing up. He was always around on Friday when I came home from school. But the biggest benefit came in the summer, when we left Portland every Thursday afternoon to spend three days at a second home on a lake near the Oregon coast. Some of my fondest childhood memories are of swimming, sailing, waterskiing, walking the beach, and playing at our lake house. I wanted to replicate that life exactly. As I built my real estate sales business, that desire drove my success. It led me to build a vacation home in Bend, Oregon, where Joan and I spent three days a week for more than five years.

Although my *why* happened to come from a positive childhood experience, keep in mind that reasons can just as easily come from a negative place — either way, they're motivating factors to keep you pressing on. Thousands of success stories have germinated from the seeds of abject poverty or personal tragedy. My father's *why,* for example, was born out of his love for my mother, who was diagnosed with multiple sclerosis when I was three years old. By the time I was in the second grade, she never took another step. My father's goal was to earn enough income as a dentist to provide my mother with the most extraordinary life possible: to travel in a wheelchair to Mexico, Asia, Hawaii (annually), and many other locations — always with three sons in tow. But mostly, he wanted to be able to care for her in her in the home where she raised her children and to give her the best quality of life imaginable for someone in her condition.

As a coach, I can only ask questions and guide you to your unique *whys*, regardless of whether they come from happy memories, adversity, or the love and commitment to another. After you determine which 12 goals you'll start on, evaluate why each one is important to you and write it down. Why did you choose these 12 goals over the others? What will these goals accomplish for you? What are you going to feel like when you accomplish them and cross them off your list?

Reading your goals list aloud is a great way to assist your subconscious processes. This action reinforces the message in your brain. Regular repetition and review, coupled with your solid grasp of the *whys,* keeps your goals front-of-mind — even when they're at the back of your mind!

Pinpointing Your Resource Needs

Achieving your goals requires resources, be they money, contacts, knowledge, skills, time, and so on — or all the above. Some fortunate folks may have an abundant supply of all resources, but most are short on at least a couple. I may have the income to allow me to train to become a world-class figure skater, but because I lack the skill, I'm unlikely to have enough time to become good enough to achieve the goal of qualifying for the 2014 Winter Olympics in Sochi, Russia.

Even if you approach your goals with an imbalance of resources, by carefully leveraging those that you have at your disposal, you can overcome many shortfalls. If you're lacking in one or more resources, you may have to invest more of the resources you have. Take my Olympics example: I'm short on time and skill, so I may need to invest more money to devote myself to full-time training, or I may have to borrow time and aim for the 2018 Olympics, instead.

As you read through the following sections, evaluate the resource requirements for achievement for each of the top 12 goals that you identify earlier in this chapter. When you complete this step of the goal-setting process, you'll have an effective set of goals that you can integrate into your time schedule, which I discuss in depth in Chapter 4.

Accruing funds: A capital idea

Most goals, if they aren't *about* money, seem to require money — building your dream home, taking a cruise, sending your kids to an Ivy League school, opening your own coffee shop. Even a goal such as landing a job at a high-powered corporation, which seems to be about earning money, may require you to get some additional education or purchase suitable interview attire.

If you find that your goal requires capital, do your best to quantify the amount. Then determine whether you have enough money to achieve your goal or whether you need more. Ask the following questions:

✔ Do you have time to earn the amount needed to fund your endeavor?

✔ Can you borrow the money?

✔ Can you leverage another of your resources to balance the shortfall?

Expanding your knowledge

Knowledge can dramatically increase the prospects of attaining your goal in the time table you've established. Trial and error is a costly means to reach your destination — especially when it comes to time investment. So if you assess your success-list goals and determine that you need more information to succeed, ask the following:

✔ What, exactly, is the knowledge you need to realize your goal?

✔ What's the best way to attain that knowledge? Formal study? Online research? Talking with experts?

✔ How long will gaining this knowledge take, and does it fit in with your goal's time frame?

Honing your skill set

For the fulfillment of many goals, additional skills are required. Don't confuse knowledge with skill. *Knowledge* entails the gathering and processing of information in a way that you can use to gain a deeper understanding of a subject. *Skill* involves putting that understanding into effective action. You can study the heart and understand how it works — even know how bypass surgery works to prevent heart failure — but you don't want to perform such a procedure without having the skill of an experienced surgeon.

Examine your success list again to evaluate where additional skills may be necessary:

✔ What skills are required for each goal?

✔ Are these skills that you already claim, or do you need to acquire them?

✔ Are these skills that you can learn within the time frame? If not, then how can you make up for that skill shortage? Can you find someone who has the skills and ask for his or her help?

Tapping into human resources

Most people have accomplished what they have because someone else helped them along the way, so don't overlook the *people* component as you tally up your resources. The right contacts can be valuable in helping you attain your goals. Consider that dream of working for the high-powered corporation, for instance. Knowing someone who works for the company — or who has inside connections — is one of the best ways to get your foot in the door. But people resources can help in achieving other types of goals as well, from buying that cabin in the woods (Uncle Sydney always believed that real estate is the best investment) to learning to play the saxophone (the waiter at the local coffee shop is only too happy to earn some extra money giving lessons). Here are some questions to ask yourself as you evaluate your human resources:

- Do you know anyone who achieved a goal similar to yours, someone who may be willing to advise you?

- If you need additional schooling but are short on funds, do you know people who may be able to help you acquire the knowledge you need, or can you utilize their talents?

- Do you know someone who has the knowledge, skill, connections, or money that you need to reach your goal?

- Can you tap into your people resources and use the skills of someone else to compensate for skills you can't attain yourself?

- Do you know someone who knows someone else who may be able to help you?

Think of ways that the people you plan to approach can benefit if you attain your goal. Can you compensate them monetarily for their help? Can you offer something in trade that has value for them? Even just asking for help and saying thank you in advance is enough for some people. (Though many times, people are more willing to help when there's something in it for them.)

If you can't find anyone to help, you're forced to take the personal education route. The good thing, though, is that lots of books, classes, and seminars are available to help you, so take advantage of them.

Chapter 3

Putting a Value on Your Time

epending on your values, different kinds of numbers may be important to you: To some, it's cholesterol count and blood pressure figures; to others, it's the number of years they've been married. To many, the sum total in the retirement account is the number-one number, and some people zero in on the amount left on their mortgage.

But I contend that your per-hour worth should be among the top-of-mind numbers that are important to you — no matter what your values or priorities are — even if you don't earn your living on a per-hour rate. Knowing the value of your time enables you to make wise decisions about where and how you spend it so you can make the most of this limited resource according to your circumstances, goals, and interests.

Obviously, the higher you raise your per-hour worth while upholding your priorities, the more you can propel your efforts toward meeting your goals, because you have more resources at your disposal — you have either more money or more time, whichever you need most.

In this chapter, I guide you toward optimizing your value so you can reap the rewards and attain what's most important to you. I start by showing you why your hourly value is crucial to effective time management. From there, I help you calculate the overall value of your time based on your employment income. (If you have an hourly job, you can skip that section.) Then I help you decide how to leverage your time and money, both in your career efforts and in your personal choices, so you can boost your hourly value and get the most out of your time investment.

Getting a Good Grip on the Time-Equals-Money Concept

Your per-hour value translates to your quality of life, both now and in the future. Not only does your income influence how you spend your nonworking hours, but it also determines how much leisure time you have to spend.

As you can imagine, your hourly value reaches beyond the basics: It impacts your health, too. For instance, studies show that lower-income earners have more health problems, including heart disease and diabetes, which are often attributed to poor diets and a lack of medical care. Additionally, the challenge of trying to make ends meet can cause great stress, leading not just to physical illness but also to depression and other mental health problems.

And though it's important to live in the present, it's also important to keep an eye toward the future. How well you prepare does have an impact on your quality of life right now. Making enough money to be able to save for retirement and other major life expenses — including a child's education — results in a sense of comfort and safety about your future.

Your personal time has value, too. And by having a grip on the value of your work hours, you gain a better grasp on what your downtime is worth. After all, most people work so they can make the most of their personal time, whether they're devoting it to family, hobbies, volunteer work, travel, or education.

When you recognize that your free time has a monetary value just as your work time does, you gain the perspective you need to make choices:

- ✔ Is the extra money you'll gain by working overtime worth giving up your holiday with your family?

- ✔ Could you go part-time and stay at home with your small children?

- ✔ Can you afford to take a leave of absence to do a volunteer stint in Haiti?

- ✔ Should you take on a freelance project that means giving up all your free time for three months to fund your dream trip to Bali?

But what is an hour of your personal time worth? Well, that's not a question you can easily answer. How do you put a price on time with your young children? Or apply a dollar value to travel experiences that bring you in touch with new worlds? Or equate the quiet therapy of a walk in the woods with the stress of a work presentation?

The harsh truth is that you don't get paid for not working. But that doesn't mean your personal time has no monetary value. Just thinking about your time as a commodity with a value helps you sort through and recognize the activities that are most important to you. (For information on valuing your personal time, see the later section "Making Value-Based Time Decisions in Your Personal Life.")

Calculating Your Hourly Income

No matter your occupation, everyone sells time for a price; it's just a lot more transparent in some situations than others. Most obvious are individuals who receive a wage or a fee based on the hours they work, including minimum-wage workers and self-employed individuals such as tutors, house cleaners, and consultants.

Other people advertise their prices based on a per-project basis, but in reality base that fee on an estimate of project hours the job takes. Freelance writers, for instance, may charge $1,500 to write a promotional brochure, but that amount is likely a reflection of the writer's value of his or her time at a certain figure — say, $75 per hour.

Some businesses and professions charge customers based on an hourly rate, although workers don't directly receive that per-hour fee. Instead, their salary or compensation is based on the revenue the company can bring in based on those hours. Law firms and plumbers, for example, may charge for their services on an hourly basis and pay their employees a salary or a per-hour rate.

If you earn a salary, you may not perceive yourself as having an hourly rate. But everyone does. Here's how to calculate your hourly income. This number doesn't affect how you're paid, but it puts you in touch with what an hour of your work time brings you.

1. **Calculate the number of hours you work per week.**

   Work hours/day × days/week + overtime = hours/week

   To be completely accurate, calculate your hourly rate based on the hours you actually work. If you consistently put in more than 40 hours a week (most salaried folks aren't paid overtime for additional hours worked), add those hours to your total. Here's an example:

   8 hours/day × 5 days/week + 2 hours overtime = 42 hours/week

2. **Figure out how many hours you work per year.**

   Work hours/week × weeks/year = hours/year

   Make sure you subtract time off. For instance, if you take three weeks of vacation each year, subtract that from your total number of weeks worked. If your salary is based on a three-week vacation and an average 42-hour work week, here's how many hours you work per year:

   42 hours/week × 49 weeks/year = 2,058 hours/year

3. **Divide your gross salary by the number of hours you work per year.**

    Salary ÷ hours/year = hourly income

    For instance, $80,000 divided by 2,058 hours is $38.87.

Boosting Your Hourly Value through Your Work Efforts

Money isn't the scarcest and most valuable resource; time is. There are plenty of ways to make more money, but there's no way to add more minutes to an hour. You have a limited amount of this precious commodity, so you want to protect it and spend it as if it's your own personal trust fund.

Most people think that if they work more hours, they'll automatically make more money. That's faulty thinking: You can devote more hours to work, but if you invest the hours in the wrong actions, you gain nothing — and you lose time.

The solution may be to ask more money for your time. Some workers have a good deal of control over their hourly income and can therefore charge more per hour for their services. The freelance writer can raise her hourly rate from $65 to $70 and bring in an additional $50 on a 10-hour project. A tax accountant can increase the fee for income tax preparation from $450 to $510. If he needs six hours to prepare the average income tax return, the accountant just gave himself an increase from $75 to $85 an hour.

However, the simple fact is that most people don't have the luxury of raising their income at will. So what's the next best step? Change how you use your time so you get the best return on investment — after all, what you do with your time leads to greater prosperity.

To increase your hourly value, you have to decide whether you'll work toward earning more money or earning more time. Then focus on performing high-value activities to achieve that goal; the process of discovering the really important actions or items you can invest your time in can help you change your hourly rate. The decision of how to increase your hourly value — whether to work toward generating more money in the same amount of time or generating the same amount of money in less time — depends on your circumstances:

✔ If you're in a commission or bonus compensation structure, you can increase productivity to earn additional income.

✔ If you're in a salary-based position, you can find ways to be more productive within the 40 hours week and reduce the additional hours you put in.

If, however, your job doesn't enable you to increase your hourly value, whether in terms of money or time, then you have bigger decisions to make. Other changes you can make to directly impact your income are to simply do the following:

- Find a similar job at a company that pays a bigger salary or offers more freedom with your work hours.

- Improve your performance and earn a raise or a promotion. Know, however, that the success of your efforts toward a raise or promotion is ultimately up to the higher-ups.

When evaluating time-for-money trades, be sure not to limit your definition of *return* to money: Ask yourself whether the exchange improves the quality of your life. Look at how your life would change outside of work if you were to double or triple your hourly rate. If what you're trading for dollars does any of the following, it's a good trade:

- Increases your ability and opportunity to earn more money

- Increases your amount of family time

- Decreases your work hours

- Enhances your physical and mental fitness

- Provides an opportunity for someone who needs it

- Removes something you don't enjoy or don't do well from your life

So that's a simple look at the overall strategy behind improving your return on investment. Chapter 4 takes you through the specifics, helping you schedule your to-do list each day so you make sure all your efforts align with your goals, which you outline in Chapter 2.

Making Value-Based Time Decisions in Your Personal Life

When you consider the way you live your personal life, divide your focus in two: chores/responsibilities and leisure time. Although personal time may seem straightforward, there really is a difference between chores and leisure activities, and the way you approach your time-management decisions hinges on that difference. But however you spend your personal time, you can assign that time a value equal to your work worth — even though no one's paying you — to help you decide how to spend it.

ANECDOTE

Helping kids understand the time-versus-money balance

Business travel can eat up a lot of the personal time you count on for recreation and renewal. You may still tie up your workday at 5:30 p.m., but instead of going home to the family, you retreat to your hotel room for the night. And your weekend may be consumed with long travel days to get home.

I know the price of a job that requires business travel. It's a price that I pay, my wife pays, and my kids pay. By the end of the year, I'll have traveled to five different continents speaking to sales organizations in countries around the world. I'll be away from my family for days — and in some cases, weeks — at a time.

When my son Wesley was 5, I was getting ready to leave for a week of speaking engagements. He was crying and begging me not to go. When I see my children cry, I'm a pushover, but I knew I couldn't *not* go, so after I saw that all my reassurances weren't working to stop his tears, I went out on a limb and tried to reason with my son.

I explained to him that I already promised the people that I'd be there and it wouldn't be right for me not to show up. I assured him that if he wanted me to, I'd be willing to stop speaking and spend more time at home. But we'd all have to make some changes: We'd have to sell our home and buy a smaller one because Daddy would be making less money. We would need to cut some things out of our budget like some vacations, eating out, toys — the new bike he'd been asking for. I wound up my explanation and asked him gently, "Do you understand?" He looked at me thoughtfully for a second and then said, "Bye, Dad. See you later." And off he ran.

Deciding whether to buy time: Chores and responsibilities

When you have a handle on the value of your time in hourly increments (see the earlier section "Calculating Your Hourly Income"), you have the information you need to make better time choices. The chores have to be done, whether you do them, or delegate, or even pay someone else to do them. The question with chores is whether you want to do them yourself or to exchange dollars for someone else to do them. You have to ask, "Is the cost of the time this task would take me greater than or less than the cost to hire someone to do the work?" Here, you're simply comparing numbers. Think of the laundry list of household chores and personal errands that can eat up every bit of personal time you have. If you could pay someone to do some of those tasks at a rate equal to or well below your hourly rate, wouldn't that be a good return on investment?

For example, paying $50 to have your grass cut each week may have been a cost barrier you couldn't get over before. But if you've determined that the hourly value of your time is $50 per hour and it takes you 3 hours to mow your lawn, you've just bought yourself $100 worth of time ($150 worth of your time minus $50 to outsource the work). On the other hand, if you have all kinds of free time on the weekend — and you enjoy being out in the yard — paying someone else to cut your grass may be a money-time trade that has no value for you.

If you love to garden but hate cleaning the house, and cleaning the house takes you 4 hours ($200 if your time is worth $50 per hour), why *not* pay a housecleaning service $70, $80, even $100 to buy back the four hours it'd take you to do it all? And you buy yourself four blissful hours puttering over your zinnias and scarlet runner beans.

Making time-spending decisions: Leisure activities

With leisure activities, your decision simply hinges on whether you want to do them at all. Unlike chores, which you have to deal with in some way, you can get away with forgoing certain pastimes. When you're faced with decisions on whether to accept an invitation or volunteer for a committee or do any other activity, that can affect your leisure time.

Looking at rewards

A leisure activity has to bring you as much joy or value as your hourly income rate. Some things you do will be priceless, but others are worthless or even less than worthless because they drain you rather than fill you up. So with leisure activities, you aren't comparing numbers — you simply decide whether a given activity is worth your hourly value. Consider the value of the activity in terms of

- ✔ Your personal enjoyment
- ✔ The service you want to do for someone
- ✔ The support to those who are less fortunate than yourself
- ✔ The desire to pay it forward
- ✔ The legacy you want to leave to others

Factoring in monetary and time costs

Another factor to consider when choosing leisure activities is the cost of your free time. Often, that time isn't so free — you undertake activities that require some recreational funds. When you have to pay to enjoy certain recreational or leisure activities, take the cost of the activity and add it to the monetary time-cost you'd have to pay for the activity. In short, would you pay the cost in your hourly value (plus any costs of the activity itself) to participate in that activity?

Say your income equates to $35 an hour. If an acquaintance you're not all that crazy about invites you to her jewelry party on a weeknight, you'd be looking at, say, a 2-hour cost of $70, plus any money you'd spend while there. Should you go? Probably not, if this acquaintance really isn't someone you prefer to spend your time with.

Or how about this scenario? A local nonprofit asks you to be on a committee that requires an average of 10 hours per month. Total value: $350 worth of your time each month. Is the value earned from your time donation worth the cost to you? How does it factor into your overall goals? Do you enjoy being on the committee and do you feel passionate about the nonprofit's mission? Do you have other more important things you have to tend to first?

The money-to-time-value consideration extends to even the seemingly most mundane of activities — for example, dining out. Going out to a 2-hour dinner with a family of four may rack up $80 or more. If you earn $80 in one hour, this may seem like a fair trade — you're paying $80 for something that would cost you $160 in time. But if your income is $20 per hour, you're essentially paying $80 for something that's worth only $40 in time. That may seem steep for a midweek convenience grab; however, if you're celebrating your child's first straight-A report card, it may feel like a fairer trade.

How about a week of vacation? Travel, hotel, and food on the road can add up fast. If you and your partner total up $3,000 in expenses for a beach resort getaway, at $80 an hour, that's not quite a week's worth (37.5) of work hours — not a bad deal, you may think. The fact of the matter is this: The decision of whether an activity is worth its cost is completely subjective. That idea is certainly empowering and freeing, as long as you make conscious choices about where you dole out your hours.

Staying open to experiences and using time wisely

The process of evaluating your leisure time is meant to help you use your time well, not to limit your experiences. If you're unsure about a certain activity but you had fun and found it worthwhile in the past, you should probably go. Also consider going if it's part of your current or future goals. If you enjoy the people but not an activity, you can suggest a change of venue and make the outing more worthwhile.

If you give up activities and find yourself mindlessly wasting the time you gained in front of the TV or online, you likely need more clarity in your goals. Or your goals may not be compelling enough. Chapter 2 can help you sort out your goals and pinpoint the activities you find most fulfilling.

Part II
Establishing a Good System

The 5th Wave   By Rich Tennant

"The funny thing is he's spent 9 hours organizing his computer desktop."

In this part . . .

Like complex mechanical operations, effective time management is based on a well-engineered system. Of course, that system requires the right tools so you can keep it in the best working order. Consider Part II your toolkit for time management.

With the valuable 80/20 rule and time-blocking techniques detailed in Chapter 4, you're well-armed to take control of your schedule, make time for what matters most, and achieve your most precious life goals and dreams. In Chapter 5, I tackle organizational skills, starting with your workspace. (After all, if your file drawers qualify for disaster relief, it's hard to get much done.) I offer a technology makeover in Chapter 6, taking dead aim at computer, database, CRM, and electronic filing systems. I also present the 411 on PDAs. And finally, for those who have to travel for work, Chapter 7 contains a veritable toolkit of tips for time management on the road.

Chapter 4

Focusing Your Efforts, Prioritizing Tasks, and Blocking Your Time

*W*hat you do with your time is more important than how much time you have. Just as recognizing and understanding your life goals helps you achieve successful time management skills, the effective use of your time goes a long, *long* way to shortening the journey to those goals. By investing your time with care and consideration, your journey toward your dreams is certain to be a smoother road. In fact, an old time-management adage says that for every minute you invest in planning, you save 10 minutes in execution. Spend an hour planning your trip, and you'll free up *10* hours — to achieve better business results, reduce stress, and add quality time at home.

The best way to achieve your goals is to prioritize them and develop an ordered plan to reach them. A universally recognized method for maximizing productivity, called the *80/20 rule,* has proven successful time and again, for more than 100 years. In this chapter, I explain the general concept and show you how to apply it — at work, at home, in your relationships, and beyond.

People who are most productive have another common trait: They treat everything in life as an appointment. These people value their time and the activities to which they commit, whether business or personal. They lend importance to their duties, commitments, and activities by writing them down and giving them a time slot, whether they're one-time occurrences or regular activities. They even make appointments with themselves.

To ensure you act on your priorities in the order that's most important to you, you need to follow a method to your scheduling — and that's what this chapter is all about. Here, I help you match your overall time investment to your goals (which you outline in Chapter 2), prioritize your tasks, and create a schedule to take you safely to your destination.

Focusing Your Energy with the 80/20 Theory of Everything

In 1906, Vilfredo Pareto noted that in his home country of Italy, a small contingency of citizens — about 20 percent — held most of the power, influence, and money — about 80 percent, he figured. That, of course, meant that the other 80 percent of the population held only 20 percent of the financial and political power in the country. Pareto found a similar distribution in other nations. In the 1940s, Joseph M. Juran applied the same 80:20 ratio to quality control issues, and since then the business world has run with idea of the "vital few and trivial many."

The basic principle that in all things, only a few are vital and many are trivial is known as the *80/20 rule* (also referred to as the *Pareto principle*), and you can apply it to almost any situation. I've heard it used in the workplace ("20 percent of my staff makes 80 percent of the revenue") and even by investors ("20 percent of my stocks generate 80 percent of my income"). You can also apply the 80/20 rule to time management, as I explain in this section.

Matching time investment to return

Generally speaking, only 20 percent of those things that you spend your time doing produces 80 percent of the results that you want to achieve. This principle applies to virtually every situation in which you have to budget your time in order to get things done — whether at work, at home, in your relationships, and so on.

The goal in using the 80/20 rule to maximize your productivity is to identify the key 20-percent activities that are most effective (producing 80 percent of the results) and make sure you prioritize those activities. Complete those vital tasks above all else and perhaps look for ways to increase the time you spend on them.

In this section, I show you how to implement the 80/20 rule.

Step 1: Sizing up your current situation

Before you can do any sort of strategizing, you need to take a good, honest look at how you use your time. For people who struggle with time management, the problem, by and large, lies in the crucial steps of assessing and planning. Start your assessment with these steps:

1. **Observe how you currently use your time.**

   Through the observation process, you can discover behaviors, habits, and skill sets that both negatively and positively affect your productivity. What do you spend most of your day doing? How far down the daily to-do list do you get each day?

2. **Assess your personal productivity trends.**

   During which segments of the day are your energy levels the highest? Which personal habits cause you to adjust your plans for the day?

3. **Take a close look at the interruptions you face on a regular basis.**

   During what segments of the day do you experience the most interruptions? What sort of interruptions do you receive most frequently, and from whom?

Later in the chapter, in "Blocking Off Your Time and Plugging in Your To-Do Items," I explain how to control and plan for your time through time-blocking your day.

Step 2: Identifying the top tasks that support your goals

Some folks tend to follow the squeeze-it-in philosophy: They cram in everything they possibly can — and then some. These people almost always end up miserable because they try to do so much that they don't take care of their basic needs and end up strung out in every possible way. The quality of what they do, as well as the amount of what they do, suffers as a result of their ever-increasing exhaustion.

To work efficiently, you need to identify your 80 percent — the results you want to achieve. Break out your list of goals (which I help you think through and record in Chapter 2). Take a good look at your top 12 goals and identify the tasks you need to do that align with those goals. If your number-one goal is to provide your kids with an Ivy League education, for example, then your priorities are less likely to center around taking twice-yearly vacations to the Caribbean and more likely to revolve around investing wisely and encouraging your offspring to do well in school (can you say "full-ride scholarship?").

After you identify what you need to do — your vital few — spend a bit more time in self-reflection to double-check that you've correctly identified your goals and essential tasks. One of the biggest wastes of time for people is changing direction, priorities, objectives, and goals. Successful people and successful time managers take the direct route from point A to point B.

Here's what to ask yourself about these key tasks:

✔ How much time do you devote to those activities? Twenty percent? Less? More?

✔ What are you doing with the remainder of your time?

✔ How much return are you getting for the investment on the remainder?

Step 3: Prioritizing your daily objectives

After you identify the tasks and activities that you need to accomplish to achieve your goals, assign a value to those goals so you can decide how to order your daily task list.

Take the send-your-kids-to-an-Ivy-League school scenario that I bring up in the preceding section: Even though another of your priorities is to be home for your kids, you — as a nonworking parent who values the type of education you can provide for your 3-going-on-18-year-old more than the short-term joy of being a stay-at-home parent — may decide to return to the workforce as you see tuitions skyrocketing. You can make this decision because you have a clear idea about how you rank your priorities. This clarity may help direct you to a job with hours compatible with your kid's schedule.

To personalize how you prioritize your goals at work, follow these steps:

1. **Look at your long-term career goals.**

   Do you want to advance to a particular career level? Do you want to achieve a particular income? Or is your goal to fine-tune your skill set before figuring out where you want to go next?

2. **Review your company's priorities.**

   Having a solid understanding of the company's priorities, goals, objectives, and strategic thrusts guides your own prioritization so you can get the edge on the company's competition. To get a global perspective, review your company's mission statement, review its published corporate values and goals, and see how they pertain to your position. Ask your direct supervisor for further elaboration on these statements and on his or her priorities so you can make sure yours align yours accordingly.

The vital 20 percent: Figuring out where to focus your energy at work

Used effectively, the 80/20 rule can increase your on-the-job performance. From boardroom to lunchroom, executive suite to mailroom, this time-management principle can help you accomplish the most important tasks in less time and help you advance in your career.

The 20-percent investment in the 80 percent of results remains relatively constant. In more than a decade of working with business leaders to improve performance, I've witnessed it firsthand: What's truly important for success changes very little within a given profession. The two global objectives of any successful business are profit and customer retention. What differs among professions is how those global objectives translate to match individual objectives.

For example, here's how the 80/20 rule factors into some major job categories:

- **Ownership/executive leadership:** As an executive or owner, your most important role is to establish the vision, goals, and benchmarks for the business. What are the core values and core purpose for the business? What are the goals for the year and then next quarter? What are the most pressing problems that need to be solved? What are the strengths, weaknesses, opportunities, and threats the company or marketplace is experiencing? You then have to convey those answers consistently in clear terms for your lieutenants to follow and hold the lieutenants accountable to the standards.

- **Sales:** For sales professionals, lead generation leads to 80 percent of your return. Without new leads and new prospects to sell to, your customer and prospect base remains fixed to your current clients. So in sales, your most important tasks are prospecting and following up on leads; you should put a priority on securing and conducting sales appointments and building personal relationships.

  Don't forget your existing client base as well. They usually follow the same 80/20 rule, where 20 percent of them contribute 80 percent of the revenue. Spend your time with this group to increase sales and referrals.

- **Management:** For those in leadership positions, your vital 20 percent is the coaching and development of people. You use coaching strategies to encourage and empower your employees, and you monitor your staff's adherence to the company's strategic plans. In addition, you help your employees acquire the knowledge, skills, attitude, and actions to advance their careers.

✔ **Task- or service-based roles:** This group of people varies the most because it's the broadest. To identify your vital tasks, take a look at your company's objectives, your department's objectives, and your own objectives to get a well-rounded picture of how your role fits into the bigger picture. Then decide which of your job responsibilities increase sales or improve customer retentions.

After that, consider the value of the product or service you offer, and weigh the importance of quality versus speed or quantity — your ultimate goal is to serve your customers better so you retain and grow your relationships with them. (If you're not sure how much weight each element deserves, talk to your supervisor about where you should focus your efforts.)

- If quality takes higher priority, ask yourself how you can deliver a better product or service in the amount of time you're given.

- If delivery speed or quantity is more important, ask yourself how you can deliver that product more efficiently while maintaining quality.

✔ **Administration:** If you're in an administrative role, your goal is to enhance the company's performance, whether you're supporting front-line sales staff or assisting the corporate leadership in steering the business toward profit. If you're in sales support, how can you help free up the salespeople to do more selling? Can you fill out reports for the salespeople? Research new market opportunities and get contact information? Can you repeat that help for the sales manager in reports and better tracking of the salespeople's numbers so the manager can do more coaching and shadowing of the salespeople?

If you're working in customer service, is there a recurring customer service problem that needs to be solved? Can you identify it? Can you find at least two solutions to the problem and bring them to your boss for review? You can make yourself an indispensible asset to the company with these actions and save time for yourself and your superiors as well.

Personal essentials: Channeling efforts in your personal life

The 80/20 rule isn't strictly business, so don't lose sight of its influence on your personal life. In fact, the 80/20 rule can have the greatest impact at home. For most, personal and family life is the realm that matters most. But with all the demands of work and the outside world, it often takes the back seat. By categorizing and ordering your personal priorities, you can customize your approach to the people and priorities in your home life and make the most of your time spent with family, hobbies, leisure, and friends.

When factoring in your personal priorities, think of a variety of areas, such as time with loved ones, a worthy cause, your faith, education, and future plans. In this section, I cover the two areas of prioritization that affect most people (for other situations, follow the general process I outline earlier in "Matching time investment to return").

Investing wisely in your personal relationships

One of the great things about the 80/20 rule is that it doesn't apply only to task-oriented items — it's also about the quality of your time and the energy you put into what you choose to do with it. If you have a significant other, for example, consider how 20 percent of all the time you spend with him or her shapes 80 percent of your relationship with that person.

ANECDOTE

Setting up family traditions

My wife, Joan, and I adhere to two traditions that don't take much time but reap huge dividends in the closeness we feel with one another and the partnership in responsibilities that we share. The first is that Friday each week is date night. We have a standing babysitter, and even with my travel schedule, we rarely miss our Friday-night date. In addition, we go away together — without kids — once per quarter. We usually take a two- to three-night trip so we can make up the connection time that often gets crowded out by parenting two active children.

My children and I also have a couple of long-standing traditions to foster nurturing relationships with each other. With my son, Wesley, I have Boy's Breakfast Out at least two Friday mornings per month. We spend about 90 minutes talking and laughing, and then I take him to school. He looks forward to it, and so do I. Annabelle, at 2½, loves to have tea parties, so I set aside time to sit among her stuffed animals and toys while she serves me tea in doll-sized cups. We don't spend as long (fortunately —

sitting in a low stool for longer than 45 minutes is murder on my back!) because her attention span is limited at her age. But she, too, eagerly anticipates tea time with Daddy.

Saturday morning means breakfast out with the whole family. It helps us all reconnect and strengthen our communication for the rest of the week. Sunday night is game night: We turn off the television and play board games as a family.

Your 20-percent time traditions may differ from ours, depending on the age, interests, and unique traits of your loved ones at home. The important thing is to find out what brings the biggest return, greatest connection, and best memories. Of course, I have to confess that applying the 80/20 rule in relationships is much easier to write about than to execute. Although you may understand how the 80/20 rule applies to your home relationships, putting it into practice remains a challenge. Work on this with each passing day.

Outside of work, personal relationships are number one, so always consider them first, before you even start thinking about chores. Evaluate your connection with each of the important people in your life, both family and friends. In this way, you can customize your approach to the people and priorities in your home life instead of lumping everything into the generalized category of "home" and perhaps not giving any individual or activity its due attention. When dealing with people, ask yourself these questions to help you identify the 80/20 balance:

  ✔ How can you invest your time with this person to create a better relationship?

  ✔ What's most important to this loved one, and how can you serve and support these needs?

Many other questions can help get you to the root — or the 20 percent — of actions that produce a bumper crop of love, security, appreciation, and experience that build meaningful relationships at home. For example, if you're raising children, you may ask yourself these questions as well:

  ✔ How can you invest your time to nurture this child's developing interests?

  ✔ How can you show that you value this child in a way that he or she understands?

  ✔ What do you need to do each week to teach this child an important life skill?

  ✔ What shared activities allow you to serve as a positive example?

  ✔ What can you do to create a positive family memory?

Balancing crucial household tasks with at-home hobbies

Face it: Your days are filled with tasks that really don't bring much return on investment. Whether it's doing the laundry or filling out paperwork, there are loads of those necessary-but-not-monumental duties that you'll never be able to eliminate. And in your personal life, these activities may include housework, home maintenance, or walking the dog.

However, you can apply the 80/20 rule to help balance how you invest your time in chores so it aligns with your hobbies. Which activities bring you the biggest return? For example, do you spend every summer evening and weekend on your back patio, entertaining or simply admiring your backyard and flower garden? Then for you, trimming, mowing, planting, and weeding may be a wise way to invest that vital 20 percent of your time. If, however, you get more enjoyment from traveling to new places, you may allocate that time to budgeting for and planning exciting vacations.

Cooking, cleaning, shopping, laundry, yard work, bill paying, and other tasks are essential, but that doesn't mean that *you* have to do them — sometimes, the added cost of hiring help is worth the time it frees in your schedule. If you gain no joy or fulfillment whatsoever in cleaning or household maintenance, or feel you simply don't have the time or energy to do all this without sacrificing your most important priorities, hire out those responsibilities. Sure, there's a cost involved, but you buy back time to spend on the activities that mean the most to you. So send out the laundry if it frees you up to explore new menus in the kitchen, or bring in a personal chef if you'd rather be out in the garden planting tomatoes.

If you can hire someone who makes far less money than you do to do something you don't enjoy, hire out the task immediately. If you can work a few more hours and increase your pay or set yourself up for promotion sooner, then work the extra hours and hire the help. In the end, you'll be doing something you enjoy rather than something you despise.

Yard maintenance will never be on my vital 20-percent time investment list. In my adolescent years, I mowed, clipped, trimmed, and hedged a lifetime's worth of yards to earn money. I don't own a lawnmower and never will. And frankly, a prizewinning lawn is not tops on my list of life satisfactions. However, I do enjoy presenting my family and friends with creative meals, so I put my time into grocery shopping and cooking. It gives me a chance to help lighten the load for Joan, and it offers another 20-percent time tradition with the kids. They love to get creative in the kitchen — especially baking cookies — so we do it together.

The 80/20 rule doesn't stop there — you can also apply it to the quality of those tasks or hobbies and the results they have on your well-being. If you're a gardener, for example, think about the 20 percent of your efforts that bring forth the 80 percent of your pleasure and satisfaction from gardening. For example, maybe you don't need to sculpt a perfectly arranged flower garden to reap the personal benefits — the very act of digging your hands into the earth may give you the greatest sense of joy. So focus on the act of planting more than on the planning and shopping.

Don't forget to include those activities that support and improve your physical, mental, and emotional health. Those activities that keep you sane, happy, and fit may seem insignificant when taken one at a time. But if they start getting squeezed out of the schedule, you just may start to see that sanity, happiness, and health start slipping. Be sure to account for all those little pleasures that add texture to your life — reading, study, yoga, your weekly facial.

Getting Down to Specifics: Daily Prioritization

After you identify the vital few tasks you need to accomplish to meet your top 12 goals, break them down a bit further into daily to-do items. Then prioritize them to make sure you accomplish the most important tasks first, identifying which ones you must do on a given day. In that way, you progressively work through all the minor tasks that lead to the greater steps that, in time, lead you to achieving your goals. Here's how:

1. **Start with a master list.**

   Write down everything you need to accomplish today. Don't try ranking the items at this point. You merely want to brain dump all the to-do actions you can think of. You may end up with 20, 30, even 50 items on your list: tasks as mundane as checking e-mail and as critical as presenting a new product marketing plan to the executive board. Or if you want to fill work on your personal to-do list, the items may range from buying cat food to filing taxes before midnight.

   Remember to account for routine duties that don't have a direct effect on your company's mission or bottom line: turning in business expense reports, typing up and distributing meeting minutes, taking sales calls from prospective printing vendors. Neglecting to schedule the humdrum to-do items creates a destructive domino dynamic that can topple your well-intentioned time-block schedule.

2. **Determine the A-list.**

   Focusing on consequences creates an urgency factor so you can better use your time. Ask yourself, "What, if not done today, will lead to a significant consequence?" Designate these as *A activities*. If you have a scheduled presentation today, then that task definitely hits the A-list. Same goes for filing your tax return if the date is April 15. Buying cat food probably doesn't make this list — unless you're totally out or have a particularly vindictive cat.

3. **Categorize the rest of the tasks.**

   Now move on to B-level tasks, activities that may have a mildly negative consequence if not completed today. C tasks have no penalty if not completed today, followed by D tasks: D is for *delegate*. These are actions that someone else can take on. Finally, E items are tasks that could be eliminated, so don't even bother writing an E next to them — just mark them out completely.

4. Rank the tasks within each category.

Say you've categorized your list into six A items, four B items, three C items, and two D items. Your six A tasks obviously move to the top of the list, but now you have to rank these six items in order: A-1, A-2, A-3, and so forth.

If you have trouble ordering several top priorities, start with just two: Weigh them against each other — if you could complete only one task today, which of the two is most critical? Which of the two best serves your 80/20 rule? Then take the winner of that contest and compare it to the next A item, and so on. Then do the same for the B and C items.

As for the D actions? Delegate them to someone else! Everyone likes to think they're indispensable, but for most people, the majority of their duties could be handled by someone else. That's where the *85/10/5 rule* — first cousin to the 80/20 rule — comes into play: You tend to invest 85 percent of your time doing tasks that anyone else could do, and 10 percent of your time is devoted to actions that some people could handle. Just 5 percent of your energy goes to work that only you can accomplish. But whether at home or at work, this doesn't mean you can kick back and leave 95 percent of your responsibilities to someone else. It simply helps you home in on the critical 5 percent, allocate your remaining time to other activities that bring you the greatest satisfaction, and recognize those tasks that are easiest to delegate.

Now you're ready to tackle your to-do list, knowing that the most important tasks will be addressed first (see the nearby sidebar, "Rocking out: Putting the A-list tasks in place," for the importance of prioritizing). Don't expect to complete as large a number of cross-offs as you may be used to. Because you're now focused on more important items — which likely take more time — you may not get as many tasks completed. In my view, however, the measure of a great day is whether you wrap up all the A-list items. If you follow this system and consistently complete the As, I can assure you success. Why? Because the B and C items quickly work their way to As — and you always get the most important things done.

Don't assume that you just move the Bs and Cs up the next day. You need to complete the whole process each day. Some of the Bs will move up, but others will stay in the B category. Some of the Cs — due to outside pressure, your boss, or changed deadlines — may leapfrog the Bs and become the highest priority As.

Rocking out: Putting the A-list tasks in place

Steven Covey and A. Roger Merrill illustrated the importance of prioritizing tasks in their book *First Things First* (Simon & Schuster) with a simple metaphor. In short, a guest lecturer was speaking to a group of students when he pulled out a 1-gallon, wide-mouthed Mason jar, set it on a table in front of him, and began filling it with about a dozen fist-sized rocks. When the jar was filled to the top and no more rocks would fit inside, he asked the class whether the jar was full, to which they unanimously replied, "Yes."

He then reached under the table and pulled out a bucket of gravel, dumping some of it into the jar and shaking the jar, causing pieces of gravel to work themselves down into the spaces between the big rocks. He asked the group once more whether the jar was full, to which one suspicious student responded, "Probably not."

Under the table he reached again, this time withdrawing a bucket of sand. He started dumping in the sand, which sank into all the spaces left between the rocks and the gravel. Once more, he asked the question "Is the jar full?" "No!" the class shouted. "Good!" he said, grabbing a pitcher of water and pouring it in until the jar was filled to the brim.

He looked up at the class and asked, "What is the point of this illustration?" One eager beaver raised his hand and said, "The point is no matter how full your schedule is, if you try really hard, you can always fit some more things into it!"

"No," the speaker replied. "The truth this illustration teaches us is if you don't put the big rocks in first, you'll never get them in at all."

Blocking Off Your Time and Plugging in Your To-Do Items

After you identify and order your priorities (see the preceding sections), you place them into time slots on your weekly calendar, broken into 15-minute segments — this process is commonly called *time-blocking*. I've discovered no better system for managing time on a daily, weekly, monthly, yearly, and life-long basis. I've seen miracle-level transformations in the lives of my clients — successes measured in income, health, relationships, personal growth, spiritual transformation, and wisdom.

Like exercise, time-blocking can be tricky because it requires a lot of thought and adjustment, both in the initial stage where you're doing it for the first time and for a while thereafter, when you're developing the skill. Everybody knows what day two after the beginning of a new fitness program feels like: Stiff joints and sore muscles have you moving like the Tin Man after a rainstorm. At first you may feel like you'll never achieve the goals you've set, but sticking to the daily program eventually brings the results you want. Figuring out how to best manage your time depends on two things:

✓ **Consistent, diligent practice:** If you want to build those time-blocking muscles, not only do you have to work them regularly, but you also need to increase the weight, stress, and pressure as you progress. Understanding the key to managing your minutes, hours, days, weeks, and so on takes repetition.

I was first exposed to time-blocking at a business seminar more than 20 years ago, and for the past 10 years, I've coached hundreds of thousands of people. In all this time, I've yet to meet anyone — including myself — who doesn't need some ongoing reinforcement, repetition, and refresher course of the time-blocking principles I share with you here.

Don't panic when you find yourself a little stressed or sore from all your time-blocking exercises. It's simply a sign that your efforts to build up those skills are working.

✓ **A span of time to improve:** Achieving a level of time-blocking mastery does take time — a minimum of 18 months and as much as 24 months. Why so long? Because you're developing a complex skill. A typical day has you switching from refereeing an argument between your kids to making an important presentation to the corporate executives; from putting together your department's annual budget to paying for your groceries in the checkout line. That's a lot to orchestrate, and even Handel didn't write his *Messiah* overnight. If you accept that time-blocking skills require time to develop, you're more likely to remain motivated. Your objective is to make measureable progress in reasonable time.

Implementing time-blocking to help organize your schedule takes a bit of time, but you reap huge dividends on that initial investment. This section walks you through a general outline of the process I follow.

Step 1: Dividing your day

To start, you need a daily calendar divided into 15-minute increments. Why such small bites of time? Because even 15 minutes can represent a good chunk of productive activity. Losing just two or three of these small blocks each day can diminish your ability to meet your goals, from finishing that project at work to writing your bestselling (you hope) memoir.

On that blank schedule, begin by dividing your day; draw a clear line between personal time and work time. When you take this step, you're creating work-life balance from the start. Don't take it for granted that Saturday and Sunday are time off just because you work a Monday-through-Friday work week. Block it into your schedule, or work activities may creep into your precious downtime. The more you take action on paper, the more concrete the time-block schedule becomes.

Apprehensive about drawing a line between work and personal time because you're wary of having to tell a business associate you can't attend a business function that extends into personal time? Not to worry. You don't have to tell a client that your Tuesday-morning workout is more important than a breakfast meeting with her — simply say you're already booked at that time. That's all the explanation you owe, and my experience shows that professional colleagues who want to do business with you respect your boundaries.

Step 2: Scheduling your personal activities

Blocking out personal activities first gives weight to these activities and ensures that they won't be overtaken by obligations that have lesser importance in the long run. Personal obligations are almost always the first thing most people trade for work; because of that, I recommend that you hold fast and tight to the personal area so it doesn't get away from you. Another advantage? You help establish a reasonable end to your workday. If you're scheduled to meet at a friend's for Texas Hold 'Em on Thursday nights, you're more motivated to wrap up your project in enough time to cut the deck.

Scheduling personal activities is twofold:

1. **Schedule routine activities you participate in.**

   Do you have dinner together as a family every night? A weekly date night with your significant other? Do you want to establish family traditions? Don't just assume these activities will happen — give them the weight they deserve and block out the time for each one. Don't forget to include your extracurricular activities here: All those PTA groups, fundraising committees, nonprofit boards, and other volunteer commitments get plugged in as well.

2. **Schedule personal priorities that aren't routine.**

   Put those personal agenda items first before filling in your day with tasks and activities that don't support those priorities.

Step 3: Factoring in your work activities

Begin with the activities that are a regular part of your job and then factor in the priorities that aren't routine. Whether you're a company CEO, a department manager, a sales associate, an administrative assistant, or an entry-level trainee, you're responsible for performing key tasks and activities each day and week. They may include daily or weekly meetings. Or maybe your responsibility is scheduling meetings for others. You likely have to prepare for these appointments. Perhaps you have to write and turn in reports or sales figures on an ongoing basis. You may have to call someone for information routinely. If you report to work daily and always spend the first hour of your day returning phone calls, time-block it into your schedule.

Step 4: Accounting for weekly self-evaluation and planning time

Your goals — whether a one-year business plan or long-range retirement vision — warrant routine checkups. Consider them as rest stops on your journey: Are you still on the right road? Is a detour ahead? Have you discovered a more direct route?

Use weekly strategic planning sessions — ideally for Friday afternoon or the end of the work week — to review your progress toward those near-future business projects as well as your larger career aspirations or personal goals. This is an opportunity to review the previous week and jump-start the upcoming week. I recommend spending 15 to 30 minutes daily and then taking a 90-to-120-minute session on self-evaluation and planning at the end of the week.

Time-blocking: Making small investments in big success

Time-blocking doesn't require a huge commitment to produce results. A few years ago, one of my clients, a top sales performer in her region, exploded her sales by more than 125 percent in one year! I knew that time-blocking had played an important role in her success. I asked her what percentage of the time she had managed to adhere to her time-blocking schedule. She confessed that she'd stuck to the schedule only 35 percent of the time. The undeniable truth is that *a little goes a long way.* As you continue to use your time-blocking skills, that percentage increases, and your productivity grows accordingly.

I also have a client named Sam, a salesperson, who increased his contacts by ten per day after adopting time-blocking. These ten additional contacts led to an increase of five leads per week. He averages one appointment for every 2.5 leads and has a 50-percent close ratio on appointments. So from ten contacts per day, he gains one extra sale a week. At an average $5,000 commission per sale, he has the potential to increase his income by $250,000 a year. How's that for results?

This strategic planning time is probably your most valuable time investment each week. It gives you a tremendous wrap-up for the week and a good start to next week, and it reinforces your vision for your long-term success. It also enables you to go home and spend time with your family in the right frame of mind.

Years ago, I booked a weekly appointment with myself to analyze the numbers, sales ratios, and business activities in progress. I found the results of my performance as well as that of my staff improved dramatically. I'd wasted weeks and months as I agonized whether to include this activity into my schedule. My advice? Book an evaluation and planning session first and ask questions later.

Step 5: Building in flex time

Plug segments of time into your schedule every few hours to help you to minimize the fallout from unplanned interruptions or problems. About 15 or 30 minutes is enough time to work in at strategic intervals throughout your day. Knowing that you have this free block of time can help you adhere to your schedule rather than get off track.

As you begin to build your time-blocking skills, insert 30-minute flex periods into your schedule for every two hours of time-blocked activity. This may seem like a lot of flex time, but if it allows you to maintain the rest of your time-block schedule and maintain or increase your productivity, it's worth the investment. My experience is that the best time for flex time is after you've put in a couple of hours of your most important work — whether sales calls, report-preparation, or meeting a deadline.

Don't schedule flex time right before you go into an important activity time: You're more likely to get distracted and fail to get started with your critical business. Schedule it after the work — then you can use it, if necessary, to resolve any unforeseen problems.

Assessing Your Progress and Adjusting Your Plan as Needed

Becoming comfortable with time-blocking takes time, and achieving a glitch-free schedule that you can work with for a stretch may take a half-dozen revisions. Even then, routinely evaluate your time-blocking efforts and adjust them periodically to make sure you're getting the desired results. It's not a huge time investment — you can check yourself with a few minutes a day or use 15 to 30 minutes of your weekly time to review your results. Ask yourself the following:

- ✔ What took you off track this week?
- ✔ What interruptions really affected your success with your time?
- ✔ Is someone sabotaging your time-block?
- ✔ What shifts would help your efficiency?

In this section, I discuss this review in detail.

Surveying your results

One way to determine your effectiveness at time-blocking is to check results. In as little as two weeks from when you launch your time-blocking schedule, you can probably see where you need minor adjustments. The best way to keep tabs on results is to track them on an ongoing basis. I suggest both a weekly review that focuses on the past week and a periodic review of where you stand in relation to your overall goals.

The weekly review is a time for you to replay the tape of the week, looking at the highs and lows. I guarantee you'll have days where you want to pull your hair out because you face so many problems and distractions. You'll also have days that are smooth as silk. What were the differences in those days besides the outcome?

As for the periodic review, review your job description, key responsibilities, and the ways in which your performance and success are measured. Then ask yourself these questions:

- ✔ Are you moving closer toward achieving your goals?
- ✔ Can you see measurable progress in reasonable time?
- ✔ Are you monitoring your performance well enough to see improvement?
- ✔ What changes do you need to adopt now to increase your speed toward reaching the goal and reduce the overall amount of time you invest?

Your success in meeting your objectives tells you whether the time-blocking is working for you.

Looking at measurable goals

If you can measure your goals in terms of numbers (dollars or sales, for example), then checking your results is a cinch. As a salesperson, for example, you may follow your sales numbers or commissions results over several months in order to get a good understanding of the effectiveness of your time-blocking efforts. Or say you're a magazine editor who's evaluated on consistently meeting weekly publication deadlines; if your goal is to publish three articles per month in national magazines, you can assume that your time-blocking efforts require some tweaking if your review reveals that you're getting only one story in print.

Evaluating qualitative goals

If your goals aren't easily measured in terms of dollars or sales, you may need to get creative in developing your own tally for results. Family and personal goals are difficult to measure, but you can likely gain a good sense of how your efforts are tracking by just paying attention to your daily life and how you feel about it, rating your day on a 1-to-10 scale. Are your kids comfortable in talking and spending time with you? Do they look forward to being with you? Are you on friendly terms with the people in your community activities? Do you and your spouse laugh together more often than you argue?

You can also turn to other measuring sticks, which are especially useful in the workplace:

- What went well this week? What could you have done better?
- Did you accomplish what you really needed to do? How many high-priority items did you carry over to the next day or week? (See the earlier section titled "Getting Down to Specifics: Daily Prioritization" for more on prioritizing.)
- How would you rate your week on a 1-to-10 scale, with 1 being utterly overwhelmed and dissatisfied, and 10 being completely in control of and happy with how you spend your time?
- How do you feel you performed at work? How does your supervisor feel you're performing?
- Did you meet your goals at home?
- Has what you've accomplished this week positioned you better to achieve your long-range goals?
- What are the key improvement areas for you next week?
- What adjustments to your long-range plans do you need to make?
- What's diverting you from your schedule?
- Were you unrealistic in your time estimates for tasks?
- What segment of the day or activity is tipping your schedule off track?

As you're reviewing your results, be careful to do so with an open, observant mind, not a judgmental one. Give yourself a couple of weeks before you resolve to change your schedule. Doing so helps you get through a long enough period of time to account for anomalies.

Tweaking your system

Looking back at your personal behaviors and skills and the interruptions you routinely face, identify two or three steps you need to take in order to increase your success. Here are a couple of tips to point you in the right direction:

- ✔ **If you're not completing the most important tasks or working toward the most important efforts each day:** Weed out some of the trivial tasks to make room for the most important ones. (I help you do that in the "Making a Daily To-Do List and Ordering Your Priorities" section, earlier in this chapter.)

- ✔ **If your most productive times of day are filled with trivial tasks:** Shift the tasks and the time slots you fit them in. (Your trouble is time-blocking, which I help you with in the earlier "Scheduling Your Time" section.)

After you figure out what you need to change, you can adjust your schedule accordingly. Unfortunately, I can't give you a one-size-fits-all set of answers to help you figure out what to change — those decisions depend on your job requirements, your personal strengths and weaknesses, your personal goals and desires, and the amount of control you actually have over those aspects you'd like to improve. I can, however, help steer you in the right direction.

Remember the old adage "Grant me the serenity to accept the things I cannot change, courage to change the things I can, and the wisdom to know the difference"? You can apply it to the way you manage your time. If you can balance the results you expect to achieve (more productivity, greater efficiency, reduction in time worked, and greater sales) with the results you need to achieve, then you'll be successful.

Following are some examples of quick evaluation questions that can help you make the most effective, results-oriented changes to your schedule:

- ✔ **What's the standard?** Do you have a sales quota that needs to be met? Are you getting your boss's priorities done? Going home, how are you feeling about your progress?

- ✔ **How accurate does the time-block schedule need to be?** In time-blocking, a little goes a long way. The real question is how well you did this week with the most important activities — the vital 20 percent of the 80/20 rule.

✔ **How much have you improved?** How have you improved since you started working your time-block? How large is the improvement? Would you be happy if you improved each week for a year at this level?

✔ **With additional revision, how much additional productivity would you gain?** Before revising a time-block schedule, look at the anticipated return on investment. Is this change going to bring significant benefit in productivity, efficiency, or personal satisfaction?

✔ **How good is good enough?** Where is the point where you'll achieve diminishing returns on your effort? At some point, further refining your schedule can lead to reduced results. Where do you think that'll happen?

Perfectionism is a scourge of people who are trying to achieve more with their time. The obsession with revising, redoing, and readjusting one's time-block schedule every few days — or even hours — leads to frustration. In your time-blocking, clearly define the line of success so you can achieve your goals without going overboard.

Chapter 5

Setting Up and Maintaining a Productive Workspace

1 wish you could've heard my staff and my wife when I started writing this chapter. They howled. Okay, I admit it: What I share here is easier to write about than to *do*. Nonetheless, even if you're not 100-percent successful with every one of the techniques, tools, and strategies in this chapter (I'm speaking from experience here, folks), adopting even some of them can increase your productivity and vastly improve your overall time management.

One study I saw indicated that most people waste an hour per day trying to find papers lost on their desks (at least, that's where they think the papers are lost). That's not so bad, you say. But an hour per day adds up to 250 work hours per year, or more than 31 wasted days per worker annually.

Multiply that by the number of executives, professionals, and sales and administrative employees in this country, and you're talking a significant loss of time. (And that doesn't include hours spent at home trying to find misplaced eyeglasses, scissors, library books, keys, needle-nose pliers, cellphones, gym shorts, earrings, pacifiers, and so on.) Think how productive you'd be if you spent all that time, well, being productive!

If your work area is a parking lot for everything from C-level "someday" tasks to hotter-than-hot, this-project-can-make-my-career assignments, you're the Titanic heading for an iceberg. Ask yourself the following:

✔ Do you know all the tasks you have to get done, complete with time lines?

✔ Do you have all the materials, documents, and tools you need right now to take each project to completion without putting out an all-points bulletin?

✔ In short, do you have everything you need to do an exceptional job in record time?

If you can answer all these questions with truthful and unequivocal yeses, you can skip this chapter. Everyone else, read on.

Streamlining Your Workspace

"Don't touch my desk! I know exactly where everything is." I've heard that line endlessly, and I've used it myself. If you're like me, however, most of the time, as you stare at the forest of papers on your desk, you *are* clueless. You may have known where that phone number was yesterday, a few weeks ago, a month ago — or even a few minutes ago — but more stacks have since been added to the mix.

It's not enough to know which chart, report, or snippet of paper is on which pile, whether it's on the left or right side of your desk, or whether it's stashed in the catch-all drawer of your filing cabinet. This is your career you're talking about. Get a handle on it!

Make way! Clearing off your desk

Repeat after me: My desk is not a parking lot. My desk is not a parking lot. My desk is not a parking lot. If you want to get your desk under control, remember: Less is more. The more pictures, notes, boxes, tools (staplers, paper-clip holders, books), and so on that occupy your desk, the greater your odds of being distracted and the more cluttered your desk feels.

You also have less room to spread out if you're consulting multiple sources of information, using a laptop in addition to your desktop computer, or studying oversized charts or graphs. What's more, a topsy-turvy desk translates into greater stress and the misleading feeling that you have all the time in the world to complete your projects.

Remove everything that isn't absolutely necessary from your desk. Be brutal. Here are some ideas to get you started:

✔ Move family photos to your credenza or bookcase, where you can still see them throughout the day (and remember why you're working so hard) without their distracting you.

✔ If you have other pictures — perhaps of you with mentors or celebrities — hang them on the wall.

✔ Store extra tools, supplies, and items you use weekly in desk drawers and filing areas.

✔ Don't allow items you rarely use or haven't looked at since slipping them into a pile to take up desk space. Put those items away in a filing cabinet, storage box, closet, or other less-accessible area.

As for your workspace, forget the Boy Scout be-prepared motto. It's a recipe for desktop disaster, especially if you're one who likes to prepare for flood, earthquake, alien invasion, and every other conceivable catastrophe. The cleaner and clearer your desk, the better you can use your time.

Assembling essential organizational tools

Having the right tools for the job is really the start of great organization. If you haven't already done so, get all piles off your desk, even if you have to put them temporarily on the floor. Then gather these tools:

✔ **A desk organizer:** You need some way to keep the standard office fare — staplers, paper clips, pens, calculators — handy at your fingertips.

✔ **Inboxes and outboxes:** You need some type of organizational flow to your work that's based on an in-and-out system. Too often, interruptions happen when someone drops off something you don't need right now or stops by to pick something up. Setting up inboxes and outboxes outside the door of your office or cubicle keeps your desk clear and reduces chitchat.

✔ **A quality filing cabinet with space for growth:** You may be surprised at how much filing space you need if you're a piler-turned-filer. I prefer lateral filing cabinets: They're more costly but can save a lot of time because you can see all the files at once. (Ah! There's that yellow folder for my volunteer project — and the blue one for my customer service committee.) If you prefer, use stacking, modular filing systems, such as those in many doctors' and dentists' offices.

✔ **Colored file folders:** Ban bland manila! I suggest using the rainbow of colored folders available today. Consider a color-coded filing system, such as a stoplight approach with green for new business and other money-generating items, red for problem issues or customers, and so on. I also find that colors jog my memory when it comes time to find the files.

✔ **File folder labels:** Labeling files is paramount to organization, efficiency, and time savings, even if you use colored folders. Labels can also be color-coded to further differentiate one file from another.

For more tools and tips you can use to organize your desk, check out *Organizing For Dummies,* by Eileen Roth and Elizabeth Miles (Wiley).

Setting up a timely filing system

Before you start going through papers, think about how you're most likely to search for the documents you need. You can choose from numerous file-labeling strategies, but here are some possible categories:

- ✔ Customers (alphabetically)
- ✔ Past clients you no longer serve
- ✔ Due dates and project timing
- ✔ Pending projects
- ✔ On-hold projects
- ✔ To-dos, miscellaneous, or a similar catch-all type of label

 You can choose to file by subject, client name, importance, or a number of other ways, but if time is of the essence, setting up a tickler filing system may be ideal. *Tickler* or *reminder files* have been around for ages. They make sure you remember to deal with delayed or deferred items at the correct times. Here's how they work:

1. **Establish two complementary tickler files, one labeled *monthly* and the other labeled *daily*.**

   Your monthly tickler can be as simple as a 12-slot expandable folder with the months written on each slot. Your daily tickler can be a 31-slot accordion file folder or even 31 hanging file folders, each labeled with dates 1 through 31.

2. **As you receive new documents, place them in the appropriate slots of your monthly file.**

   If a document you receive in December requires no action until March, place the document in the March slot of your monthly tickler file.

3. **When you enter a new month, move documents from that month's slot into the daily folders.**

   When March rolls around, pull all the papers from your March tickler and place them in the appropriate days of the month in your daily tickler file.

This system is tremendous for both home and office. I use it to pay bills: I write our bills twice monthly and place them in my daily tickler file so I remember when they're due and when to mail them (if a bill is due on July 25, for example, I write the check, put it in the envelope, add a stamp, and place the envelope in the July 15 slot to be sure I mail the bill well ahead of its due date). Best of all, I've invested minimum time.

Note: For many businesspeople, powerful software programs called *customer relation management* (CRMs) have replaced tickler files. Turn to Chapter 6 to find out more on CRM software and organizing computer files.

Going paperless

One way to clear your desk is to reduce the amount of paper you handle altogether by increasing your use of electronic files. In today's technology world, you can scan most documents and create a digital version; many computers then allow you to apply optical character recognition (OCR), which changes the scanned image into text that you can edit and search through. You can also have your faxed documents turned into digital documents that can be shared by all in your department and e-mailed to others.

Electronic versions are especially useful when you need to retrieve files. You can organize the digital or electronic files in multiple places at one time. For instance, you can keep a prospect's information in a *prospect file* as well as in a file under the prospect's name — it's like being two places at the same time. You can also search for files or have your computer do the search while you're working on something else — the only true multitasking one can do!

If your filing skills are truly abysmal, have someone who's a natural filer help you develop your filing system. I'm far more effective when I hand papers, reports, and memos off to an assistant. Whether a document is paper or electronic, I find I can also retrieve information more efficiently when someone else has filed it (because that person can help me find it!). Of course, only you can file some items (confidential personnel reports, salaries, information you want to keep personal, and the like). But as for the rest, use your team's strengths and gifts so you can make better use of yours.

Tackling piles systematically

To de-clutter yourself, you need to remember this simple rule: Put the important things where you can remember where they are and where you can get to them quickly. Here's how the de-cluttering process breaks down:

1. **Figure out what you can get rid of.**

   Here are a few simple questions to ask yourself:

   - Do you really need this? *Really?*

   - Is there value in saving this item? (If the answer isn't a definitive yes, toss it.)

   - What happens if you don't keep this?

   - What's the worst that could happen if you throw this away?

Never throw away important documents, such as tax returns and business receipts. The IRS requires you to retain tax records and all supporting material for seven years. Before you toss, think carefully about whether an item has future value and whether copies are filed elsewhere so you can access them if you need to.

2. **Condense the offending material into smaller piles by selecting items to go into a single master important pile.**

   Many piles are simply files in disguise: documents that haven't been put away where they belong. By collecting the most important items into a single pile, you get an idea of how much time you need to dissolve this pile into nothing.

   At first, you may not be able to do much more than create your master important pile. After all, you still have meetings to attend, e-mails to respond to, and work to finish. However, the master file ensures that you tackle the important stuff first; the smaller, less-important items have to wait.

3. **Schedule an appointment with yourself in the next 48 hours to rid yourself of your master important pile.**

   You don't need to be in tip-top mental form to file. I suggest setting your filing appointment toward the end of the week, preferably in late afternoon when your energy level is low. Friday afternoons are a good time to file with comparatively few interruptions. (If you're struggling with interruptions, turn to Chapter 9 for help.) Don't worry about your other piles yet. Using the filing system you chose (see the preceding section), focus on the most important pile until it disappears.

4. **After making your master important file disappear, go back to your remaining clutter and repeat the process.**

   Start a *second* most-important master file and move all most-important items into that pile; then file them. Then make a third most-important master file. By now, you can probably see the surface of your desk, and you may even have a substantial area cleared.

Keeping Clutter from Coming Back

Not so long ago, a handshake or verbal agreement sealed the deal. No more. Today, you need paper to confirm an agreement, assure mutual understanding, and even organize tasks. Paper has taken over people's lives.

Whether you're at home or at the office, maximizing your time means that all paper has to quickly find its way to the proper place, even if that place is the recycle bin or shredder. The key to controlling paper before it controls you is to decide quickly where to put it (for tips on making decisions, see Chapter 11).

The best strategy for maintaining a clutter-free workspace is to avoid creating piles in the first place. You need to be more strategic in your work time to circumvent pile explosion. This section gives you two quick starts to circumvent the explosive growth of piles on your desk (or credenza, bookshelves, filing cabinets, extra chairs, window ledges, floor, or any other flat surface).

Letting the mess get away from me

When I was a kid, my bedroom was a mess. My parents asked me to clean it, and I did; but like Pigpen in the *Peanuts* comic strip, I seemed to carry my mess with me everywhere I went, and my bedroom started re-accumulating clutter the minute I entered. Mere hours after I'd tidied it, it was a disaster again. In fact, my bedroom once led my father to believe we'd been burglarized:

Seeing my room in complete disarray, he ran to his and my mother's bedroom to see what the thieves had taken! I've since left most clutter behind, but like mushrooms after rain, it creeps back when I'm not paying attention. I now lead a (mostly) well-organized, efficient life, and so can you.

Handling papers once

Those who master paper have mastered single-handling. These people touch a paper and take action. They don't pile, table, ponder, check, reconsider, or delay. They get rid of the paper the first time they handle it.

If you want to become a single handler, follow the five Ds: dump, delegate, detour, do it, or depot. Otherwise, you confront a less-productive list of Ds: dawdle, daydream, deliberate, and deceive — all of which lead to your demise.

Dump it

The dump-it principle is simple: Do you need it? If you don't, dump it or dispose of it. Say no to any of the following questions, and you can feel comfortable sending it to the shredder or recycling bin:

- ✔ Do you really need to act on this or keep it?
- ✔ Is this new, relevant information you need now or in the future?
- ✔ Does this information benefit a colleague or client?
- ✔ Are there consequences for not keeping it?
- ✔ Will this increase revenue or customer service?

Sort your mail over the recycling bin or waste basket. Everything that swirls into the bin or basket is no longer your problem.

Delegate it

Do you have an inner pack rat that wants to hold onto everything, including every paper that crosses your desk? One way to shut down this impulse is to delegate papers to someone else. Even if you *know* you could complete the task with two hands tied behind your back, that doesn't mean it's the best use of your time. Delegate and give yourself more time to work on high-value tasks while building the skills and confidence of people you delegate to.

Detour it

Handling every sheet of paper once is a fantastic goal, but sometimes it's impossible. Maybe you need more information before you can delegate or dispose of a paper, or perhaps the paper raises significant questions that need to be answered before you act. If you can detour and park the paper for later follow-up, you've saved time deliberating *now*.

Don't park paper permanently! Create a detour file for delayed papers, but be sure you get the information you need and deal with the paper. Don't let your temporary file grow into a pile hidden in a file.

Do it

Do it is the easiest and most straightforward of all the Ds. Take action, either to get the task done quickly or because there's a high level of urgency associated with it:

- ✔ **Tend to urgent matters.** If the task moves to the top of your priorities list after you read the paper, the best course of action is to do it now. Change your priorities and work until the new priority is completed, even if it takes you the rest of the day.

- ✔ **Get the task done quickly.** Follow the five-minute rule: If the necessary task, phone call, response, or clarification is something only you can do, and it'll take fewer than five minutes, do it yourself right now. By the time you detour it, pick it up again later, reread it, and refocus, you'll have invested far more time than the five minutes required now.

Depot it

A *depot* is a place where something is deposited or stored. You can find essential tools for filing earlier in this chapter in "Streamlining Your Workspace," so you can establish an effective depot for papers you need to keep (and *only* the papers you need to keep).

Filing regularly

Because the task of filing is mundane, it's all too easy to allow other tasks, people, and priorities to creep into the time you set aside to deal with your piles and files, and in a few short weeks, the weeds can take over your garden again. Don't let that happen! Daily filing may not be necessary, but waiting a month or six weeks is too long. Make your time spent filing a priority. At the end of filing, your desk is devoid of piles, and you can begin filing once a week — for a much shorter time — and still keep on top of your paperwork. Keep up with your filing, and you won't find it so tedious.

Schedule a weekly filing appointment with yourself and put it on your calendar. As you look ahead to assess your week and see your filing appointment, you begin mentally preparing for it. When you're prepared, you're more likely to keep your appointment with yourself, and when the time arrives, you'll be more efficient. You may find yourself throwing away more marginal items throughout the week and completing the task in less time.

When you're facing a few hours of filing, set a goal or benchmark. If you can't complete the whole project, break it down into a portion you can complete and commit to finishing that part without fail. (For more information on completing projects by chunking, see Chapter 10. Look for my Swiss-cheese or salami-slice methods.)

Taking notes that you can track

In business, most people overlook the simple skill of note-taking as a time-saving tool. Most people think anyone with a pen and paper can take notes: After all, everyone learned how in junior high, right? And if you're like most people, you probably take notes on whatever's handy: sticky notes, slips of paper, cocktail napkins, envelopes, or even important documents. Wrong approach! You can face significant time-loss and embarrassment when you later find out you lost the slip of paper where you took notes.

Whether you're using specially designed and cut pads printed with "from the desk of," a full 8½-x-11-inch pad that's a color other than the standard white or yellow, or a smaller white or yellow notepad, you need to use something that stands out.

If you know you'll need to file the notes, make sure you go with large paper so you can find it later. When you finish writing, add action items to your priority list for the following day and then drop the notes into the appropriate file for record-keeping. If your action items make it to the A level during the next day's priority sort, all you have to do is pull out the file folder and find your notes there as you left them, safe and sound.

Although sticky notes are great for attaching quick reminders to your computer screen so you don't forget to buy ice cream and pickles for your pregnant wife, they're one of the worst places to jot down information. Here's why:

- **They're too small for extensive notes.** You run out of room and have to transfer information to a larger note pad or, worse, to a second (and possibly third) sticky note. Then you have a sticky note stuck to a sticky note stuck to a sticky note, and if you lose one, you lose them all.

- **Sticky notes tend to sprout legs, sticking where you don't want them to: to the wrong document headed to the wrong file.** Then you're on a frantic mission to find your all-important sticky notes (and when they've hitched a ride on an unknown document going who-knows-where, your chances of finding them are slim to none).

- **Aged sticky notes lose their stick over time.** More than once, I've lost important information because my sticky note came unstuck and fluttered into oblivion.

If you're not sharing a document with others, consider taking notes directly on the document rather than on a sticky note. You can take notes in the margins around the key issues in the document or use the white space at the beginning or end for summaries or more-general points.

Limiting the Paper You Receive

Many people receive more material via snail mail and e-mail in one day than they can read in year. No one wants to miss news or seem out of it, but few people have time to read, let alone organize, the printed gridlock paralyzing their inboxes and mailboxes.

The question isn't how to handle the information, because you can't. All you can do is decide what's important and try to limit what you receive. You may have an information-overload problem if you

- Have stacks of periodicals around that you intend to read but never do.

- Buy books that sound good, only to get home and find that they're already on your shelf.

- Get frustrated because you haven't read your weekly news magazine in six months.

Here's how to cut down on the paper overload:

✔ **Cancel subscriptions that you don't read regularly.** Don't immediately renew subscriptions to magazines you read infrequently — take a break for a couple of months and see whether you really need them or miss receiving them. I can assure you that the publishers are eager to have you back and may make you a sweeter deal than if you were a regular renewal.

✔ **Move to Internet-based subscriptions.** Most quality publications now offer Internet-based subscriptions. They save time because you can search issues by topic and you can read only the articles that interest you. You can also search topics by date.

✔ **Get off mailing lists.** If you're like me, unsolicited correspondence easily makes up 60 to 80 percent of your daily incoming mail. If you're on one mailing list, your name is bought, sold, and bartered to numerous others before you can say "spring catalog."

Most reputable firms belong to the Direct Marketing Association (DMA). Write the DMA (Mail Preference Services, P.O. Box 643, Carmel, NY 10512) or visit online at www.dmaconsumers.org and ask the DMA to remove your name from its lists.

✔ **Take a sabbatical from the news.** The news can be negative, biased, and sensationalized to attract an audience. Don't let that be you. If you're interested in a topic, research it in depth (remember books?). You may find that your news sabbatical turns into a permanent vacation. (If you do need a news fix, look for the online version of your newspaper of choice.)

✔ **Create a tear file of all the articles or papers you do want to read.** I've been using a tear file for almost 20 years, and it's saved me countless hours. A tear file helps you decide quickly what's worth your time and what isn't.

It's simple: Tear out articles you want to read from trade publications, magazines, newspapers, and so on and file them in your tear file. Throw the rest of the publication into the recycle bin. Carry your tear file with you all the time, so whenever you're waiting — in traffic, at the doctor's office, at the car repair shop — you use your time productively. If the same article remains unread in your tear file for more than a couple months, pitch it.

Accounting for Ergonomics and Aesthetics

Not all time-saving techniques pertaining to your workspace are directly related to organization; elements such as comfort and positive energy also affect your productivity. Two of the most important and often overlooked areas are *ergonomics* (a fancy term for fitting the job tools to the worker, rather than vice-versa) and aesthetics (how you decorate your space to make the place where you spend your time enjoyable and uplifting).

An ergonomic workspace increases your productivity, reduces your work hours, and prevents workplace injuries by placing your body at optimal angles and at distances where productivity increases and fatigue decreases. (Many work-related injuries can be traced to poor posture, poor work practices, and badly designed office chairs, desks, workstations, and computer keyboards.)

Likewise, aesthetics plays an important part in time management because it encourages you to be more productive. By surrounding yourself with things that inspire you, you help yourself keep all things in perspective, particularly the balance between your work and personal life so you can make better decisions and — on those days you feel like you're drowning — remember why you're doing what you do.

As I tell my wife, Joan, when she chooses her shoes based on style rather than comfort, ergonomics plays second fiddle to aesthetics all too often. If we're going to walk around town for an afternoon, and Joan wears her fashionable (and very attractive) slides rather than her walking or athletic shoes, I know that sooner or later, she's going to pay for her choice. The same is true in your workplace — so tend to your needs before making adjustments that are helpful but not crucial.

Setting up a proper workstation

Although today's desks are more likely to be designed to accommodate PCs, many desks are still manufactured first and foremost for writing, note-taking, phone conversations, and getting organized.

The standard desk is a couple of inches too high for comfortable computer use, so if you spend a considerable amount— say, 50 percent — of your time on the computer, a keyboard at desk height can lead to problems with your back, shoulders, and neck. You probably know someone who's had carpal tunnel syndrome — numbness, tingling, and pain — in his or her wrists because of repetitive and incorrect computer use. That's only one ailment resulting from non-ergonomic work stations.

You probably spend the bulk of your office time sitting. To avoid fatigue and injury, invest in a good, ergonomically sound chair. Features to look for include the following:

- Adjustable height and tilt
- Adjustable back rests for your lower back
- A rotating seat
- At least five wheels

Be sure you align your keyboard and monitor, too, instead of letting pieces jut left or right.

Decorating your space

Productive people create workspaces where they enjoy spending time. You spend many hours working, so make your work environment a place where you can focus and be productive for long stretches. You may have a strictly utilitarian view of your work area (it's Spartan but functional — what more do you need?). Or it may be important to you to dress up your space a bit. Whatever your preferences, keep them in mind as you begin planning your work area. Consider the following aspects of your workspace:

- **Walls:** Do you work better if your walls are a softer, more comfortable color than the harsh white of most offices? Consider painting or hanging wallpaper or swatches of fabric.

- **Images:** Are pictures, art, and photographs important in your surroundings?

- **Floor:** Should you buy a rug to add color and form or give your office a warmer feel?

- **Lighting:** What's the lighting like? Most people work beneath the low hum of fluorescent lighting. To give your area a warmer feel, you may try a desk lamp or even a lamp on your credenza behind you to create better ambience.

- **Furniture:** Do you need to upgrade your office furniture? If it's okay with your boss, can you add a couch for afternoon cat naps or creative brainstorming? Do you need a small table for meetings with your team?

Here are a few points to remember as you personalize your space:

- **Limit the items on your desk to the more utilitarian variety.** Remember: The top of your desk is not a decoration zone. Use the walls, floor, and credenza to bring the environmental influence in your workspace.

- **Pay attention to placement.** If you're someone who dreams about better times as you toil away, right behind your desk may not be the best place for a large photo of your last trip to Hawaii. Instead, you may consider putting on your credenza so you can look at it during a moment of relaxation and envision what you're doing all the hard work for.

- **Be careful not to add anything that'll add to the responsibilities you have to tend to each day.** After all, the point is to increase your productivity, not give you more to do. Consider this scenario, which I advise against in your own space: I once worked with a woman who had fish swimming in a tank on her credenza. Although her mini-aquarium was beautiful and soothing and drew plenty of attention, I often wondered how much work time she spent cleaning it — and how she persuaded her co-workers to feed her fish when she went on vacation!

Maintaining a Productive Environment in the Home Office

With gas prices skyrocketing and technology booming, the number of people working from home continues to grow. You can cash in on big savings in both time and money if you work from home. Here's how:

- ✔ You can redirect the daily time you used to spend commuting into work, exercise, and family.

- ✔ Flexible hours give you almost total control over your work schedule. If you need to get up early or stay up until midnight to meet a deadline, it's doable, and you're minutes from bed.

- ✔ You spend less on lunches, dinners, and snacks, not to mention what you save on departmental gifts for holidays, parties, and other special occasions.

- ✔ You chalk up lower costs for clothing.

- ✔ Transportation expenses such as gas, car maintenance, tolls, parking, and train or bus fare drop.

On the other hand, beware of perceptions and misperceptions that can cause your productivity at home to fizzle. In this section, I explain how to set up your office away from the office.

Creating an environment that fosters solid focus

When choosing a location for your home office, you want a place that affects your productivity and your ability to manage your time in a positive way. When the space is less than ideal, or when you struggle to focus on work even when your location is ideal, consider trying these tips to nurture your productivity:

- ✔ **Choose an out-of-the-way locale.** Look for an area that's yours alone, removed from general traffic and noise, where you can shut the door and hang a do-not-disturb sign on the knob. The more out of the way your office is, the better use you'll make of your time.

  Setting up your home office in Hub Central — the family center of your home — without physical boundaries is unwise. Today's typical den off the entry doesn't provide enough physical distance. It is right in the middle of the home, so noise from both ends of the house reaches you clearly. Your family walks by numerous times, and in newer homes, the office doors are often glass, providing no visual barrier whatsoever.

I once had an office that was nearly ideal. It was above our detached garage, which created a short commute of 47 steps from our side door up the steps and into the office. Believe it or not, those scant 47 steps substantially decreased the number of interruptions.

✔ **Employ other physical barriers if your office location isn't ideal.** If your home office isn't off in a private area of the house and your doors are glass, your best defense is a shade or visual barrier. When children see you "not working" (that is, thinking), they may figure it is playtime. The other necessary item is a lock on the door, which announces that you're busy and uninterruptible.

✔ **Use white noise to block out other household noises.** You can establish auditory boundaries by blocking household noises with white noise. *White noise* is a constant low-level background sound, such as static or a whirring fan, which quickly becomes inaudible but drowns out other, more disruptive noises.

✔ **Drown out distracting noise with music.** The best background music for me is Baroque piano. It's simple because it's only one instrument; also, studies have shown that Baroque music stimulates the creative side of the brain. I advise against the radio because of the constantly changing style and tempo of songs, the newscasts, and disk-jockey monologues (though some people claim to work better with this sort of background noise). I also suggest instrumental music rather than songs with lyrics — words can be distracting. I listen to orchestra and symphonic music, such as classical or easy listening.

Establishing boundaries and getting yourself in the work mindset

I can't emphasize enough how crafting and adhering to a set of rules for you as well as your entire family and friends increases your chance of success when you're working at home. By drawing lines between your work time and your personal time, you allow yourself to be fully present with each — and presence is a key component of productivity. To establish a solid set of boundaries for yourself, follow these suggestions:

✔ **Treat a day at the home as you would a day in your office.** Start your day the same time you'd begin your commute to home-away-from-home and end it at the same you'd end your work day. Take only a half-hour lunch (but be sure to take that half-hour lunch). Regular start and stop times and set lunch breaks allow everyone to recognize your schedule and abide by it.

✔ **Start early.** If you work at home, you may find, as most office workers have, that you're most productive before others arrive. In the home office world, that's before your household wakes up for the day.

✔ **Dress for success.** Because you don't have to shower, shave, and don office clothes, you lose the empowering feeling you get that makes work seem like work. If you need formal dress to perform better and are negatively affected by staying in sweats or pajamas most of the day, by all means, get up, shower, and get dressed, just as you would if you were heading to the office. If you *feel* successful, you'll be successful, regardless of where you work.

✔ **Set goals for yourself.** Set goals in terms of work completed and reward yourself for achieving them, just as you would at the office.

✔ **Don't answer personal calls during your workday.** Using a home office to increase your productivity is an act of discipline. Others sometimes adopt the attitude that you're not really working; people who wouldn't imagine interrupting you at the office call to chew the fat, simply because you're home. Parents are often guilty of this. Be polite but firm: "Mom, I'm sorry. I'd love to talk, but I'm working right now. I'll call you back at five, as soon as I'm finished, okay?"

✔ **Control interruptions from your family members.** Patiently train your family on your work schedule and etiquette. You may want to establish set times when you allow for interruptions.

Setting these boundaries can be challenging, especially with the pre-school set. When we were blessed with children, I decided that my work time would be "interruptible" when it came to our kids, and I stand by that philosophy. (I have to say, however, that both Annabelle and Wesley have uncanny abilities for selecting the worst possible times to inter-rupt!) Here's the one exception I make to the come-on-in rule: Absolutely *no* interruptions when I'm on the phone. You, too, may want to set some inviolable rules. Make them few, but enforce them rigorously.

Bartering can empower both you and your family. For example, while trying to finish a chapter a few days ago, I offered Wesley a trade: No more interruptions for the rest of the morning in return for an hour of fishing together. He let me complete the chapter (which took me at least an hour less to finish than it would've otherwise). Then I quit a little early, and we had our fishing contest in the golf course pond in our backyard. I lost one to four, but in spite of that, I managed to get my work done — and have a winning afternoon with my son!

✔ **End on time.** Being available to work extended hours can diminish the quality and quantity of family time. Set boundaries. When the office door closes, let voice mail pick up work calls. Leave the office behind.

✔ **Allow yourself uninterrupted time each day to compress.** A commute allows you time to shift gears. On your way home, you move from CEO, salesperson, manager, assistant, or customer service representative to Daddy, Mommy, husband, wife, partner, or Fido's master. When you exit the door of your home office, the shift is over, and you're on! So when you're done for the day, take ten minutes to decompress before you walk out the door. You may even play some relaxing music so you can leave the troubles of the day behind.

Chapter 6

Fine-Tuning Organization Skills with Technology

*P*icture this: I'm getting ready to go on vacation, when a critical client asks me to make a sales presentation to one of the largest sales networks in the country. For a moment, I panic — the event is scheduled immediately after my return from my vacation. If I'm to be prepared, I'll have to disappoint my family and cancel our getaway. Ah, but then I remember — I have a similar version of that presentation wrapped up on a PowerPoint program. A few tweaks and some minor revisions, and I'll have a new and customized presentation in a couple of hours. I put in some research time, modify my PowerPoint, and head out for a week of fun and sun.

I'm a prisoner of technology, and I'm delighted. I love what technology does for me and for my business, Sales Champions. The computer is the lifeblood of my organization, from communication and data storage to organizing projects to dealing with clients, suppliers, and prospects. It must be love, or I'd never tolerate the terrible, awful fits technology occasionally gives me.

In this chapter, you discover what the love affair is all about. I point out the efficiency provided by electronic scheduling and using a personal digital assistant (PDA). I help you eliminate excess baggage on your computer, organize and name the files you save so you can access them quickly, and archive files you may need to refer to in the future in a way that minimizes the time you spend searching for them. I also show you how a customer relationship management (CRM) program can help you organize your client information and increase business. Read on.

Plugging into Electronic Scheduling

Electronic tools can help keep your time and schedule under control. A quality PDA, for example, acts as your electronic assistant on the road or in your office. It's an easily writable, very compact computer that takes only seconds, not minutes, to boot. This section outlines your options for electronic planners, whether you're looking to use calendar software on a desktop computer or to pull out your smartphone when you're on the go. I also discuss the pros and cons of PDAs and considerations to keep in mind before deciding which one to use.

The calendar-sharing benefits of electronic scheduling tools

One of the biggest benefits of using electronic scheduling tools is that you and your co-workers have access to each others' schedules *without* making a phone call or pestering administrative assistants. This slashes the time you need to set up a meeting because the software also informs you where others are, what they're doing, and when they're available. Electronic scheduling saves time on the recipient's end, too — because others can see your schedule, you receive meeting invitations only at times you're available and you don't have to consult your schedule to see whether you can attend.

Say, for example, you've been trying to reach Bob Smith for two days. Every time you call him, he's in a meeting, and every time he calls you back, you're out in the field. You cut through the time-wasting telephone tag, check into your network scheduling system, and schedule a time for both you and Bob to talk. You can see that he's in the office but free of meetings between 2 and 3 p.m.

Scheduling systems, such as Microsoft Outlook, are great for setting up meetings for the convenience of the majority. For example, suppose you need to set a meeting next week for the ten people on your budget task force: Your attendance, as well as those of three department heads, is required. By using Outlook to schedule the meeting, you can see others' schedules before you even send a meeting invitation. You can search through the week to find the best time for the most people, ensuring your numbers and the attendance of those critical to the meeting.

And when you're not available? Don't worry: No one knows that you're actually getting a haircut at 3 p.m. Thursday — they just know you're not available to meet.

The utility of portable planners

Portable planners have an incredibly wide variety of uses. When traveling via air, I frequently see executives turn their handhelds to airplane mode as soon as the chime signals that the plane has risen above 10,000 feet, and many barely slow down until the chime sounds a few hours later on descent. When the plane lands, they fire up their PDAs, and all their hard work goes out via e-mail before the plane is parked at the gate.

A PDA allows you to carry your calendar — and every one of your client and prospect contacts — in one hand. You can even put your time-block schedule, which shows what you're doing at each moment of each day and keeps you on track, into your electronic planner (see Chapter 4 for in-depth guidance on that crucial time-management tool). In most programs, you can copy your time-block for years into the future with a few keystrokes. And when you want to share your schedule with others, you can quickly and easily upload it to your computer network.

A PDA also serves as your multimedia center: It can function as an MP3 player, portable flash drive, electronic photo album, or video player. You have instant Internet access for stock quotes, news, sports, and so on.

The last ten years have brought an explosion of options in this area: You can choose from Palm handhelds, Palm Treo smartphones, Apple iPhones, and BlackBerries (not to mention numerous other "berries"). Your cellphone carrier may influence which make and model you select because the make and model can affect coverage, service, and reception.

Most PDA companies partner with cellphone companies, so when you get your first PDA or upgrade an existing one, keep an eye on what your cellular provider recommends as well as any specials the company may be running.

Where you use your PDA influences your choice as well. Many PDAs offer global coverage. You can use BlackBerries, for example, in more than 90 countries, so when you land in Hong Kong, London, Sydney, or Los Angeles, you can send and receive e-mail. However, if you travel nationally or internationally, some PDAs are more effective than others. I was in Australia a few weeks ago, and another U.S. speaker at the conference couldn't get his PDA to work Down Under.

Beware: Some PDAs don't work with some brands of CRM software (see the later section "Managing Contact Info with a CRM Program"). Be sure to check whether your PDA is compatible with your CRM before investing in either. Also check whether you can sync from remote locations or whether you need to physically be in your office to sync. In addition, some PDAs, as well as some CRM software, won't sync if you're connected remotely. This means e-mail you send and receive, calls you make, notes from those calls, and appointments booked by your staff won't show up in your PDA — or in the server containing your CRM — resulting in missed appointments, duplications, wasted time, and lost revenue.

Despite all their benefits, PDAs do have drawbacks: You get married to the technology; you can be too accessible; if you lose the PDA, it's as if you lost your whole life and database. Although most of the world has embraced the PDA revolution, at times you may want to be *less* accessible.

When deciding whether a PDA will save or cost you time overall, consider your job and the level of concentration that you need to perform well. Do you really need to be accessible at a moment's notice? Are you the type of person who can put it off or down? Do you answer all the phone calls that come to your home? If you're unable to screen calls at home, you may have a hard time screening your PDA.

De-cluttering Your Computer (and Keeping It That Way)

Is your computer a junk drawer, collecting everything you don't have time to deal with? Your computer has limited space, and sooner or later, you'll be forced to clean it or find another drawer (and computers are far more expensive than drawers!). The more junk on your computer, the harder it is to find what you're looking for. And just as an overflowing drawer gets harder to open and close, an overstuffed computer also works less efficiently.

The best way to tackle an overburdened computer is to sort its inventory and then purge what you can from it, whether you back files up to a disc and delete them from your computer or simply delete them once and for all.

Naming files and organizing them with an electronic tree

Start by creating categories for your electronic files, with one folder for each of your major areas of responsibility. Typical categories include *sales, marketing, human resources, promotion,* and *current projects,* as well as categories based on your products and services. You may also include folders for key customers. Again, just as you create subfolders under these headings in your file cabinets, create electronic subfolders for smaller, more specific categories.

Build your *filing tree* — an outline of major folders and the subfolders to go beneath them — in your computer before you begin to file individual documents. Don't start filing and *then* try to organize your files. It's difficult to see all your files at once on a computer, so that strategy rarely works. Having at least a rough outline of the files and folders on your PC, and perhaps even on paper, before you begin eliminates a lot of copying, cutting, and pasting. Result: greater efficiency and significantly less frustration.

The most challenging part of organizing, whether physical or electronic, is developing a system. The key to being able to retrieve information without wasting time is to file it correctly in the first place. The following subsections present some questions to help you devise a system that works for you.

How do you usually need to access information?

Do you need to retrieve information by date? Subject matter? Company? Project name? Everyone has different priorities based on the type of business, job description within that business, and personal preferences. If you're the keeper or primary resource of spreadsheets, reports, correspondence, or contracts, you may have to be able to pull up files quickly for others or communicate or share this information. In that case, you may need to tailor your filing system to what works best for someone else. Think about how your boss or colleague asks you for a document. Does he usually remember the name of the contact he was working with, the location he travelled to, or the time of year that he was working on the project?

If your projects are very large, break them into smaller, more easily accessed files. Here are a couple of basic breakdowns for your filing system:

- ✔ **If you do the same set of projects for several different clients, you may want to file under client names.** If you're going to file by name, decide whether to file by last name, first name, or the name of the company that person represents. (Does your client Mike Wallace of ABC Company go under *m, w,* or *a?*) Whatever you decide, stick with the system for all your files so they're grouped together and easy to retrieve.

- ✔ **If you're prone to look for files by date or if your files are continually evolving with newer versions each time they're used, structure your system so that the date information is always part of the file or folder name.** If you primarily access information based on when it was created, regardless of the client or project, the date it was created is the most important item in your document or folder title. If due date is more important, make that part of the file name.

Inconsistency and even spelling or punctuation errors can send your folders and files to unintended locations, which can make them difficult if not impossible to find later. Your computer organizes files in alphabetical and numerical order, so set some guidelines for how you plan to name your files before you start. For instance, regardless of where you place a date in your document or folder name, you need to create your date the same way each time. July 29, 2008 ends up in a different location than a document titled with 7-29-2008 or even 072908. Also be consistent in whether your date comes at the end of the file name or the beginning.

Because of all the information you want to include in the file name, your documents may have names that create a file path that is too long. An overly long file path can also prevent you from moving the document to another location, or in some cases even e-mailing the file. Abbreviations can help, but be sure to be consistent. If you abbreviate Joe's Coffee Shop as JCS on one project and Joe's CS on another, they won't show up next to each other in your computer.

If you work in a fast-paced environment, set aside a blocked-out period of time each month to go through your current files and make sure they're correctly labeled and filed. As time passes, it's easy to forget which file belongs to whom and where it should go. Files can easily become lost forever, creating a huge time loss when you launch into an endless search and end up having to re-create a file from scratch. (Of course, you can always use the search function on your computer to look through a single document, subfolder, file folder, or your entire computer. After you find your missing document, check to see why it was misfiled in the first place and then correct the error.)

How far back must you keep files?

Depending on your business, you may have years' worth of files you need to keep on your computer for a longstanding client or project. How often do you call up archived or non-active information? If you keep data and detail for a long time, you may set up a system that gives you quick access to "closed" files without cluttering your screen.

You may want to try keeping the current year or the last two years in your everyday files; by the time you need to look up those files only occasionally, create a subfolder where you can combine information for each past year — then put that folder in a different area. You may even be able to move this seldom-used information out of your personal files and into your company's main folders on the server, which can keep your current computer files less cluttered and save you time.

How do you create new documents?

Do you work regularly with documents based off a template? For example, do you send out client contracts? Put together a weekly status report? Submit expense reports or check requests? Generate form responses? Think about the best system for pulling up the appropriate templates and revising them accurately and efficiently — and storing them so you can find them quickly.

If you create documents from scratch regularly, look for a way to create templates for frequently created formats to avoid reentering the same information for each version you produce.

Do you work on projects that generate multiple versions of documents? For example, do you have proposals that are reviewed, edited, and revised by numerous people? If so, you want to incorporate a system that allows you to easily track the history of changes and pull up what's been done in the past. For instance, when people save new, updated versions of a document, you may have them alter the file name by adding their initials, adding an abbreviation to indicate a certain stage of a project, or dating everything so you don't end up searching through proposals that are so old and outdated that you'll never use them again. Make sure every knows the naming system.

Are most of the new documents you create specific to one issue or one client? When you spend time producing documents for specific clients, your organization method should make it easy to call up a client and identify everything related to that client.

If you're constantly creating new documents, the job of organizing is more challenging. Your document load is heavy and constantly increasing. Consider setting up your organizational system by client or having an archive file where you store master contracts, proposals, letters, templates, checklists, and other regularly used items. You may also set up folders so these frequently used master files are easy to access.

Offloading excess by archiving or deleting

The more files your computer has on its hard drive to search, the more slowly it works. As with paper files, a key part of organizing your computer is removing what you don't need to keep, including duplicate files. Electronic clutter is hard to see because unlike the physical stacks piling up on your desk, it tends to be invisible — until your computer slows or balks. I've found numerous copies of the same programs on my computer because I forgot that I'd installed earlier versions.

You know you need to archive when the icons proliferate on your desktop until it looks like the parking lot at a busy superstore. *Archiving* files doesn't mean deleting those old files; it means backing them up to a CD, DVD, or other storage device. Whether you have a few desktops or a large server, archiving frees up hard-drive space and speeds your computer's performance. To weed out excess, follow these steps:

1. **Search your computer to make sure that the programs installed are ones you need and that you're using the most recent versions.**

   Save the data in the old versions onto a CD or DVD, or update the program and transfer it to the new version. Then send the old versions to your computer's recycle bin or uninstall them.

2. **Create a permanent archive directory or folder and get in the habit of archiving any files you don't use regularly but want to keep.**

Always label your CDs or DVDs. Don't just throw them into storage in anonymous jewel cases. If nothing else, print hard copies of the disc's contents, fold the paper to the size of the case, and secure the package with a rubber band. That way, if you come back to it five years from now, you'll know what the disc contains.

Be sure to keep CDs and other storehouses in a safe place. Buy a fire safe that's rated for electronic storage (read the label before you buy because not every safe protects CDs, zip or flash drives, or floppy disks). Store particularly important records, such as periodic complete system back-ups, in a safe deposit box. Also use multiple backups so you're well-covered for a catastrophe — if one disc is corrupt, you don't want to lose all your data. We used to back up daily at my companies with a different CD for each day, but we've since gone to mirrored servers. With *mirrored servers,* you always have a backup — if one server goes down, you can be up in minutes on the other server without losing data.

After you've purged the excess files, periodically defragment your computer. The process helps increase the speed of your computer so the data is compressed and organized in a manner in the computer that it can find it easily.

Saving new files strategically

The Save As feature on your computer is one of technology's greatest functions — for personalization, for producing numerous letters with only minimal changes, or for tailoring presentations to specific groups without losing your original documents. When you save without Save As, you replace one file with another, losing potentially valuable information that could save you time later should you need that information for a similar situation in the future.

I had an assistant a number of years ago who never used the Save As function. When I customized a presentation based on an industry's or client's needs, my assistant typed and formatted workbooks and PowerPoint presentations and saved the customized information over previous versions of the file. In essence, she replaced every presentation with the most recent version. I lost at least a year's worth of new ideas because my assistant didn't make strategic use of Save As.

For all its benefits, the Save As option can also be your hard drive's demise if you don't use it judiciously — it's too easy to create (and store) numerous documents that are almost identical. For example, if you have a master file of a letter to customers, Save As makes it a cinch to personalize the letter from your master file. But do you need to keep copies of all your personalized letters? You may want to save the letter into the appropriate customer file, but you probably don't need to keep a copy of every personalized letter in the master letter file (unless each version is different enough from the original that you may use the new version periodically in the future).

Cleaning up a hand-me-down computer

You may inherit hand-me-down computers filled with old files. If and when that happens, check organization dates or last-edit dates. Often, files have been passed on for generations of employees. Instead of sending the files out to be carbon dated, do the following:

✔ Store the file in an interim file so you can research it when you have time or archive it so it's out of your way.

✔ Print out a hard copy and ask your boss or the computer's previous owner whether you should save it.

✔ Save the file on a CD, zip or flash drive, or floppy disk and purge the file from your computer.

Managing E-mail Correspondence

If all the e-mail correspondence you've ever received, sent, saved, responded to, forwarded, and deleted were turned into paper mail, your output alone could probably fill a U.S. Postal Office. Of course, you don't keep it all, but if you're like me, you let your e-mail accumulate at times, perhaps until your system notifies you that your mailbox has exceeded its limit.

A good tool is only as good as the person wielding it. If you know how to use e-mail properly, it makes your productivity hum. If not, you can end up sabotaging your efforts to get things done. This section helps you rein in the all-too-often unwieldy paperless communication system.

Filtering what comes in

Even militant time masters can lose hours of productive time to e-mail — and much of that e-mail isn't even work-related. Sometimes it's not even something you *want* to receive, yet you still have to dig your way through the sludge.

Spam is only one factor that adds to the deluge of e-mail you find in your inbox on a daily basis. If you're like most people, you probably authorized or even requested most of the promotional e-mail you receive. Here are some tips to slow the flow of spam and other incoming e-mail that only clutter your inbox:

✔ **Unsubscribe from newsletters or mailing lists that you no longer read.** When you were starting up your organic garden last spring, a weekly e-mail about composting tips seemed like a great idea. Now you find that you almost always delete without opening. Time to put that idea to bed.

- ✔ **Think twice before signing on for new mailing lists.** You may appreciate a monthly newsletter about one of your hobbies. But instead of bulking up your inbox, why not add the Web site to your Favorites list and visit when it's convenient for you?

- ✔ **When ordering online, seek out the checked box that confirms your agreement to receiving e-mail — and *un*check it.** Called the *negative option* response, many merchants include a box on the order form that indicates, "Yes, I want to receive regular notices about your company's special offers." That box is already checked off, for your "convenience." In order to get *nothing,* however, you have to take action and get rid of that mark.

- ✔ **When visiting or leaving personal or contact information on a Web site, always check the privacy policy to confirm that your information won't be sold.** You can usually find a link to the privacy notice at the bottom of the Web page or next to where you enter your information.

- ✔ **Install spam-filtering software on your computer.** Remember, though, that these programs typically don't remove the spam; they simply filter it to your junk folder so you can review or simply delete.

Don't ever respond to spam. You may hope that your polite request to remove you from the mailing list will stop the mailings, but most often the opposite happens. Your reply confirms that your e-mail address is a valid one. You may start getting even more mail, and your address may be sold to other annoying spam-senders. Clicking on an opt-out link can also put you at risk if the e-mail is spam, so let your spam software do its job and leave it at that.

Employing an e-mail response system

During my formative years, I watched the TV show *M*A*S*H* with my family. I remember that when the wounded would come into the medical unit, the doctors would perform *triage*, the process that determined patient priority. Does this wound need medical attention now? Will this soldier die without immediate care? Will this one die even if he receives attention? In this way, the medical team could most efficiently prioritize their work in a situation of chaos.

Performing triage is an excellent way to approach your e-mail responses. Some mail you get is dead on arrival, other messages are of interest to you but not critical to address immediately, and others need your attention right now. Those of you who can turn on your computer to find as many as 100 new messages need the critical care of a good e-mail management system.

Here's what works for me: When I open up my mailbox, I resort to the three Ds: *delete, do it,* or *defer.* Every e-mail fits into one of these categories.

Hit the delete

Although your computer doesn't take up any more space if you have 10 e-mail or 10,000, the clutter of useless, obsolete, irrelevant correspondence in your inbox can *seem* like a mile-high stack of stuff you have to carry with you.

Keep your inbox clean by discarding any e-mail that's unimportant or long-obsolete. As for the advertisements, forwarded jokes or urban myths; and the string of thanks, you're-welcome, have-a-good-day, see-you-after-work correspondence, read 'em (or don't) and delete immediately.

Also delete without opening any e-mail with a subject line that seems too good to be true or seems like a marketing pitch from an unknown sender. How realistic is it to think that some company has sought *you* out to offer you an opportunity to make millions? And if a deal is really so incredible, would the advertiser really need to tell you that? Probably not. Beware any e-mail with subject lines containing misspelled words or words with symbols in place of letters (such as *Fr** Mon!y*).

Knowing how to delete helps everyone in your company. When employees share a network, the server fills up when everyone retains all e-mail, which can stop the flow of inbound e-mail for the whole company. Most networks establish a limit to the size of individual inboxes and send notices when you get close to the limit. Then it's time for some major housecleaning. Better to keep up with the cleaning rather than let it build up.

Just do it

Just down the street from my high school in Portland, Oregon, is the headquarters of Nike, the company that coined the phrase "Just do it." That's not bad advice for e-mail management, either. Of course, this *do it* response is critical if the matter is urgent or must be done today, but it's also a sound strategy for most other e-mail, too. If a message warrants a response, do it. Now. Answer the question. Forward the message. Transfer the to-do to your task list or schedule. Send a response. If you need little more than a click or a minute or two to respond, file, or forward, then don't waste time by keeping it for later.

Just as with mail or papers in your inbox, the best strategy is to handle it once (see Chapter 5) and then get it off your plate.

Defer until later

For those e-mail messages that aren't critical-care matters, it may make sense to set them aside to address after you pass through all your correspondence. So you *don't* forget and leave them buried in your inbox to be remembered too late, immediately place these e-mail messages in an appropriate folder so they'll pop up later for your attention. Messages that fall into this category may include personal e-mail that you want to read carefully and to which you want to take time to craft a response. They can also include flexible–time line projects that don't have to be done today or even this week.

Actually, I just thought of a fourth D: *delegate*. It falls in the defer category. Although you can simply hit the Forward command and send the message along with instructions for carrying out the requested action, the reliability of e-mail is suspect enough that you want to remind yourself to follow up if you hear nothing back from the delegate.

Automating your responses

The ability to plan ahead with e-mail communication saves you loads of time. If you regularly field the same FAQs numerous times during the week or day, it may make sense to craft template e-mails of standard responses. Place these templates in a folder where you can easily access them and you're ready to cut and paste your reply, using the form language and making the personal tweaks as necessary. For example, if you get queries from clients about the status of their projects, you may put together a standard response informing them that you're attending to their project and will get in touch with them by such-and-such a date.

Don't forget about the automated message function when you're out of the office. Set up a message with the pertinent details: when you'll return, whether you'll be checking e-mail, when people can expect to hear from you, and who they can contact if they need immediate assistance.

Organizing and storing e-mail

Managing, organizing, categorizing, and filing your e-mail is a practice that can serve you as well as maintaining a well-organized paper filing system does. Many of your e-mail messages are probably important to you as reference, especially business correspondence. And you, like me, have probably searched in vain for that important e-mail you know you received, oh, maybe eight months ago.

Fortunately, you don't have to print off every e-mail and stick it in a filing cabinet. Your e-mail program includes many valuable tools that help you keep information as close as a click of the mouse. Most e-mail programs include various folder and filing systems that serve, in a way, as a virtual lateral file cabinet — but searching and finding what you want is a lot easier, with just a little experience. You can sort and store your e-mail by a number of categories, grouping them by sender, date, project, importance, or subject. Here are just some ways you can use the features your e-mail software provides:

✔ Set up so that certain messages — periodic newsletters, for example — automatically route to a specific folder. (This tool works on the same concept as spam blockers, except these items go in a folder you actually want to see.) With the help of filtering software, you can flag specific e-mail addresses and automatically send them to a folder — or even delete them — before they hit your inbox. I find that most people use only a small portion of what their filtering features in their e-mail software can do. Take a few minutes to explore your options — filtering takes very little time to set it up.

✔ Create a new-arrivals folder, defining *new* as a day, a week, or whatever you determine.

✔ Establish a *dump* folder that you clean out once a month or as often as you choose.

Don't look at all the e-mail in the dump folder before you dump them. That takes too much time. You've filtered them enough to be able to let them go.

✔ Make specific project folders where you can save relevant e-mail, providing a record of all conversations for the future. When you no longer need the file because the project is long-complete, you can delete it. This setup also presents a great backup system.

✔ Employ the search function to track down any correspondence about a certain topic. For example, if you're looking for an e-mail outlining details for a trip to the Bahamas, you can type "Bahamas" in the search field and all inbox e-mail with *Bahamas* somewhere within the body or subject line will come up.

Managing Contact Info with a CRM Program

If you're in business, you already know the profit to be tapped from existing customers. They're already yours! In countless customer service studies I've read in the last 20 years, I've seen one conclusion over and over: It takes many times more effort, energy, and time to acquire a new customer than it does to retain an existing one.

No matter what your business, the ability to contact existing customers easily and frequently — with the inside knowledge of someone who knows them well as customers — is invaluable. Add the ability to send customers personalized communications at the exact time they're in the market for your product or service, and you're in business: *profitable* business. Even if customers won't need to replace your product for many years, you may be able to offer them related items or garner a referral to their friends.

One of the most valuable tools in business is a customer relationship management (CRM) program. CRM helps you maximize the service, communication, sales, and relationship-building with prospects and existing clients — the lifeblood of any business — by providing quick access to critical customer information, whether you're selling, serving, or invoicing.

Additionally, CRM enables your office practices to become nearly paperless, especially if you have compatible software that changes faxes into electronic documents. You can even enter notes into your CRM software while you're on the phone with prospects and customers, allowing you to keep records of discussions in one centralized place, banishing sticky notes and random slips of paper. This automation saves time and money and provides practically unfettered access to documents and client files from anywhere in the world. What's more, it's kind to trees.

Looking at software and services

Most computers come with simple CRM systems. In Microsoft, it's Outlook. However, Outlook isn't powerful or customizable enough to keep more than basic client and prospect data, so I recommend ACT! (www.act.com) or GoldMine (www.goldmine.com). These two programs are affordable (around $500 for a single user) and readily available, and they've stood the test of time as high-quality CRM programs, so they're reasonable tools for businesses big or small. They offer powerful abilities to customize your business data, and they also help segment your customers and clients so you can tailor your communication, service, and sales strategies to particular groups. (For information on using the program features, check out *ACT! 2007 For Dummies* or *GoldMine 8 For Dummies* [Wiley].)

If you need multiple users, then you'll need to establish a network for the CRM programs to run on so all people in your company have access. Another option is the *SaaS* (software as a service) model, in which you access the program online. In this case, a separate company houses the data and software, charging you a monthly service fee per user for their CRM and all the servicing. Programs that operate that way include www.salesforce.com and www.sugarcrm.com. You have some options in what you use, but as a businessperson, not having a CRM program shouldn't be an option at all.

Unleashing the capabilities of a CRM program

I can personally testify that, having used a CRM for nearly 18 years, a CRM can provide the following:

✔ More revenue in slower months

✔ Better service to current clients

✔ Increased referral business

✔ High levels of customer satisfaction

✔ More time for technicians to take new customer service calls

This section covers some of the ways you can use the program to make it happen.

Categorizing clients

You can use a CRM program to segment your clients, which is a tremendous strategy. All customers are important, but some are more important than others. Your most important customers

✔ Do more (and more profitable) business with you.

✔ Send more of their friends, neighbors, business contacts, family members, and associates your way.

✔ Hold strategic positions in companies or organizations you'd like to do business with, meaning they can send even more business your way.

You can use CRM to reach out to clients based on their relationship with you. You can, for example, segment your customers and clients into three distinctive categories:

✔ **Platinum clients:** These are your best customers. They're delighted with your service, are likely to send you referrals regularly, and wouldn't think of going anywhere else. CRM helps you stay in touch with them through newsletters, phone calls, or special correspondence on a regular basis.

✔ **Gold customers:** These people may not be as excited about you and your company as the platinum people, but they continue to do business with you, even if you get raves and referrals only when you ask. CRM helps identify gold-level clients and reminds you to communicate frequently — with the goal of raising them to platinum level.

✔ **Bronze customers:** These are folks who may only sporadically do business with you, switching to other sources from time to time; or they're individuals and businesses who haven't called you for a long time. You can use CRM to help you make a more concerted effort to build a stronger relationship with them.

In addition to current customers, you can also segment prospects and customize your communication with them. A strategic CRM program helps you categorize and organize your prospects as well as separate them from suspects. (*Suspects* have a less than 50 percent chance of using your products or services. *Prospects* offer you a better than 50 percent chance of creating a new business relationship.) Using the technology of a CRM effectively, you can increase the frequency and effectiveness of contact and move the prospects up what I call the *loyalty ladder* more quickly.

Contacting target groups all at once

When you group your prospects, customers, and clients, you can communicate with them with a few keystrokes or clicks of a mouse. If deliveries of your pressure washers are back ordered, for example, you can easily notify all your pressure-washer customers. Or if you're changing the pricing on the half-page ads in your magazine, you can contact all your customers and let them know. You may tell them that, beginning at month-end, ad prices go from $4,000 to $5,000 (but as valued customers, they can lock in the lower price by signing a one-year contract now).

Most CRM programs can merge information, including inserting customer and company names in both greetings and bodies of letters. This allows you to craft a generic e-mail or business letter, but use customer and company names in strategic spots so the letter is more personalized. It also saves you from writing 20, 50, or even 300 separate customer letters.

Putting customer contact on auto-pilot

After you categorize your customers and clients, you can take the final step to saving time with a CRM: automating customer contact. The companies and people who use CRMs most effectively automate *everything*. They have documents, communications, letters and systems, troubleshooting communications, and so on in the CRM. This allows the program to find the document, write the letter or e-mail, attach the document in a PDF file, and keep it in the current client record — all electronically. After you design an automated process (who, what, where, when, and why), the CRM does the rest. You can even set up some programs, such as ACT! and GoldMine, to dial the phone for you.

CRMs let you set up long-term communication systems delivered through automation. After your customers receive their 5,000 tongue depressors, an automated thank-you note goes out. The following week, you (automatically) offer a special on gauze. The week after that, you may (automatically) send a customer-satisfaction survey. You can set this system up in advance for customers, clients, prospects, and suspects in platinum, gold, and bronze groups (see the earlier "Categorizing clients" section for more on these groupings).

The CRM program can also integrate the notification for calls from different people in your company or department as well as e-mail and faxes. You can establish a system in which each person gets his or her marching orders from the CRM. For instance, you can tell Susie in accounting to send the invoice and tell Bob in sales to make a follow-up call at 3 days, 7 days, and 14 days after the delivery; and the CRM will also generate a thank-you letter that Sally in administration can send out tomorrow. And finally, Penny in customer service gets the notice make a call in five days to check in on any training needs the customer has with the new product.

Creating effective client profiles

The building blocks of a profitable customer file are standard: name, address, phone number(s), e-mail address, and (if applicable) administrative assistant's contact info. These five or six bytes of information provide you with the start of a great customer record. To take customer communication to the highest level, however, you need more information.

The more you know about your customers, the easier it is to deter defections — times a client chooses to do business with someone else or refers business to another company or agency. That's a killer for your business: Just think of the enormous time you've invested in getting and keeping your customers!

Figure 6-1 shows a chart you can use to increase your knowledge of your customers and create more personal connections with them. You can program this information into your CRM by customizing the fields:

Say you've collected this information about your customers over time and you've entered it into your CRM. The next time you come across a couple of extra tickets to the golf tournament in town, you search your CRM for customers who are golf fanatics and give them the tickets. Of course, it doesn't hurt your relationship that the tickets came from you!

Another example: You see a great article about the University of Alabama. You search for University of Alabama alumni on your customer list and e-mail them the article. What have you invested? A few minutes of *really* listening to your customers (and you do that anyway, right?) and a few minutes of data entry. What have you achieved? You've brought your relationship with this customer to a new level and spent minimal time doing it.

If you really want to impress a customer, take great notes in your CRM and start the next call with something like the following:

- ✔ *"How did (the wedding, your party, the conference) go?"*
- ✔ *"How was Bobby's soccer game last week? Did his team win?"*
- ✔ *"What did you do with* X? *Last time we spoke, you said* Y.*"*

Take a few moments of your time to note nuggets of information in your CRM, use that information to make your prospect or customer feel valued and unique, and watch your customer relationship grow and solidify.

Date: _____

Customer Profile

1) Customer Name _____
Nickname _____

2) Company Name _____
3) Company Address _____
Home Address _____

4) Telephone Numbers _____
Business _____
Home _____

5) Date of Birth _____
Place of Birth _____
Hometown _____

Education

6) High School _____
Year Graduated _____
College _____
Year Graduated _____
College Fraternity/Sorority _____

7) _____

8) Sports _____
_____

Family

9) Spouse name and occupation _____
10) Spouse education _____
11) Spouse's interests _____
12) Anniversary _____
13) Children _____
names/ages _____
_____

14) Children's education levels _____
_____

15) Children's interests (hobbies, problems) _____
_____

Special Interests

16) Clubs, fraternal associations, service clubs _____
_____

17) Community activities _____
_____

Lifestyle

Figure 6-1:
A sample
customer
profile.

18) Favorite place for lunch _____
Favorite place for dinner _____

19) Favorite spectator sports _____
Favorite sports teams _____

Putting a CRM program on a server to maximize accessibility and backup

My rule: Everyone in the company must be able to access public information in real time at all times. All employees who serve or sell to customers need access to client documents and information. This is true for all departments: sales, marketing, administration, accounting, and so on. And you can set up a CRM program so all employees can tap into the data. Putting CRM on a server has security advantages as well.

Not only does having company data spread around on various computers create an organizational nightmare, but it also represents a security flaw — you can lose valuable customers in a keystroke. For example, if you have a salesperson who has given notice or, worse, one you've terminated, that person may have 200 customers — and all their customer information — saved on his or her computer. Before leaving, that person can easily delete every customer file in the computer.

Ouch! You just lost the history and possibly the contact information for 200 customers. You also lost customers that current salespeople were hoping to close in the next 30, 60, or 90 days. Now you have to try to reconstruct which customers the salesperson sold to, what he or she sold to them, and what the customer-salesperson relationships were like. And you're back figuring out how you can increase sales and service to these customers in the future.

If you have multiple independent computers with company data stored on each, I highly recommend that you connect your company's computers in a network run by a server. Server-accessible CRM data ensures that your business can avoid data-loss nightmares. With the CRM program, you can immediately lock an ex-employee out of the system and have system backups to reconstruct data as needed.

Some companies may be reticent to open access to this information because of client confidentiality or simply the risk of corrupting or deleting important data. If you want to protect accounting, personnel, and other private information, you can do that no problem. The programs offer password protection so that only certain employees can access the most confidential information. You can also set it up so employees can *see* the data but not delete or modify it in any way.

Chapter 7

Taking Time Management on the Road

The life of the road warrior is anything but a vacation. With airline congestion, weather delays, cancellations, lost luggage, overbookings, botched reservations, unreliable wake-up calls, and other increasing frustrations of travel, careful planning and effective use of time on the road lay the groundwork for a productive trip — and a smooth and enjoyable homecoming.

In this chapter, you discover how to prepare for your trip, minimize packing, make your flight productive, sail through airport security, and get to work in your room — all in good time. I also explain how to maintain your health routine on the road so you're ready to go in the morning. *Note:* My wife, Joan, was a flight attendant for eight years, and she can testify to the grueling, frustrating nature of travel for work — and to the importance of careful time management on those trips. I have to acknowledge Joan's valuable contributions to this chapter.

Organizing Trips for Peak Productivity

Just as I encourage you to plan out your hours, days, and weeks on a regular basis, I recommend the same strategy for the times you're on the road. By planning ahead, you're able to maximize your time, squeezing every drop of productivity from your trip. For each and every business trip you take, sit down in advance and be sure you address the issues I set out in this section. By following this process every time you travel, you reduce the potential for glitches, delays, and loss of productivity.

Scheduling multiple engagements for one trip

I meet businesspeople whose travel schedules put them on the road as often as twice a week, sometimes sleeping at home for only a night before flying out for another one-day or two-day trip, often to a destination close to the one they just returned from. That makes about as much sense to me as stopping off at home between trips to the grocery, the gas station, and the dry cleaner.

Whenever possible, group your business trips together, creating one weeklong schedule instead of scattering several small trips over a couple of weeks. It's bound to reduce your commutes to and from the airport and possibly your total travel time, and you allow for a longer stretch of home-base time for yourself.

Even if your destinations aren't close to each other, it may still make sense for you to book multiple engagements for the same trip. You may do a little zigzagging in the skies, but overall, you're using your time more efficiently. Why *not* fly from Chicago to Atlanta to Phoenix and back home to Dallas? Combining your three meetings into one weeklong travel-thon instead of spreading them out over two or three weeks keeps you home for a bigger block of time.

As you plan a scheduled business trip, ask yourself these questions:

- ✔ Do you have other upcoming travel obligations that you can take care of on this trip?

- ✔ Can you reschedule this travel commitment to a time when you have other meetings or events in that location?

- ✔ What else can you do or whom can you meet with in this destination or region?

- ✔ Can you perform some tasks *there* that you typically may not travel for, such as meeting with a client or vendor?

Identifying trip objectives

In the process of making polite chitchat on a flight, the same questions crop up with virtually every person I sit next to: "Flying for business or pleasure?" And "What brings you to fill-in-the-blank?" When my seatmate establishes that the trip is for business, he or she typically responds to the second question with something like "Oh, I have a meeting with a client" or "Going to a conference." Well, I don't expect or *want* fellow travelers to tell me all the details about what they hope to accomplish, but I can tell you it's critical to their success that they've answered the question for themselves long before they slide their laptop cases under the seats in front of them.

Identify your objectives *before* your trip. By getting a handle on your objectives, you can do a better job of preparing for your trip. For instance, say you're heading up a meeting of colleagues at the company headquarters to address a recurring communications problem and come up with a viable system that ensures all offices receive corporate directives in the same manner at the same time. By nailing down some specific objectives, you're then able to identify other preparations necessary to accomplish your goals, such as closing the big sale on a new prospect or meeting with your best customer to resolve delivery issues.

And no, when naming your objectives, "going to a meeting" or "attending a seminar" isn't enough. What do you want to accomplish by the time you return home? Depending on your responsibilities and the purpose of the trip, your answers may look like some of the following:

- ✔ I want to learn everything I can about the client and her company.

- ✔ I hope to turn the prospect I'm meeting into a client.

- ✔ I intend to learn how to operate *X* software program so I can effectively perform a new function in my job.

- ✔ I'll make a minimum of ten networking contacts for future business relationships during the workshop breaks.

- ✔ I plan to resolve the issue with the home office so we can return to our successful production levels.

Your objectives raise questions that allow you to effectively prepare. (See Chapter 13 for info on meeting and appointment preparation.)

Packing a full agenda

After you establish the *who*, *what*, *where*, and *when* of your trip, the next step is to determine the *how* — how you're going to work all of this into your travel schedule. The solution is to pack each day to the fullest. Follow these tips:

- ✔ **Schedule your day tightly.** Don't pad the time when you're on the road. Factor in meeting length, travel time, preparation time, and even when you wake up, have meals, and get your exercise in for the day. When someone else is arranging or has influence on your schedule, ask for a specific time parameters so you can schedule your other obligations accordingly.

- ✔ **Be firm about your time — don't allow time overruns.** When you need to be done, be done with what you're doing. You may even tell anyone involved in advance when you have to be done with this meeting, discussion, or appointment. That'll increase the odds that you finish on time.

✔ **Wind it up before winding down.** Devote some time to a daily debriefing process. Review the day's events and the information you gathered and take care of follow-up paperwork or wrap-up reports. Do this early enough in the evening so you can accomplish the necessary wind-down time before you head for bed. Otherwise, you may have difficulty sleeping, which can lower your productivity for the next day.

Right before bed is a good time to write thank-you notes to the people you've met with. Yes, thank-you notes — even before you get back to the office. Always travel with note cards or stationery and stamps. Your contacts will be impressed when they receive your note with a postmark from their location. You can drop the mail at the front desk as you check out from your hotel the next morning.

Tickets, Please: Making Plans to Go the Distance

Before you head out your front door, you need to book your hotel and set up your transportation. In this section, I discuss how to choose an ideal hotel, how to decide on a mode of transportation, and how to book the best flight.

When making reservations, I find that using a travel agent has its advantages, even though you pay a fee for the service. Many agents are able to compare all forms of transportation to give you the options you need to make the best choice. If you're more of a do-it-yourself person, then I suggest going to the source directly. In recent years, I haven't found much of a difference in price between booking a ticket directly with a major airline and going to a Web-based service such as Expedia or Orbitz. The problem with online services is that they almost give you too many options, and looking at all those options takes a lot of time. I've also found that many of the options aren't ideal for a business traveler because they have you coming back on the day following your trip or require an additional overnight stay.

Selecting a hotel

Selecting a hotel for its convenience is key. If you have an early morning meeting, there's no substitute for staying a few minutes away rather than 30 minutes away. Most of my speaking engagements are in hotels and conference centers, and I stay at the hotel where the convention or event is being held. The ability to walk downstairs and be on the platform far outweighs the advantages that other hotels may offer.

When you do have a choice of hotels, here are the time-saving amenities to look for:

✔ **Internet access:** High-speed Internet service, preferably wireless, is a must.

✔ **A concierge:** A concierge can help you select restaurants and make reservations there. I've even had a few concierges track down clothing or personal items that I forgot and needed.

✔ **Late night or 24-hour room service:** As a road warrior, work constraints or even travel issues may prevent you from arriving at your final destination at the dinner hour. Room service ensures you stay fed.

✔ **A good business center:** It's hard to bring all the tools that you need on the road with you. After all, a good photocopier is hard to get into an overhead bin. A business center with a computer you can use with a printer can really be a lifesaver at times. It also helps you check in and print out that boarding pass for tonight's flight before you leave the hotel this morning.

✔ **A quality workout facility:** I prefer staying in hotels that have actual athletic facilities rather than a retrofitted hotel room with a few machines stuffed in it. It ensures that a machine is available for you to use when you want to exercise — you're not stuck waiting for someone to finish.

Planes, trains, and automobiles: Choosing your mode of transportation

Deciding whether to travel via plane, train, or automobile has a tremendous effect on the use of time in today's security-alert society. With the Transportation Security Administration (TSA) issues at the airport, the savings you get from air travel is limited for travel that'd take less than two hours by train or automobile. By the time you arrive at the airport 60 to 90 minutes in advance of a flight and actually travel by air, you could've driven there or taken the train.

One advantage that air travel has over the automobile is that you can use the time for work. Reading a report to prepare for your meeting while driving is pretty hard! At least with airline travel, you can get some work done in the airport awaiting your flight and on the flight.

A train can be a good choice, especially if you live in a big city on the East Coast. The frequency and schedules for commuter trains tend to be much better between large cities on the East Coast than other places. The security and check process takes much less time than at the airport, so you can save that time while still having a comfortable seat to work from for the duration of your travel. Additionally, most train stations are located in downtown areas or close to them, reducing the commute from the train station to your client's downtown office.

Booking a flight

Booking a flight for the middle of the day is a helpful strategy for avoiding rush-hour traffic and long lines at the airport, which is busiest in the early morning and early evening.

Also check the connections and airports that you'll be traveling through. You don't want to feel like the airport is your new campground, but you also don't want a connection so tight that you have to run through the airport, either. I think that an hour connection time between flights is about right. It means that you're not stuck for three hours between flights in limbo, but if your inbound is delayed, you still have a reasonable chance of making your connecting flight. If you have the minimum connection time of 35 minutes between flights, one weather delay can leave you scrambling to secure a seat on a later flight. And with airlines dramatically cutting their schedules, more people will be stranded due to weather and much fuller planes than ever before.

Seat selection is important for peak productivity. More than a curtain separates first-class seating from coach. Space, boarding privileges, stowage, meals, amenities, and service are *all* better. For me, the extra seating space is reason enough to fly first-class anytime I can. With room to comfortably open my laptop, I can easily turn a cross-country flight into a five-hour work session. And when I fly internationally, especially if it's an overnight flight, I arrive at my destination much more rested and ready to get down to business.

Cashing in on frequent flyer status

If you travel via air or are starting fly more often for business, signing up for frequent flyer programs can improve the experience dramatically. The more miles you travel, the more points you earn, which convert to more perks and benefits. Differences between a top-tier flyer and low-mileage flyer can be dramatic — the more miles you've racked up, the better the seating, boarding, flexibility options, and extra benefits.

It pays to funnel as much of your flying to one carrier as possible so you can leverage more miles for more perks. Based on your typical business travel patterns, identify the airline that offers you the most routes and best connections for those destinations. If the choice is between a couple of different carriers, study the benefits and programs to see which gives its members the most services for their miles.

Are first-class upgrades an important benefit to you? If so, check out the type of planes that typically fly to your frequent destinations — how many first-class seats do they hold? Eight or 24? Obviously, your chances for an upgrade increase with the number of seats available.

The price of admission for first class or business class passage is significantly more than a super-saver fare in coach. And for many businesspeople restricted by corporate travel policies, paying as much as five times more for the luxury isn't an option. But if you've racked up enough frequent flyer miles, you may be able to gain admission without breaking the bank.

Some airlines offer special, roomier sections that cost less than first class but still provide perks. For instance, United Airlines has an Economy Plus section in some of its aircraft. The first ten rows or so offer about five inches more legroom. Typically, these seats are reserved for travelers who chalk up more than 25,000 miles a year with United. You can also purchase a yearly pass for $299 to book these roomier seats.

Booking your flight online allows you to view the plane's seat availability and then book your preferred type of seat, if any are left. Here are some considerations as you make your selection:

✔ Do you need to be able to disembark as quickly as possible? Go as far forward as possible.

✔ If you have a lot of laptop work or reading to do, a window seat means you won't have two seatmates nudging past you when they make a trip to the restroom. Nor will you be disturbed as the drinks, snacks, and trash are passed back and forth under your nose.

✔ If you're tall or you just prefer a little more legroom (so you arrive better rested and have more space to work), choose an aisle seat. If an exit row seat is available, you gain a few more inches, although some airlines add $25 to $50 to the price of exit-row seats.

Lightening the Luggage Load

I recently was on a multi-city weeklong tour with several speakers who traveled together. As one of the newest speakers joined the group at check-in, we watched as he struggled with three large suitcases. The rest of us had regulation carry-on bags or a single bag to check. We shook our heads and smiled as we anticipated his end-of-tour exhaustion after wrestling with those bags at every airport and hotel. "He'll learn," our glances at each other seemed to say.

Anybody who has spent a good amount of time on the road — be it for business or pleasure — has picked up a singularly important lesson: The lighter your luggage and the fewer pieces of luggage you have, the better you can react to travel troubles and opportunities. Carrying the equivalent of a steamer trunk is only going to slow you down, wear you out, and likely cost you more money in overweight fines and extra tips to porters. This section explains how to lighten your burden.

Picking the right luggage for your travel needs is an important step. Invest in some good bags — at least two and possibly more. Short trips require the minimum of clothing and work materials, so a rolling carry-on with laptop compartment may do the trick. Extended travels may require a bigger bag with a garment section. Whatever your needs, pick sturdy pieces.

Sticking to carry-ons

In times when your luggage is likely to end up San Francisco, leaving you sleepless in Seattle, it's no surprise that more travelers are opting to keep their possessions with them. I find that limiting my luggage to carry-ons also offers tremendous time savings. Even if I have to leave my luggage at the door to be stored underneath (with overhead-bin overload, flight attendants often call for passengers to leave their bags at the door for storage), my carry-on is waiting for me when I disembark, saving me that wait at the baggage claim and eliminating the possibility that my bag will be diverted to another destination. Also, sticking to carry-ons may be cheaper: Unless you're a top-tier flyer, you have to pay to check a bag or two on most air carriers.

Sticking to carry-ons gives you more flexibility to make last-minute flight changes. Since 9/11, security regulations have required travelers and their bags to travel on the same plane. So after you've checked in your luggage, you can't make a last-minute change to your routing — even if weather, delays, or other circumstances make it a sensible option.

If you do plan to check your luggage, consider choosing nontraditional colors and shapes of luggage — and save some time at baggage claim eyeing yet another black soft-side bag like everyone else's. You can also tag your bag with ribbon or a unique luggage tag to make it stand out.

Checking your baggage does allow you a more relaxed travel experience. (Who wants to feel like a Sherpa wheeling an unwieldy carry-on and weighed-down backpack?) But weighing the pros and cons, carry-on wins out over check-in.

Addressing clothes quantity

I used to overpack for my business trips, anticipating every possible scenario: What if I needed to go out in the evening with clients? What if I spilled mustard on my jacket — at each meal? What if I ripped my pants? So I carried the equivalent of nearly two changes of clothes a day. And I used the same strategy for my work-related materials, loading up a virtual library of books, reports, correspondences, and saved-up reading into my briefcase.

Well, experience taught me that I rarely go out in the evening, so the most casual attire is just fine for the room-service delivery person. And I turn out not to be the slob I feared — on the infrequent occasion that I spill something, a little water and soap usually removes the stain. And if not, hotel services can take care of the cleaning or even sew up a pair of ripped trousers.

As you pack for your trip, consider every item and ask, "Is this critical to either my success or comfort?" If not, leave it home. Here are a few tricks I've picked up over the years:

- ✔ Color-coordinate your clothing and shoes so you can mix and match items, expanding your wardrobe without packing more.

- ✔ Fold and place all your dress shirts in a box (instead of hanging them) for more efficient packing — and less ironing when you unpack them.

- ✔ Carry ties on a caddy that rolls them up. You can find these in most travel magazines.

- ✔ Stick socks or other small items inside your shoes to maximize space.

- ✔ Those plastic bags that shrink-wrap clothes to take up two-thirds less space really work — especially for bulky items.

- ✔ Find out what items your hotel makes available. You may be able to leave behind your bathrobe, slippers, hair dryer, cotton swabs, and more.

Carrying work materials: A case for being brief

In addition to choosing a travel wardrobe, the business traveler has to pack all the necessary work materials for a productive trip. The modern "briefcase" holds a laptop or Blackberry, a cellphone, business cards and contact information, relevant files, reports and research materials, PowerPoint presentations, and more.

As soon as you're on the road, you want to have absolutely everything you need to guarantee a successful trip — but it's still a good idea to strive for a minimalist approach. Consider these ideas:

- ✔ Invest in the smallest laptop model that you can comfortably use and that meets all your storage needs.

- ✔ Keep reports and research files on your computer instead of carrying printouts.

- ✔ Start a tear file for your travels. Instead of stuffing a stack of magazines into your bag, quickly flip through your periodicals before the trip and tear out the articles you want to read.

✔ Store your books on an electronic reader. I recently purchased a Sony Reader, a ½-inch-thick, postcard-sized device that lets me store 160 books. I used to travel with two or three hardback books. What a difference this technology has made!

Compiling your travel details

You can cut a lot of items from your luggage, but a collection of your travel details isn't one of them. On-time flights are becoming rarer — and that's on top of all the possible trip-ups at check-in, security check, and boarding. And after you arrive, there's all the hassle with car rental reservations or securing transportation and hotel check-in. Each step of your journey seems to require its own special password, code, document, and procedure. Fumbling at any one of these steps can send your progress screeching to a halt.

Whenever you travel, carry a comprehensive itinerary — which I call a *travel map* — that includes every airline record locator, reservation number, transportation detail, hotel location, time table, and contact phone number that you may need. Place all your info in chronological order for easy access. That way, if you run into a problem, say, with the hotel check-in (they lost your reservation!), you can pull out your reservation detail showing the time of booking, your reservation number, what kind of room you requested, and — *voila!* Everything is settled and you pick up your room key.

Some of the details captured in your travel map may include the following:

✔ **Airline information:** Include flight numbers, departure and arrival times, record locators, seat assignments, and the airline reservation phone number.

✔ **Terminal information:** If you're connecting to other flights, this info tells you whether you have to hustle from one terminal to another to make your flight.

✔ **Ground transportation details:** Gather car rental reservation numbers or car service information for each leg of your trip. Include the costs you were quoted when you made your reservations in case there's a dispute about the rate.

If you're driving, you need directions to where you're going, as well as some idea of traffic issues, rush-hour times, road construction, and areas to avoid before you arrive. Plenty of Web programs, such as MapQuest, can give you that information in advance. Plot your route and print out the map before you leave home.

✔ **Hotel information:** Include the reservation number, address and contact details, a map if you're driving to the hotel, shuttle details if applicable, room type or preferences requested, and the room rate you were quoted.

> ✔ **Meeting details:** Include the location, directions to, start and stop times, and contact information (in case you are unavoidably late or lost).

The other option is to download all that information into your PDA schedule. This allows you to avoid the paper altogether (depending on the length of your trip and the complexity of your travel schedule, you may have a *note-book's* worth of paper).

Carry your confirmation printouts from the airline, hotel, or transportation service in paper. In case there's a question whether you actually *have* a reservation, you want to have proof.

Taking Wing: Making the Most of Travel Day

When you travel by air, you have to resign yourself to the fact that you've given up some control for the convenience of a swift journey. Weather, mechanical delays, overbookings — you can't do much if these situations occur. The best way to make a travel day as smooth as possible is to take control of what you can: being packed and ready to go well before flight time is a biggie — and checking in for your flight from home is another.

Confirming flight status before you leave for the airport is another way to take control and avoid sitting around the airport needlessly. Many airlines and travel booking sites now provide electronic flight updates by e-mail and telephone, even text messages to your cellphone. You can request notification about changes or delays to your flight; such alerts can give you an hour more at work or a little more family time at home.

In this section, I give you some other suggestions to make getting there as smooth and productive as possible.

Navigating the post-9/11 airport

The world of air travel changed dramatically after 9/11. The lines got longer, patience got shorter, and travelers were forced to do the half-Monty at security checkpoints. You can minimize the snags and slowdowns of airport check-in and security, but it does require a little planning.

Flying through check-in

If you want to bypass that interminable wait while the check-in person seems to type a college thesis into the keyboard before generating your boarding pass, check yourself in via one of the electronic self-service kiosks that most airlines have available. In fact, the self-check-in is now the rule rather than the exception. If you have bags to check, you still have to deal with one of the attendants after you've generated your boarding pass, but the wait is usually short.

Even better, most carriers allow you to check in up to 24 hours in advance from your home computer. Print your boarding pass at home, and if you don't have check-in luggage, you can skip the entire process and go straight to security check. If you do have luggage to check, you still save time; you simply have to go to the counter for them to check your ID and take your bags.

Online check-in offers many benefits:

- You can respond to problems with seating and flight changes earlier.
- The earlier check-in reduces your odds of getting bumped from the flight. (Although you can still volunteer to give up your seat and earn future travel benefits in case of overbooked flights.)
- You can get to the airport a little later. Most airlines cut off check-in at least 30 minutes before departure, so passengers are advised to arrive anywhere from an hour to an hour and a half early. Checking in at home buys you a little more time.

You may be able to take advantage of off-site check-in for your return flight as well. More and more, hotels are setting up lobby computer kiosks for guests to check in prior to leaving for the airport — definitely an amenity worth asking about before you book your hotel reservation.

After you confirm that your flight is on schedule, leave for the airport in plenty of time, padding a bit for possible traffic congestion or construction detours. If you've checked in from home and only have carry-on luggage, plan to arrive at the airport 60 minutes before your flight. With check-in bags, schedule 90 minutes for domestic flights and 2 hours for international departures. In most cases, this should get you to your gate without sweating it, even allowing for a check-in snag or security jam.

Don't arrive at check-in less than 30 minutes before your flight is to depart: The airline is likely to deny you boarding — and it has every right to! Get to the check-in desk with less than a half hour before departure, and you just may find that your seat has been given to a standby passenger.

Arriving early gives you a chance to put your name on a list for a better seat assignment. Passengers may have missed connections or simply don't show. And other passengers may have received upgrades, leaving a roomy exit-row seat or an aisle seat up front open.

Passing through security

With ongoing concerns about safety, you still can anticipate potential congestion at the security checkpoint. Allow plenty of time for this step. Depending
on your flyer status and airport, getting to the gate for departure can take
upward of 90 minutes — especially if you're selected for a search. Don't cut it
too close.

To avoid being part of the security slowdown, follow these guidelines:

- Visit www.tsa.gov and review guidelines from the TSA before you pack.

- Choose shoes and a jacket that slip off easily — you're expected to
  remove them.

- Leave behind or pack any jewelry that's prone to set off the metal detector.
  Unclasping necklaces and slipping off bracelets can hold you up.

- Limit electronics and pack them neatly. A tangle of too many wires,
  cables, and gizmos in your carry-on is likely to trigger a search. And of
  course, any electronics you do bring should be easily accessible — you
  have to pull your laptop computer from your carry-on.

- Pack your quart-sized plastic bag of liquids and gels in an outside pocket
  of your carry-on so you don't have to dig for it. And don't take more than
  the 3-ounce limit per container. They *will* confiscate your regular-sized
  shampoo. And remember, tubes of toothpaste are considered liquid, too.

If you have frequent flyer status, ask the customer service representative at
check-in or a TSA employee whether there's an express security line. In many
airports, the express lines aren't well-marked. If they don't have one, consider
sending a complaint to the airline to get working on it with TSA.

Taking advantage of airline clubs while you wait

One of the best ways to use your wait time at the airport is to spend it in an
airline club room. By joining United's Red Carpet Club, American Airlines'
Admirals Club, or Delta's Crown Room, for example, you can relax away from
the crowds in the gate area and enjoy a number of amenities.

Snacks and beverages are available to members. The seating is much more
comfortable, with cozy chairs and lounge areas, as well as work spaces with
Internet connections — some carriers such as Alaskan Airlines provide free
access. There are even conference rooms. If you have a lot of time between
connections, you can work while grounded, sending e-mail and forwarding
documents you may have completed during your flight — or at least enjoy a
quiet place to read, relax, and recharge your batteries.

Some of the airline clubs have reciprocal privileges with other carriers, so be
sure to check on this if you're flying another carrier.

Boarding early

I'm a believer in early-bird boarding. I know a lot of people like to wait until everyone else is on so they don't have to sit in sardine-formation any longer than necessary. But if you're one of the last to board, you probably won't be sitting near your carry-on because the overhead bins in your section may have filled up. As soon as the gate agent begins calling for passengers, board at your earliest opportunity.

Preempting delay disasters

If you travel with any frequency, you'll inevitably find yourself at the gate or aboard the plane, listening to the announcement that the flight has been delayed or cancelled. After the collective groan, get ready for a stampede of passengers desperate to secure whatever remaining seats there may be on the next flight out. If you're sitting at the back of the plane when this occurs, you may find yourself at a distinct disadvantage.

Don't despair when you find you're likely to miss a connecting flight due to delays. While still making your way along with the rest of the pack, turn on your cellphone and start dialing the airline's toll-free reservation line (program the number into your cell before you leave home). Of course, other passengers are probably doing the same thing, but you still improve your chances of rebooking on the next flight. Although only one or two gate agents may be reticketing customers, there are likely many more operators doing the same thing over the phone. Cover your bases, though: Stay in the customer service line — you may find yourself listening to a medley of hold-music greatest hits and actually reach the live agent first.

Making good use of flight time

Advance planning ensures that you make the most of your flight time. To begin with, don't attempt any serious work or reading during the boarding and take-off stages of the flight — too much competition. If you're on a longer flight, wait until the onboard entertainment starts, the hustle and bustle of drink delivery is over, and the cabin is quieter.

Now is the time to get out what you really want to get done. Be realistic about what you can accomplish under the circumstances. For example, writing a book chapter requires a level of focus that I simply can't achieve while flying. Nor can I develop strategic plans with my laptop on my tray table. But I *can* write articles for magazines or online publications. I can analyze data, ponder problems, contemplate ideas, and discover solutions.

Take a look at this list of productive activities you may be able to devote yourself to while flying, depending on your energy level, focus, and concentration level:

✔ Catch up on the news.

✔ Review reports.

✔ Write e-mail messages to send later.

✔ Read your tear file.

✔ Plan sales strategies.

✔ Write performance evaluations.

✔ Review your presentation for tomorrow.

✔ Tweak your PowerPoint presentation.

✔ Escape into a good book.

Many veteran business travelers report that it's easier to accomplish work on outbound flights. A higher energy level, a measure of anticipation, and perhaps even more pressure to be successful during the upcoming meetings seem to motivate these professionals. So with this in mind, try to take full advantage of this drive and make the most of your outbound travels.

I usually bring light reading for the homebound trips at the end of the week. I find that my brain is anticipating getting home to be with family, so reading a lighter book for pleasure allows me to slow down and transition from Dirk, the business owner and driven sales professional, to Dirk, the doting family man.

Of course, work success or even a nice nap isn't a possibility if you're easily distracted by all the activity around you. Pilot and flight attendant announcements, chatting seatmates, crying babies, drink service, and possibly even a movie all compete for your attention in the air. So a must-have, in my view, is a noise-canceling headset that cuts down the ambient background noise. The roar of the engines goes down to a dull roar or hum. The headsets are available in numerous forms and price ranges. Carrying your own music can also help you block distractions. I've found that classical music is an excellent selection for productivity, focus, and background noise abatement.

Soaring through the Rest of the Trip

Tray tables are now in the upright and locked position, landing gear is engaged, and all electronic devices have been turned off. You're coming in for a landing and ready for the next chapter of your journey. Although you've made it to your destination, you still have a lot to do before you can deem this business trip a success — and I cover that in this section.

So put your books, games, laptop, reading glasses, and any other possessions in your bag and get ready. (Though you may want to keep that magazine in the side pocket for easy access, just in case there are delays in taxiing to the gate and disembarking.)

Moving on: The ABC's of ground transportation

I admit it: When it comes to getting around in a strange city, I'm a snob. I go for a car service over a taxi, shuttle, or car rental. First, with a car service, the driver meets me as I exit the gate area — from that point on, I have less to think about. The driver, holding a sign with my name on it, directs me toward baggage claim (if I've checked in luggage), grabs my bag, and guides me out toward the car. I don't have to look for the car rental shuttle or search for the taxi line and make my way to a hotel on roads that I'm unfamiliar with. I'm probably exhausted from a day of travel, it may be late at night by the time I arrive, and I most likely have an important meeting that I want to be fresh for first thing the next day.

A car service strips the experience of stress and provides comfort and convenience for about $20 more than a typical taxi ride. To my mind, that's a small price to pay.

If you have to take a taxi, make sure it's an authorized line for safety and cost reasons. Many airports have a taxi queue — where passengers wait in line and the airport representative asks you where you're going, directs you to the next waiting cab, and gives you a receipt with the set rate. If you're approached outside the gate by individuals offering taxi service, pass them by — they're most likely unauthorized drivers.

If you're renting a car, you save time and money when you join a priority club from one of the major rental companies. Priority club status allows you to bypass the line that all the other customers have to go through. Your name is on the LED board, so you proceed to your car and are out of the parking lot in less than a few minutes. Many companies waive the annual club fee if you have a preferred credit card. For example, a Platinum American Express card member gets a free Hertz #1 club membership annually.

Most rental companies offer cars with a GPS navigational feature, and they're a huge time-saver. The audio warnings guide you to your destination, turn by turn. And if you do get off course, you hear the friendly and patient navigator alert you that it's recalculating your route.

Mastering hotel room productivity

Your productivity journey starts at check-in at the hotel. Being a member of the hotel brand's frequent-guest program can speed up check-in.

If you're traveling alone, request a room with a king-sized bed instead of two doubles. You end up with a bigger bed and more space in which to move about the room. Because the single king opens up more room space, you may even get better or more furniture — a sofa and sitting area in addition to a desk and workspace.

Follow a routine when you enter your hotel room after check-in. For example, I call for a bathrobe, which saves me having to pack it or other additional clothes for an evening in my room. I check the Internet connection and set up my workstation. If I'm going to watch some television, I heat up the iron to do my pressing for the next day. If I'm staying in the hotel for a few days, I do all the ironing at once.

Know yourself well enough to recognize your energy and level of focus. At times, you can really get work done when you're in a hotel room; other times, you're too tired from the day's travel. Select the right activity based on your energy, intensity, and focus right now. Don't waste your time trying to grind through a report that you know you can't focus on. Instead, take a nap or go to bed early for the evening and get up earlier, when you're refreshed and can focus better. Nothing is worse than staring at the paper, a report, or your computer screen when your head isn't clear.

Using room service to help manage your time

Room service saves you the hassle of going out to eat and can give you some much-needed alone time. I have to admit I order room service for more than 90 percent of my meals when I'm on the road. After a long day spent around people, I'm peopled out. I like nothing better than to return to the quiet of my room, read the paper while eating my dinner, and catch up on the news or the sports of the day on TV. I prefer to stay away from noisy restaurants, loud music, and boisterous crowds. And this solitary time also allows me to do other housekeeping items while I wait for my food to be delivered. I can unpack, organize, work out, or iron while the chef is preparing my meal. I can even request delivery at a certain time to coincide with the completion of my workout or tasks.

I use room service for breakfast, too. I highly encourage the use of the night-before door hanger for putting in your breakfast order, one of the greatest time-saving devices in any road warrior's arsenal. You can order your breakfast to be delivered at any time you desire. Most hotels offer this service. It beats calling room service in the morning only to find out it'll be 45 minutes before they can deliver your breakfast.

This service lets me plan my whole morning in advance. When I want to wake up, work out, spend my quiet time in prayer and reading, and shower, I can do all those and still have my breakfast in my bathrobe before I get dressed for the day. It's a beautiful thing!

Eating to win

Proper eating on the road helps you optimize energy so you're more productive throughout the day. However, eating on the road is always a challenge. Choices are often limited to tasteless prepackaged airport fare, trans fat–filled carryout, overly rich and heavily sauced chain-restaurant entrees, or the limited selection of club sandwiches, buffalo wings, and cheesecake on the after-hours room service menu.

To avoid being stuck with a growling stomach and no alternative but vending machine snack foods, it's best to have a preemptive plan of attack. Here are a few ways to eat timely meals without resorting to fast food:

✔ **Pack your own.** The demands of travel, business meetings, and work engagements may limit your opportunity for a leisurely repast and force you into stuffing down whatever sustenance you can find at odd times, so bring provisions for your stay. If not a sandwich, at least pack a couple of energy bars, nuts or trail mix, a banana or apple.

✔ **Choose airport food wisely.** More and more, airport eateries are offering to-go items such as healthy subs, wraps, salads, and fruit to buy and carry on the plane. So instead of counting on peanut packages or overpriced sandwiches that don't taste much better than the paper they're packaged in, carry your meal onboard.

✔ **Start the day off with a full tank.** Before confirming your hotel reservations, check to see whether it offers a *full* complimentary breakfast — the kind with fresh fruit, yogurt, bagels, maybe even cooked omelets and sausage. Many hotels advertise free breakfast, and it's no more than a tray of store-bought Danish or donuts and canned orange juice — not enough fuel to power your morning.

✔ **Preview hotel dining options.** Ask about room service and delivery service from nearby restaurants. What are the hours for room service? Can you order fresh and healthy at midnight? Are there healthy selections — fish or chicken with vegetables instead of fries? Do some options meet any dietary restrictions you have (low-sodium, vegetarian, and so on)? If the hotel room service is limited, do nearby restaurants deliver? And are there walk-to options?

✔ **Visit the local grocery.** A quick trip to a nearby supermarket can help you stock up on some nutritious essentials. If all else fails — room service is closed, the pizza delivery estimate is two hours, and the vending machine won't accept your wrinkled dollars — a supply of emergency rations can see you through till morning. Ask whether the hotel has rooms with a mini-fridge to keep your perishables fresh.

Fitting in your fitness routine

Whether it's taking a long walk, stretching out or practicing yoga in your room, or hitting the hotel pool, a little bit of physical activity goes a long way in keeping you fit, alert, and productive. When you're out of your routine, you tend to slip into behaviors that may not be the healthiest. You may eat fat- and sodium-heavy fast food — and more of it. You're probably sitting more and moving less. The stress of travel is likely taking its toll on your mood, as well.

Taking time to exercise while on the road helps offset these unhealthy aspects of travel. Commit to some sort of physical workout every day — it doesn't have to be your full-blown regimen. Here are some travel options:

✔ Book yourself in a hotel that has a fitness center with the sorts of equipment you like to use: treadmills, elliptical machines, free weights. If you're a swimmer, make sure the hotel has an indoor pool. (Call ahead to make sure it's open and working.)

✔ If you do yoga or a floor routine, pack your mat and other equipment (blocks or bands). More and more, hotels are beginning to stock these items for guests, so check first to see whether they have what you need.

✔ If you belong to a gym or club with a national presence, check to see whether there's a branch in your destination and whether you have reciprocal privileges.

✔ If all else fails, find a nearby mall or park and plan for a daily vigorous walk. Or do a simple equipment-free routine involving push-ups, crunches, and lunges.

Part III
Confronting Challenges to Time Management

The 5th Wave   By Rich Tennant

Cell Phones

"This model comes with a particularly useful function – a simulated static button for breaking out of long winded conversations."

In this part . . .

From a faulty alarm clock to a client who doesn't show for a meeting, unexpected time management obstacles seem to pop up every day. And then there are problems that rest solely on your shoulders: procrastinating, overscheduling, forgetting to record a task on your to-do list. Whatever their origin, most of these time vampires are hard to eliminate. But you can take precautions to ward off their evil power, and in Part III, I offer you plenty of rays of light.

The ability to communicate effectively can help increase earnings and quality of life, so in Chapter 8, I look at communication as an art form — one that you can shape to enhance your productivity. Chapter 9 gives you the secrets to warding off interruptions, whether they come from the phone, e-mail, co-workers, family, clients, or bosses. I follow this with advice on keeping procrastination and indecision at bay in Chapters 10 and 11.

Chapter 8

Communicating Strategically to Get Results — Fast

*W*hen communication goes awry, the impact is often subtle, though no less time-consuming and expensive. For instance, in a 1998 survey by a temporary agency, employees estimated that 14 percent of their work week was wasted by poor communication. That's more than 5.5 hours per week — and more than 290 hours per year! Studies also show that managers spend 80 percent of their time communicating and that 80 percent of work mistakes are due to miscommunication.

Everyone makes real efforts to get messages across to family, friends, colleagues, business associates, and supervisors. But as these figures illustrate, many of those messages fail because they're unclear, inaccurate, or too long. And for every message that doesn't succeed, you waste time: repeating, redoing, reworking, and reorganizing. In this chapter, you discover how to head off those problems by choosing your medium and using it effectively, keeping your message direct, and asking the right questions.

Choosing the Right Medium for Your Message

Whether you realize it or not, you communicate in three main ways: words, tone of voice, and body language. When you communicate with someone face-to-face, you can employ all three forms of communication, dramatically increasing your effectiveness and speeding your way to the desired outcome. When you communicate over the phone, you use two, and when you do so over e-mail, you're down to one. So despite e-mail's speed and efficiency, sometimes a face-to-face meeting or a phone call is the best way to address and resolve the situation.

How you decide which medium is most appropriate for the information or for your topic of discussion depends largely on the complexity of the information you're sharing as well as on the nature of the topic of discussion. When you have to communicate by e-mail or telephone rather than in person, you need to make these channels work for you as much as possible.

Communicating face-to-face

As companies expand, merge, spin off, morph, and spread their influence throughout the world, an increase in meetings seems to be one of the side effects. And you can't outrun meetings simply by getting transferred to a remote office. Advancements in audio and video conferencing make even telecommuters vulnerable to meeting overload.

The purpose of a good strategic meeting is to communicate goals, identify objectives, seek counsel and advice, share knowledge, solve problems, and gain cooperation from others. Although I concede that sometimes just having face time with a group of co-workers brings value, it's not a good enough reason to hold a meeting. You may be better served to build camaraderie in another way.

The value of the meeting needs to clearly meet or exceed the costs. Identifying the costs can provide a strong motivation to reconsider the *need* for a meeting when so many other communication options are at your disposal. My formula for evaluating the time cost is a bit more complex than simply adding up the hourly salary for all the attendees. I also figure the following:

 ✔ Time invested in preparation for that meeting

 ✔ Time for the meeting host to design the agenda, goals, and objectives

 ✔ Time to coordinate and communicate meeting details to all participants

 ✔ Time required to travel to the meeting, whether people are coming from across town or across the continent

After I add up all investment of company resources for even an hour-long meeting, the labor costs alone are often in the thousands of dollars for a typical meeting. So before you call a meeting, make sure that face-to-face communication is absolutely required to do one of the following:

- ✔ Solve the problem
- ✔ Make a decision
- ✔ Share information
- ✔ Plan and facilitate a project
- ✔ Launch action

Apply your "necessary" test to standing meetings as well. Sure, your department holds an update every week: same time, same place. But if you find that week after week, everyone drones off status reports or presents information others already know or can get in some other way, reconsider the value of the weekly commitment. If there isn't a significant reason to hold your meeting this week — or any week — come up with a better, quicker way to communicate.

Countless studies have pointed out the power and effectiveness of face-to-face communication. Face-to-face communication is best for situations where tone of voice and/or body language is crucial in determining how to respond. Here's some of what you can effectively do in a meeting:

- ✔ Present or sell new ideas
- ✔ Deal with emotionally charged concerns
- ✔ Carry out personal or professional evaluations or disciplinary actions
- ✔ Discuss complex topics that may require explanation or clarification
- ✔ Hand controversial situations that generate back-and-forth discussion among a group of people
- ✔ Communicate when there's a chance that meaning may be misconstrued
- ✔ Discuss sensitive or confidential issues

For instance, if you're in sales and you sell a complex product or service such as MRI machines or consulting services, a phone call can help you book an appointment, but you should make the sale through a series of face-to-face meetings. Or if you're breaking up with your boyfriend of two years, meeting face-to-face to explain why you're kicking him to the curb is more acceptable in breaking-up etiquette.

If you're hesitant to call a meeting but it fits in one of the preceding categories, consider whether you can keep the meeting small or dovetail it into an existing meeting.

Vocalizing your message over the phone

In my opinion, the telephone remains one of the greatest time-saving communication devices ever created. Certainly, the phone offers advantages over face-to-face encounters because you don't have to drive to get to where the other party wants to meet. And although many people feel e-mail has overtaken the telephone, I prefer the telephone because it's more personal, more interactive, and more adaptable. Here's why the telephone is tops:

- ✔ Calling can bring a discussion to a quicker conclusion. You can get instant feedback and response from a phone call.

- ✔ The phone reduces chances that the other party will misinterpret your words. You get a chance to correct misunderstandings in real time rather than hours or even days later.

- ✔ You send a more personal sense of warmth and caring; and you get to use your tone, volume, and selected words to convey meaning via your voice. E-mail, on the other hand, allows readers to filter the communication through their current attitudes toward business, life, and you — without your input.

Should the person you're trying to reach not answer the phone, leave a voice message — don't hang up and try a different means of communication. Voice mail offers myriad advantages e-mail messages and messages taken by other people don't:

- ✔ With voice mail, your message will be delivered verbatim. And because you're not leaving the message with a person, an overzealous assistant won't screen it out.

- ✔ Because you can speak faster than you can type (or even text), voice mail is faster than e-mail.

- ✔ Your message won't get zapped by the spam filter or mixed with the hundreds of other e-mail messages your addressee receives daily.

See the "Corresponding Clearly and Confidently via Telephone" section later in this chapter for tips on leaving effective voice messages. And if you're in sales, be sure to read my book, *Telephone Sales For Dummies,* for valuable advice on increasing your phone sales results.

Putting messages in writing: The joys (and perils) of e-mail

As with all seismic tech changes, e-mail has its infinite blessings — and its bitter curses. E-mail can help you get more work done, but it can also distract you from working. Younger readers may have only heard about the days when business correspondence was conducted through the mail. But those old enough to remember a time before computers and voice mail recall that the only way to get an immediate response from a colleague meant a phone call — and I'm not talking text-messaging. You had to actually talk to them!

It's hard to imagine a time before e-mail. Sometimes, when I've just firmed up a speaking engagement with a client in Asia after one day of e-mailing, I can't fathom how I ever got anything accomplished! Even within my own staff, I can shoot off several projects, answer questions from a dozen employees, review a critical proposal from my top manager, send my sales team an updated status report, and forward a couple of resumes to the HR people — all without lifting my fingers from my keyboard.

Indeed, the e-mail explosion has been one of the most significant advances in the world of work in the twenty-first century. The speed with which e-mail communicates and the breadth of its reach, the efficiency in the ability to store, respond, forward, copy, follow up, and conduct business online is beyond momentous.

But for all its advantages, e-mail is often misused in ways that result in inefficiencies, misunderstandings, and added time. Be sure the message is right for e-mail; some subjects are better handled by phone or face-to-face, where you can gauge responses as you're delivering the message and add information through tone of voice and/or body language. E-mail is ideal for the following:

- In straightforward situations that require a simple, direct response
- When you need a written record of communication
- When the recipient needs to see attached documents, reports, and articles
- When you need to forward information to multiple parties
- When you're unable to reach a person by phone
- When dealing with non-English-speaking people who have heavy accents that diminish understanding
- When the person you need to speak with is long-winded
- When time differences are an issue

I have clients in the Middle East and Asia, which means that while I'm busy working, they're either done with their workday or sound asleep. E-mail allows me to keep our business deals flowing without getting up really early or staying up late. I send off my queries to them and get their replies the next morning.

E-mail can be particularly dangerous in situations where your response is strong or emotional. Who hasn't received an e-mail or voice message that riled them up to the point of pounding out a ferocious e-mail response? In most cases, this situation only ends badly. The blessings of e-mail can also be its curse: Its immediacy gives little time to reflect and process. *Never* send an e-mail when you're still angry, whether to your colleague, vendor, boss, or political representative. Give yourself adequate time to completely calm down before shooting off an emotional message.

That said, I'm all for using the process of writing an e-mail to work through anger. The exercise helps you work off some of that emotional energy and serves to clear your head and think through your reaction and response. But where I put a stop to it is in clicking the Send button. Go ahead and write your e-mail response — I suggest you do it offline so you don't inadvertently send — and then park it in your draft folder until you cool down some. If you reread it the next day and still feel justified, go ahead and send. But if you review and blush at your vitriol, you're saved the embarrassment of having to apologize for your outburst.

Basic Communication Skills: Being Direct and Succinct

Your high school English teacher was right when she told you that length and quality aren't necessarily synonymous. Just because someone's lips move and sound emerges doesn't mean communication is taking place. To ensure that your audience fully receives your message, invest time upfront crafting your correspondence. Plan out questions, presentations, and even short conversations.

For impact, build your message with as few words as possible while still getting your meaning across. Keep the message short, sweet, and to the point. This section tells you how.

Cutting out the clutter in your language

Many people are uncomfortable about following a direct approach, so they fluff out their communications with superfluous information or wrap the salient points in a veil of irrelevant niceties. The problem with this fluff is that it extends meetings and phone calls, confuses important issues, and turns a fellow employee's quick stop by your cubicle into a 25-minute tale about how the weather rained out her kids' soccer game last night. You don't have to do away with social pleasantries — in fact, you shouldn't — but remember what you're trying to accomplish and what your time frames are. Gab is only as useful as it is meaningful.

Being direct doesn't mean being curt, cold, or negatively opinionated — it means that you're clear, concise, and professional; and that you convey a constructive and supportive tone, not a confrontational one. The distinction sounds subtle, but it matters greatly when you're aiming for the most time-effective response.

E-mail: A little less conversation

Research shows that the nonverbal methods of communication are far more important to the message you put out than the words you use. Consider these stats (and check out the following figure for a visual of the communication breakdown):

✔ The words you choose deliver 7 percent of your message.

✔ Your tone of voice delivers 38 percent of your message.

✔ Your body language delivers the remaining 55 percent of your message.

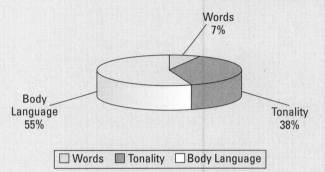

When you communicate via e-mail, you lose the 38 percent of your communication that's transmitted by your tone of voice during a face-to-face conversation; and you lose an additional 55 percent of your message because your recipient can't see your body language — and you can't see your recipient's. Compared to face-to-face communication, e-mail shortchanges you of 93 percent of your total communication! The 7 percent that's left is totally dependent on the effectiveness of the words you select.

Don't try to impress others with your use of obscure words, phrases, and unnecessary technical jargon — it only blocks communication and wastes time. The result is confusion, hesitation, misunderstandings, and alienation from the receiver. Hearers may become quiet because they don't want to admit they don't know the meaning of the words you're using. Using simple and straightforward language to communicate complex ideas will make you look smarter and more gracious every time.

Including the essential stuff

To maximize your time (and everyone else's), shoot for a succinct message but don't sacrifice crucial information in the interest of brevity. Ask yourself these questions as you craft your message: Who are you giving information to? What is important for this person to know? Then answer those questions — and don't be afraid to ask others whether you've missed anything. When you communicate directly, you let people know

- What situation you're facing
- What you want or need
- What you expect the receiver to do and what the standards of measurement are
- What the time line is

Notice how the following statements improve by adding this specific information:

- *"As a company, it looks like we need to do a little better."* (Compare: *"Our goal is to improve corporate results by 6 percent by the end of the third quarter."*)
- *"You all know what you have to do, so go out and do it!"* (Compare: *"Let's work together to cut travel expenses in each of our areas by 2 percent by year-end."*)
- *"There's a lot to be said for making our goal."* (Compare: *"We outdid ourselves this year. We exceeded our goal by 7 percent! Let's see if we can exceed our goal by 9 percent by next year. If we do, you'll all earn a 3 percent bonus!"*) (Now, *that's* communicating!)

Just saying no

One of the most crucial parts of being direct (and managing your time well) is saying *no* when you need to (and when doing so is appropriate). If you're swamped at work, for example, and someone asks you to volunteer to decorate the office for the holidays or to serve on the Thanksgiving celebration committee, the best response you can give is, "I'd really like to help, but maybe next year. I'm seriously under the gun right now to finish Project *X*. But please ask me again next year."

If a simple *no* would put you in bad favor, such as when your supervisor asks you to take a side project that you don't have time for, ask your supervisor for help in reprioritizing your work so you can make the deadline instead of responding with a flat, "No way. I have too much to do." That way, your boss sees your commitment to getting the job done, but she also knows that you're realistic with your time commitments and value your own well-being enough to set some boundaries.

Fostering Camaraderie When Meeting in Person

Almost all business situations — whether one-on-one conversations or group meetings — benefit from a beginning that's dedicated to creating or strengthening relationships. That's simply good business. Teamwork is what makes the business world go 'round, and good teamwork is built on positive interactions with colleagues, clients, and co-workers.

Use a little small talk to get people comfortable with each other and prime them for conversation. Some safe starters for any meeting or conversation include the following phrases:

- *"How was your trip?"*
- *"Did you have any trouble finding our offices?"*
- *"Is it still raining (snowing, sleeting, hailing, hot, cold) out there?"* (I know — everyone always talks about the weather, but that's because the weather always provides a safe opening gambit!)

I advise only a few minutes of conversation starters.

Use small talk only with people who have some sort of relationship with you — a current customer, client, employee, or friend. Don't ever use them with someone new. If you use these conversation starters with new sales prospects, for example, all they can think of may be "salesperson and what is he selling?" Not exactly the opening that you want to project!

During your conversation, read others and take your cue from their behavior. For example, avoid pursuing personal information if the other person is obviously uncomfortable. It's okay to let people be themselves — after all, you're working for positive relationships, which mean different things to different people.

Be sure that your body language is inviting and open. Smiling can warm up the communication with the other person.

Corresponding Clearly and Confidently via Telephone

Obviously, body language isn't front and center when your conversation is via telephone, but you do need to keep in mind how your body language affects your tone of voice and ability to focus and convey a sense of energy. Here are some options that can help you project your body language into the telephone conversation:

✔ **Use a headset.** A phone headset offers a number of advantages:

- • It reduces fatigue because you aren't holding a phone to your ear.

- • It allows you to stand and move your body while you communicate.

- • It leaves you free to take notes and record important information that you can review later.

 Warning: Do *not* get the cheapest headset you can find. Inexpensive headsets usually have such poor sound quality that the person on the other end can't hear you clearly. This defeats your purpose. Spend what it takes — possibly a few hundred dollars — to get a headset of sufficient quality.

✔ **Smile.** A smile will help your attitude and the delivery of what you're saying.

✔ **Stand up during the conversation.** Standing up helps you to use your body language to reinforce what you're saying. The listener can't see you, but when you're standing, more energy flows through the phone. You have more confidence and conviction, which make their way into your voice. If you really can't stand up, at least sit on the front edge of your chair with your back straight and shoulders back.

If the person you're trying to reach can't or won't take your call, you can get a lot of information from assistants and front-desk people by asking questions — reconnaissance can help you make a sale or get the info you need later on. You may also consider dialing the wrong number — either one higher or lower than the number of the person you're trying to reach; if you reach a person who will internally transfer you, the person you want to reach may be more likely to pick up the phone.

If you get voice mail, don't give up and send an e-mail. Leave a message so the listener gains the full effect of hearing your voice. Properly used, voice mail can stand in for a personal visit from you in a lot less time. You can easily come up with a basic voice mail template you can customize, especially when you have enough insider information to tailor it to your recipient. Here are some guidelines for a productive working relationship with voice mail:

✔ Keep your messages to 15 to 30 seconds.

✔ Be prepared. Have a script in hand; if you stumble, mumble, and bumble your message, you're worse off than if you leave no message.

✔ Launch the call by identifying yourself. State your name, company, title, and phone number.

✔ Because of the unreliable reception quality of voice mail, speak with greater clarity. Relay information slowly and carefully.

If a recipient has to replay a message several times to decipher it, he or she probably won't. This is especially true when leaving your telephone number. You must speak it slowly and at least twice. You know your phone number by heart, but the recipient doesn't!

✔ Ramp up your energy level to deliver your message with passion and enthusiasm. (If you sound like a sleep-aid commercial, delete and repeat!)

✔ Smile when you leave voice mail messages. Even if it's the 50th message you've left today, don't let your recipient know it.

✔ Take advantage of voice mail features, such as replay and re-record functions.

Writing Effective E-mails

The advent of e-mail has forced everyone to focus on keeping communications brief, if only because so many people dislike writing and typing. That's all good. But as short and straightforward as e-mail messages seem to be, they're also dangerously deceptive and easy to misinterpret. Studies indicate that more than 50 percent of those who use e-mail say their business correspondence is misunderstood.

There's no getting around it: E-mail often leads to misunderstandings. For instance, a message from your boss may translate as curt or even displeased to you, when in reality he or she was simply rushed. A remark that would pass as playful humor in person can come across as an insult in writing.

In this section, I explain how to write a clear, effective e-mail that minimizes the potential for misinterpretation.

Crafting a clear and targeted subject line

Your Aunt Edna, of course, always opens your e-mails, with or without a subject line. But a potential customer or business contact is flooded with messages from advertisers and with other highly expendable e-mail. You have between 25 and 35 characters to persuade the recipient to move your correspondence from the B pile (or the *delete* file) to the A pile. Make your e-mail a keeper by tagging it with a standout subject line after you write the body of the e-mail. Pull out a phrase or series of words that sums up the message.

As you decide what to write in the subject line, keep in mind that this line has two purposes:

- ✔ To tell the recipient the purpose of your e-mail
- ✔ To pique the receiver's interest enough to command attention from the slew of e-mail he or she is sifting through

In sales and marketing, one tactic I employ is to use a *page-turner* subject line: an unfinished thought that can be completed when the recipient opens the e-mail:

- ✔ "Just one week until . . ."
- ✔ "Our clients have increased sales by 84%"
- ✔ "Don't miss this tremendous . . ."

Spam software programs identify some key words and phrases and block any e-mail containing those words in the subject line. Steer clear of the following words and phrases (and their relatives):

- ✔ Incredible
- ✔ Free
- ✔ Limited time only
- ✔ Money
- ✔ A friend gave me your e-mail address

Keeping an eye on composition

The subject line gets readers to open the e-mail, but as with people, wine, and birthday presents, it's what's on the inside that counts. Here are some tips for composing the body of your e-mail.

Looking at structure and length

E-mails are most effective when they're short and to the point. If recipients have to scroll, the odds increase that they'll miss some of the information toward the end or feel so overwhelmed that reading your missive is a task they shift to the back burner. That's why many experts suggest that e-mail messages should be about four paragraphs long or less — definitely no longer than a screen full. If you find you have more to say than will fit on the screen, consider these alternatives:

✔ Use another mode of communication.

✔ Send the message as an attachment, including a paragraph of explanation within the e-mail.

If you know for certain that you must include all information in the body of an e-mail and that you need more than four paragraphs to house it all, remember that the first and last paragraphs carry the most punch. To make effective use of your presentation, follow these rules of thumb:

✔ Be sure that the most important information is in the top part of the e-mail.

✔ Include a call to action earlier in the e-mail rather than at the end, where it typically goes. The reader may not make it to the last paragraph.

✔ When you receive an e-mail that warrants forwarding — or one that you want to copy someone else on — delete the trailing chain of discussion so only the issue at hand remains.

✔ Use bullet points rather than narrative to call out the critical points for the reader.

What if you're on the receiving end of a litany of questions in e-mail form? Simple: Hit Reply (with history) and craft a short paragraph that explains that your responses are found below. Then respond right after each individual question — within the original message — in a professional but standout color so the original sender clearly and easily sees your responses. I frequently use red, blue, or black for my color — and if need be, green. This setup helps senders avoid scrolling up and down from their question to your responses.

Maintaining a professional level of formality

Because of their immediate nature, e-mail tends toward the informal. Between friends and family, dispensing with punctuation, salutations, and even correct spelling may be acceptable. But in the world of business, it's a huge no-no.

Although you may have congenial enough relationships with co-workers and even some clients, my advice is to keep *all* business correspondence formal. These messages reflect on your professionalism and may end up printed out and passed around or forwarded to other businesspeople. Just like dressing for a job interview, it never hurts to keep it formal.

Treat an e-mail the same as you would a paper letter, and follow these tips to maintain your professional appearance:

- ✔ Use conventional salutations and closings: *Dear* ___, *Hello* ___ and *Best regards, Sincerely,* or the like.

- ✔ Don't assume your recipient knows lingo or abbreviations common in text messages and online chats — leave them out. Abbreviations, single letters, and misspelled characters may only confuse recipients to the point they ignore the message.

- ✔ Steer clear of *emoticons,* those sideways facial expressions created from punctuation keys :-P.

- ✔ Keep vernacular and slang out of the e-mail.

- ✔ Don't use all capital letters. In e-mail vernacular, capital letters indicate shouting. True, the recipient doesn't hear you shout, but it's difficult to read long tracts of copy in uppercase.

- ✔ Always close with your name, as if you were actually signing a letter.

- ✔ Run spell-check.

Reviewing your writing

E-mail produces copies of your writing that you usually can't retrieve after you send it into cyberspace, so make sure everything you write is exactly as it should be. To ensure that you don't accidentally overlook any errors or omissions and that you'll get the response you're seeking (if any), follow these bits of advice:

- ✔ **Allow yourself time to put written communication aside; then come back to it to see it as a first-time reader would.** E-mail is a lot like a tennis match, with the Reply button serving as the ball. It's a good idea to take that button out of the game and allow a little more reflection. Have you covered everything that needs to be covered? Time spent upfront, honing your communications, can save you more "expensive" time later in the project. As for your own e-mail messages, try putting them in the draft box and come back to them later. This can help you catch any language that comes off as snippy, short, abrupt, or offensive.

  If you're in a rush to get out a lot of correspondence, go ahead and whip through them all at once. But stick them the draft box and return to each with fresh eyes before launching them.

- ✔ **Have a co-worker — preferably someone not involved with the project — look over your memos and e-mail.** Are there unanswered questions?

✔ **Proofread your e-mail for spelling and grammar errors by using spell-check *and* reading through your e-mail one last time before sending it.** Making typos and grammatical errors is common in e-mail, primarily because the communication is so fast and immediate. Again, in a business environment, you want your correspondence to reflect your high level of professionalism. Although you may not get a pay cut for misspelling a few words, others may note your lack of attention.

Preparing for the send-off

Before you hit that Send button, review your recipients and give your sending options one last review:

✔ **Give the urgent-message flag a rest.** Avoid the boy-who-cried-wolf syndrome: When every single message you send is marked *urgent,* well, you know what happens. Don't use the flag unless you need a response in 24 hours or less.

✔ **Don't overuse the carbon copy (Cc) function.** If you need to include others, terrific, but keep the list of Cc's only to the people who really need to know. If someone has only peripheral interest in the discussion, leave that person off.

✔ **Use the blind carbon copy (Bcc) for large e-mail sends.** The advantage of Bcc is that you're not sharing your list of contacts. With the explosion of spam, everyone needs to protect privacy, and people who have your address have that obligation as well. By using the Bcc feature, no one other than you knows who has received your correspondence.

✔ **Mark it *private*.** With most corporate e-mail systems in companies, you're able to send an e-mail privately. If the message is confidential or sensitive, be sure to make it *private* — for the recipient's eyes and your eyes only. Ask the IT department in your company how you can send private e-mail throughout your division or department.

Asking Targeted Questions to Get Results

The key to finding out what you need to know more quickly is asking the right questions. No matter what your job is, good questions direct your communication through the veritable maze of issues, challenges, and distractions that pop up whenever two or more people get together to exchange information and solve problems.

When you pose strategic questions, you guide the conversation to make the most of the time spent. You also gain insight that influences how effectively you can move forward. Don't be afraid to ask as many questions as necessary to completely understand the situation. And don't stop asking until you have a clear picture of what's expected.

Maybe you learned as a child that asking too many questions was impolite or intrusive. Not in business situations! By focusing on other people and keeping them talking, you gather more information — information that can make you more effective. If, for example, you're in sales, ask questions that center around the prospect's DNA[2]: *desire, need, ability,* and *authority* (see Chapter 14). To shrink decision time, ask more questions. Before you discuss products, services, or solutions, construct a clear image of who this person is and what he or she needs.

Of course, you can't ask questions willy-nilly and expect to get the information you need. You have to ask questions that get results, which I help you do in this section.

Determining what sorts of answers you need

Whether you're in management, administration, sales, service, human resources, or any other facet of business, preparation is essential. Your communication is far more fruitful if you think it through beforehand. To improve your chances of success, envision how you want the conversation to go before you initiate it. What's your ultimate goal? What information do you need to do the best job in the least amount of time? What specific questions must be answered? What are the potential stumbling blocks or choke points?

Amazingly, many people link organization and advance planning to mechanical communication. But *planned* is not *canned.* You expect the pilot who flies your plane from Los Angeles to Sydney, Australia, to be well-prepared before take-off, right? You take it for granted that he or she has checkpoints along the way. Without proper planning, the plane could end up thousands of miles from Sydney because it was a few degrees off at the beginning of the journey. It's just as easy to be off-target in important conversations.

There's a fine line between preparation and creative avoidance, otherwise known as *procrastination.* (See Chapter 10 for more on the topic of procrastination.) Five or ten minutes is typically plenty of time to organize for an important call. If you're spending a half-hour to an hour preparing for calls or conversations, chances are you're putting them off rather than preparing for them.

Starting the flow with open-ended questions

The most valuable questions early in any dialogue are open-ended questions, ones that require more than yes-or-no answers. Open-ended questions allow you to gather information, thoughts, ideas, observations, opinions, and comments. You reach agreement much more quickly and easily through open-ended questions.

When you ask open-ended questions, you force dialogue and trigger the flow of information. Starting your questions with *who, what, where, when, why,* and *how* narrows the focus, defines the standards, gives you insight into what others are thinking, and outlines expectations. Here are some sample questions:

- ✔ **Who?** Who should I consult about this? Who else will be involved in the final decision? Whose standard do we need to meet or exceed? Who else are you considering for this job or position or project?

- ✔ **What/which?** What's the best way to approach this problem? What new product are you offering? What's the deadline? What are the specific standards of performance? What's my number-one priority? What has moved this project to the front burner? Which priorities should I shift to accomplish this project? What else should I know about before I begin?

- ✔ **Where?** Where should we go from here? Where does this project fit into our strategic objectives?

- ✔ **When?** When can I expect an answer? When do you want to review the first part? When should we meet to review my progress? When are we meeting with other key people?

- ✔ **Why?** Why do you think this problem keeps recurring? Why is this change, project, or new procedure coming up? Why did you give this opportunity to me?

- ✔ **How?** How can I help you? How does your product compare with other products we offer or with other products we've offered in the past? How will this help you, our department, or the company? How will this help me advance? How would you go about tackling this project, challenge, or issue?

If you have answers to these questions, you can achieve the desired results faster — and ensure that they meet everyone's expectations. That's a powerful combination: better time management and more successful results.

Narrowing the focus with closed-ended questions

Many experts in time management, sales, customer service, and management tell you to avoid closed-ended questions. I disagree. A correctly placed closed-ended question lets you take a reading: Are you progressing toward your goal? Are you moving in the right direction? Are you earning your customer's business?

A closed-ended question — one that can be answered with a simple *yes* or *no* — serves as a temperature gauge that tells you whether to turn up or turn down the heat. If you don't use closed-ended questions to test your progress, all you're doing is gathering more and more information without moving toward a conclusion. (See Chapter 14, on getting customers to make decisions.)

Here are some examples of good close-ended questions:

- ✔ Is this what you envisioned when you delegated this to me?
- ✔ Do you believe our product is right for you?
- ✔ Do I need to run this by anyone else?
- ✔ Is the timing right for a salary increase?

Limited and strategic use of closed-ended questions can save time. However, if you don't follow a closed-ended question with another open-ended one, the dialogue often dies there. Follow that *yes* or *no* response with another open-ended question and keep the conversation moving.

Pinning down maybes and other conditional responses

Sometimes open- or closed-ended questions need clarification. This is especially true when you receive not a yes or *no* but a *maybe* — what's known as a *conditional response*.

Maybe is probably the most misunderstood response in the world. Depending on your level of optimism, a *maybe* can mean *yes* or *no*. If you're like Eeyore in *Winnie the Pooh*, you assume the *maybe* is a *no*. If you're a bouncing Tigger, you may take *maybe* for a veiled *yes*.

In fact, a *maybe* is a *maybe* until it's clarified. To do that, ask simple, direct questions that elicit a concrete response; if you're still unclear, ask direct follow-up questions until you get the definitive response that you need. The following are some examples of questions that can help you pin down "maybe" responses:

- ✔ What does that mean exactly?

- ✔ Under what circumstances do you see yourself using our service?

- ✔ Under what conditions would you consider ___ for this project? How did you arrive at your conclusion?

- ✔ So if I did ___, would that change your decision to a *yes?*

- ✔ Would you ever see yourself giving me that opportunity?

- ✔ Under what conditions would that be?

Don't be too quick to rush to take the next step without pinning down the *maybe* first.

Achieving a positive tone

No matter where you are in the questioning process, remain positive. Negativity can increase the time it takes you to mend gaffes, or it can stop the process altogether. A negative approach puts others on the defensive and squelches your ability to gather information. Asking positive questions, on the other hand, communicates that you anticipate a positive outcome. You're focused on the future, learning from your mistakes, and ensuring that you don't repeat them.

How do you put a positive spin on your questions? Here are some examples:

- ✔ *"What would you like to see improved?"* instead of *"What didn't you like about ___?"*

- ✔ *"What should I have done differently?"* or *"How could I have done better?"* instead of *"What did I do wrong?"*

Preparing to listen

People like to talk about their favorite subjects: themselves. That's good! When people talk about themselves, you glean valuable information about them, their business, how they make decisions, what's important to them, their business relationships, their goals, projects, spouses, kids, pets — in short, what they think and feel about pretty much everything. You can also discover their needs, wants, and desires. What motivates them? If you identify their challenges, you can create opportunities to help them solve their problems. You may even discover new business or career opportunities.

What's my motivation? Getting input from your key actors

The point of a dream question is to help someone envision a better time and place where results are improved, goals are achieved, and problems and challenges are reduced. When you supervise people, asking dream questions gives you unique insight into their motivations and goals. The upshot? Connecting their tasks to what they want in life can increase their production during work hours. Some examples of good dream questions include the following:

✔ Where do you see yourself in five years?

✔ What are your long-term goals for your department?

✔ What are the most challenging issues you see, now and in the future?

✔ If you could close your eyes and make one problem disappear, which would it be?

After you ask questions, remember to actually *listen* to the responses. If you're talking, you're not listening; and if you're not listening, you're missing important information, spending additional time following up by phone and e-mail, and frittering away minutes and hours you could use to work on your real goals. There's wisdom in the old adage that you "have two ears and one mouth for a reason." If you listen twice as much as you speak, you reduce the time you invest with others to achieve results for them and for yourself.

Bonus: When you ask questions and engage people by getting them to talk about themselves, you're considered a brilliant conversationalist. If you want to get invited to more galas with the movers and shakers in your town, ask terrific questions — and really listen to the answers.

Chapter 9

Defending Your Day from Interruptions

*W*ithin the past two decades, people have embraced communication technology. But in many ways, these miracles of convenience have robbed workers of their ability to control their own time. Multiplying points of access — voice mail, e-mail, instant messaging, audio and video conferencing, and of course, the cellphone — can shackle you like a house-arrest ankle bracelet, sentencing you to a life-term of perpetual availability. Business colleagues can track you down on vacation, and friends can interrupt an important client presentation. I'm not sure I'd describe this as *progress,* but it's inarguably a fact of modern life.

Consider this: Every one of these interruptions — no matter how small or insignificant — robs you of at least five *additional* minutes of productive time. Whether your spouse calls and talks to you for 30 seconds or 30 minutes, you can subtract at least five more minutes from your day. Tally up 20 interruptions over the course of your day, and you lose nearly two hours of productivity — and that totals to the loss of 36 hours a month!

Distractionitis is the scourge of time-block adherents; the fastest way to render a time block or even a day useless is not to deal with distractions well (see Chapter 4 for more on time-blocking). So now's the time to gain control of the interruption game, whether you're at risk from wandering bosses and colleagues, demanding clients, or the technological tools that can slice through your best defenses. I show you how in this chapter.

The Fortress: Guarding Your Focus from Invasion

Being successful in time management and adhering to your time-block schedule happens through controlling access: You need to limit the frequency of the interruptions you allow. Recognize that I use the word *allow* here. You're the one who controls your time and allows other people and situations to pull you away from your goals, dreams, objectives, and time-blocked schedule. You're in control, and you're the master of your time.

Think of yourself as the castle guard: Your workplace is a fortress, one that must be protected in order for it to remain a happy and productive place. Your best strategy is to establish an impenetrable wall between you and interruptions. In this section, I explain how to protect yourself from invaders on foot and how to disconnect from the electronic devices that can cut through your physical defenses. Finally, you discover how to screen your calls so only the essential information gets through.

Protecting your domain from walk-in intrusions

The biggest interruptions in your workday frequently come from within. Your co-workers pose a great threat to your effective time management. What's doubly scary is that you don't always recognize your colleagues as threats. Hey, these folks are on your team — they're the good guys, they're *there* for you! However, it's important to recognize the signs of danger from time-wasting co-workers. If not, you're at risk of falling to friendly fire.

The modern work environment is often designed on an open-office concept. Few if any employees are granted an office with a door, and most workers are parked in open cubicles, often with partitions that do little to block views (and definitely not the noise) of co-workers. It's supposed to manifest a more unified effort and team spirit, I guess. But it doesn't do much to protect you from your teammates' intrusions on your time. Unfortunately, the same open-door philosophy that allows employees to drop in on their supervisors at will is often carried throughout the workplace, so co-workers may stop by to talk about a mutual project — or the office football pool.

Creating virtual barriers

When you have little in the way of a physical barrier, defending your border from invasion becomes a challenge. But it can be done — just because you don't have a door to keep people from entering your space doesn't mean you can't create *virtual* barriers when you're unavailable:

✔ **Communicate subtly through the posting technique.** Put signs on your office door or cubicle letting others know you're busy.

The best action you can take is to post a do-not-disturb sign outside your cubicle, perhaps indicating the critical project you're working on. Your co-workers and supervisor may be more sympathetic to your plight if it's a project they're familiar with.

✔ **Verbally communicate your schedule to others so they know when you're unavailable for interruptions.** I call this *communicating the standard.* For repeat offenders, the posting alone won't work. You have to explain to them verbally and with authority that you don't have an abundance of time.

✔ **Threaten to put them to work.** If you're in sales, for example, inform the would-be interrupters that you're prospecting and that if they interrupt, they have to come in and make calls with you. That'll usually stop any salesperson from the interruption because he or she won't want to join you in the prospecting quest.

Set your unavailable time for the hours before 11 a.m. It's uncanny, but the world seems to start delivering problems to your doorstep just before midday. I've dubbed this phenomenon the *11 a.m. Rule.* If you set your "closed" hours prior to 11 a.m., you can get your important stuff done before you start to hear the buzz of trouble brewing outside your cubicle wall.

Scheduling time to manage and interact with your staff

If you're a manager, you walk a fine line: It's important to be available to staff to address issues and offer encouragement, but a manager who loses control of the border may discover that the flow of employee communication is akin to a circus parade with a never-ending line of elephants connected by trunks and tails.

Fortunately, you have a few additional ways to keep those elephant invasion forces at bay, preventing in-person interruptions while maintaining your role as a teamwork facilitator and employee go-to resource. Both management techniques center on blocking time in your schedule to interact with staff so you put constraints on the open-door policy. Creating specific time blocks to interact with the staff allows you to shut your door and focus a greater percentage of the day so you follow your schedule more readily. The times before and after lunch — when you're likely between projects — are excellent for open-door hours.

Here are some options on how to approach this scheduled time for interaction:

✔ **Making the rounds:** A popular preemptive tactic that managers have followed since the first workplace self-help books came out, *management by walking around,* puts the time control back in the manager's domain. It suggests that making the rounds on a scheduled basis allows you to establish your availability and deflect those interruptions that could otherwise come later. Instead of getting snagged on the way to get a cup of coffee, *you* proactively seek out your staff, asking how their projects are going or whether they have any concerns or issues you can help with.

Setting your rounds for the morning is a sound strategy, though it's a good idea to wait until everyone gets settled in at their desks and the caffeine kicks in so they can respond to your "How's that proposal coming?" with some clarity.

✔ **Having employees come to you:** Establish your scheduled interaction time as open-office time for staff to drop in. Or require employees to make appointments to meet with you during that time.

One danger in setting up specific drop-in hours is that it puts you in a state of waiting. You may not get any takers of your time, but your ability to focus on any other work is more challenged because you're expecting to be interrupted at any moment. To avoid this, I've implemented scheduled-appointment hours in my office. I still set aside the same time block to be available to my staff, but I insist that they make appointments. They can't just stop in without notice.

You can require whatever advance notice you're comfortable with — 15 minutes or 15 hours. That way, if some of the time goes unbooked, you can schedule something else in that slot. You can choose to limit these appointments in length — 15 minutes, a half-hour — and you can require that employees explain what they want to talk about when they schedule so you can be prepared.

See Chapter 18 for more guidance if your job involves managing others.

Scheduling time offline

Used effectively, the telephone and e-mail can enhance performance, increase productivity, boost profitability, and expedite career growth. But there's a flip-side: Because modern communication allows for easier interruptions, it creates a greater loss of production, performance, profitability, and advancement than ever before. And to a certain extent, e-mail has taken many people hostage. Do you feel compelled to open all e-mail immediately? Do you jump on to the next e-mail even before you've responded to or resolved the previous e-mail? Just as with cellphones, the fact that you *can* be reached easily and at any time seems to dictate that you must be available to anyone — all the time.

When you stop to open each and every e-mail as soon as it arrives or answer the phone every time it rings, you are, in essence, *multitasking,* trying to perform one or more tasks simultaneously. And as I frequently point out, multitasking is just not time-efficient.

To keep your focus, set aside time — daily or several times per week — during which you simply do not take calls, check e-mail, or allow other interruptions. Such prescheduled segments ensure blocks of concentration, a tactic certain to raise productivity and lower frustration. If you're concerned about being unavailable for too long of a time, then limit these periods to one or one and a half hours, with time afterward to return messages.

Letting e-mail wait in your inbox

I am a firm believer in working offline. There's no way I can resist the temptation to check my e-mail every time my computer tells me a message has arrived. During your offline time, turn off your e-mail notice or disconnect from the Internet. Schedule your e-mail time and devote a reasonable time block to take care of it. Then turn your e-mail program off so you don't see the you've-got-mail icon on your computer until your next scheduled e-mail session.

Or compose all your own e-mail correspondence in your word processing program, and when you've completed, reviewed, tweaked, polished, and made sure each message says exactly what you want, you can go online and send those e-mail messages off. If you compose your e-mail in a word processing program, you gain yet another advantage: This tactic serves as a safety precaution — you won't inadvertently shoot off a critical e-mail before you're completely satisfied with it; no more "recalls."

The toughest decision you may face is whether to check your e-mail first thing in the morning when you fire up your computer. Wait and knock out a few priorities first? Or open it up and relieve the suspense — and possibly get waylaid by some marauding issue you feel compelled to pursue? It's your choice — do what works best for you. But by staying offline for the bulk of your workday, you're likely to stay focused on the tasks at hand and get much more accomplished.

Stopping the ringing in your ears

Let your voice mail or assistant take phone messages. Voice mail is your not-so-secret weapon for dodging phone interruptions and taking back your time. If your system has a do-not-disturb button, push it or put your ringer on mute and you won't be tempted to ponder who called. If you're an executive, forward the calls to your assistant for a time or ask the receptionist to let your callers know that you're in an appointment and will call them back.

Additionally, give yourself times when you turn off your cellphone. The most brilliant innovation with these amazing devices? You can turn them off! Without missing a message, you can continue with your conversation, errand, or work without distraction and get back to the call when you're through. Of course, you may already protect yourself against uninvited interruptions by limiting who you give your cell number to. But unless you're awaiting an urgent call from your kids, your boss, or the state lottery commission, you can likely afford a period of off-time while you attend to important tasks that require your full concentration.

Screening interruptions before letting them through

You may need to make sure certain types of information can get through to you, even while your barriers shut out everything else. The solution is to screen your calls using caller ID or to have your assistant screen your calls for you.

If you're the boss, you're the wizard who turns business transactions into gold, and your assistant or receptionist operates the drawbridge, keeping out those who attempt to foil your efforts. Your administrative staff needs to adopt the gatekeeper philosophy. The first step is set your business up as a fortress, making it hard to get in to see the royalty — *you.*

The administrative staff has total control of the drawbridge that grants access to the fortress. They should have a militant approach to allowing people access to you. You need to clearly identify to your staff who is to be granted access and who is not. Only a few people should pass easily through the gate; the rest should be screened thoroughly to see whether another team member can assist them first.

Arm gatekeepers with the tools necessary to identify and keep out intruders and the knowledge to recognize whom to lower the drawbridge for. Their role in managing access is instrumental to your productivity and that of the department. A properly armed assistant is able to

- ✔ Answer most questions from callers and eliminate the need to talk to you
- ✔ Capture enough information so that you're prepared with a response, which means a shorter interaction when you do get back to the individual
- ✔ Schedule an appointment for you
- ✔ Know which issues or requests require your immediate attention
- ✔ Take messages from people who must talk with you

Taking a message is more than just noting the caller's name, phone number, date, and time of the call. A highly trained assistant finds out the specific reason for the call and tries to handle the question right there on the spot. This is one of the biggest time-saving techniques of all. If unable to handle the situation on the initial call, the assistant finds out the answer and then returns the call.

If it's absolutely necessary for you to speak to the caller, set a specific time when you'll return the call, effectively making a mini-appointment for the return telephone call.

Those who don't have a loyal staff can turn to technology. What a miraculous invention, caller ID! By glancing at the phone number ID on your receiver, you can determine in a second whether it's a call you want to take. Not only is caller ID helpful for screening out unsolicited telemarketing calls, but you can also use it to determine whether a call is critical to take *now*. And at work, if you're on a roll on that big proposal and you'd only take a call from your boss, your phone helps you make that decision.

If you're working from home, you face some unique challenges in handling phone calls (they don't call it *tele*commuting for nothing!). Not only do you have to contend with more calls from the office (if you were there, you could at least put up a do-not-disturb sign on your door), but you also catch all the solicitation calls you'd miss if you were out of the house during the day. Plus there's a strange phenomenon at work for telecommuters: Both friends and business contacts seem to feel more comfortable interrupting your workday when you work from home.

Caller ID for telecommuters is even more effective if you have two separate lines, one for work and one for personal calls. That way, you can tell by the ring which is which. When you're "at work," you can choose to disregard the personal line — and if you're sitting down to a family dinner, you can ignore your work line with a clear conscience. Only my work number rings into my home office. I can't hear our personal residence line, so it doesn't distract me. A second phone line is a small monthly investment that helps me manage my time and increase my productivity.

Limiting phone interruptions from loved ones

In some cases, family calls are the primary source of telephone interruptions. Have a frank talk with your family members about when it's appropriate to call you at work.

If you have young children, you know how they want to tell you all the cool things that happened during the course of their day, well before family dinnertime. You likely expect and welcome these calls. Certainly you want to set opportunities for them to reach you, but it's good to establish boundaries at the same time. You may, for example, ask your kids to call you and fill you in on their day at a certain time — say, after they get home from school or in the case of preschoolers, after lunchtime. Same goes for your spouse or partner.

Warning: Most job environments allow for some personal-call time, but few are tolerant of employees who receive calls throughout the day. That type of phone interruption can undermine your productivity, not to mention your career. At work, you really don't need the kinds of emotional distractions that'll dramatically affect your performance and productivity for the next thirty minutes, an hour, or even the rest of the day. Calls from family can move your mind to home even though your body is still at the office.

Secondary Defenses: Minimizing Damage When Calls Get Through

If you set up the defense mechanisms and blocking techniques I cover throughout this chapter, you can avoid more than 90 percent of the interruptions that most people experience each day. But no matter the system or strategy you use to protect yourself, telephone interruptions are certain to penetrate your defenses. When this happens, your best strategy is to accept it and go with the flow. Okay, so an interruption slipped past your perimeter: Instead of expending effort to repel the breach, just deal with it. A negative attitude or reaction is likely to cause more damage and waste more time than simply resolving the matter that made its way to you.

The most effective technique to help you adhere to time-blocking is to plan for the distractions that'll undoubtedly come. You may use the preemptive strike technique, which allows you to deal with distractions from others on your terms. In this section, you discover a few plans for handling the phone calls that make it through to you.

Delegating the responsibility

When the call penetrates your defenses, attempt to delegate the call to someone who can handle it for you. Inform the caller that you're booked, buried, under a deadline, committed, or heading into a meeting — and that you're shifting the responsibility for the call as the fastest way to resolve the problem or challenge. Assure the caller that you're bringing in someone qualified to help.

 You also convey a strong reassurance when you explain that the other person is better equipped to resolve the situation. Often, especially if you're the boss, clients and business contacts want to talk to *you*. When you confess that you aren't the best person to fulfill the request, you're more likely to gain the caller's confidence that you have his or her best interests in mind.

Shortening or condensing the conversation

When a call does sneak past the fortress guard, your best defense is to bring that call to a close as quickly as possible. Your focus has been broken, and it'll require five minutes from the point you wrap up the call to regain your momentum. You want to keep the conversation short so you can get back in the groove.

Inform the caller upfront how much time you can offer. You may, for example, explain that you're in the middle of an important project and have only ten minutes available. You can also plead an appointment — and if you've implemented the time-block schedule (see Chapter 4), you've blocked out your day, so your claim is true.

Some people feel uncomfortable about cutting calls short in this way, especially with clients or prospective customers. Giving the caller a time limit feels abrupt. But it doesn't have to. Here's one way your speech may go:

"I know we can resolve your problem, but I have an appointment in ten minutes that I have to keep. If we can't resolve the problem to your satisfaction in the ten minutes, then we can set a time to talk later today to finish up."

This approach still gets you off the phone in the allotted time but gives you an out. The customer can also feel better that you're offering more time. I've used this technique for years with high-maintenance clients. Rarely do we need the additional conversation, but they appreciate my offer all the same.

Rebooking discussions for a better time

If now's a bad time to handle the call, then reschedule. The caller certainly doesn't know your schedule, and it probably never occurred to the caller that this could be a bad time. Offer a brief explanation — you're in a meeting, on your way to an appointment, or simply tied up at this time. Then without allowing time for a response, offer two options of when you're available:

"I'm not able to give your situation the full attention it deserves at this moment. Can we schedule a phone meeting for this afternoon after three or first thing tomorrow morning?"

By offering options, you give back some control to the caller. If you've been caught without your day planner, give a general time, such as Wednesday morning or Thursday afternoon. Then don't forget to transfer the call appointment to your planner.

Handling Recurring Interruptions by Co-workers

Being very clear on your personal boundaries is essential with your co-workers. However, there's a fine balance between being viewed as a hermit, loner, or outcast and conveying your commitment to your job and the deadlines that you've been given, so you have to approach the confrontation with finesse.

Especially if the interruption outbreak is a department-wide epidemic, suggest to your supervisor that the team get together to talk about solutions. By coming together as a department or work group, each individual is more likely to take ownership of the situation. Call a team meeting to discuss workflow, distractions, and interruptions. As a group, you can brainstorm solutions and come up with a strategy that everyone can buy into. Because you're all making a commitment in each other's presence, everyone is more likely to honor it.

Time-wasting co-workers fall into a few categories, each of which can cause you interruptions that are detrimental to your career. You first have to figure out which category the offender falls into so you can respond in a way that'll effectively remedy the specific situation. In this section, I preview four of the most common colleague categories and some signs to watch out for. These individuals may be hard workers, possibly overburdened, and very productive. Unfortunately, they sap a lot of their productivity from their co-workers, often disrupting others in the office to seek assistance, whether it's emotional support or actually trying to pass off specific tasks.

The colleague with nothing to do

Face it: In most companies, the division of labor is rarely parceled out equally — not fair, maybe, but it's a fact of life. For you to survive with your time intact, you need to recognize who's not carrying his or her share of the work. Why? Because to add insult to injury, these are often the same people who sabotage the efforts of those who do the bulk of the work by interrupting their productivity. These folks often pop into your space, flop into a chair, and strike up a conversation about anything and everything.

If you get interrupted by someone who clearly doesn't have enough to do, ask her what she's working on. What are her priorities and deadlines? Inform her of yours and ask for her help. Asking offenders to help or to work sends most of them the other direction to their own cubicles — voila!

The colleague who just doesn't want to work

I may be in the minority on this view, but I think people who waste time on their company's dollar are stealing a portion of their paycheck from their company. Workers owe the company that pays their salaries and benefits their best efforts for the whole time they're working. The people who lumber along, encourage others to waste time, take two-hour lunches, and generally don't give their best effort have a character flaw. The problem is that you can't help these individuals a whole lot. Your boss needs to be the one to lay down the law.

Make sure your own responsibilities aren't at risk. In time management terms, give a few minutes, and someone will take an hour. That means you can't sugar coat the issue with co-workers. You have to be direct and firm, noting (with a smile) that you don't have time for frivolity. Better to confront your co-worker than miss a deadline and be viewed as not trustworthy of performance under pressure. Don't allow someone else's agenda to diminish you in the eyes of your boss.

If all else fails, go to your boss for help. If the time-waster is influencing your performance, then your boss will want to know. Be careful not to create a link between your frustration in telling the lazy co-worker she's lazy and talking to the boss. Give yourself a few days between each discussion so you reduce the chance of backlash.

The employee who's wrapped up in his world

Some people are excited about everything in life, especially their family and outside interests. They're constantly talking about their weekend, their date last night, their favorite team, and their family ad nauseam. Their focus is so scattered and their excitement is so high that they're almost like a Dalmatian jumping at your feet for attention. The real challenge is that like a Dalmatian, they don't get the subtle hints you drop that you're busy. It's as if you have to hold them still, bring your face to theirs, and say, "I am busy!" nose to nose. Be direct.

The person who treats work as her sole social outlet

Some people have such a limited life outside of work that they want to know all about yours. They live vicariously through your life experiences, from dating to family to your weekends past or future. Short of being their dating or activity secretary, you need to limit the interaction. The lunch hour is usually a bad option for talking with these people because it can wipe out time before and after lunch as well as lower productivity, but if you want to help them get their life in order after work, go for it.

Dealing with Interruption-Oriented Bosses

In most companies, probably the biggest offenders who interrupt the staff are people in supervisory positions. In some ways, this is understandable. These folks are presumed to have an inside track on corporate priorities and often have to call upon staff to change gears and redirect their efforts. It's no surprise when the director whips into your cubicle, announcing that you've just been tagged to take on the company's latest and greatest new program — and you're to put anything else on the back burner. However, that's a far cry from the boss who sidles into your guest chair and launches an hour rant on executive office demands, reduced budget, and upcoming weekend plans. Or the one who drops in every 15 minutes to ask you how you're coming on that report that's due in three hours.

Most bosses aren't out to find ways to deliberately disrupt their employees' work. More than likely, they're focused on their goals — whether those goals are meeting sales quotas, completing a project on time, reducing costs, or maintaining production. And in their quest to meet those goals, they're often simply not sensitive to others' need for focus.

Enlisting the cooperation of your direct supervisor can be a bit touchier than confronting a co-worker with your interruption issues. It may take some more diplomacy and tact, but it can and must be done. Meeting with your boss to discuss your time-block schedule or to ask your boss to help you with your schedule is a good opening salvo. Get your boss's commitment not to interrupt you during a certain segment of your day — it can pay large dividends for you both.

The seagull manager

It's hard to gain control of the seagull manager. These types of managers do the aerial attack of interruption by flying over, pooping on everyone, and flying back out. Their bombing run of new ideas, changed priorities, and emergency deadlines is ever-changing because their organization and skills in management are lacking.

This type of manager is generally young and inexperienced in management and motivation. These managers can also be overly aggressive and unrealistic about the results that can be achieved in a specified time frame. The truth is that in my younger days and even once in a while now, I can put myself into that category.

With seagull managers, your best bet is to play up to their desire to achieve. Point out that you understand the importance of having the department pull together to help meet these goals. Confirm with your boss that the work you're currently involved in is in alignment with those goals. (You may uncover that it's not — and that may be the reason for your boss's repeated interruptions.)

If you get an affirmative, however, you then have an opportunity to ask for your boss's help in assuring that you fulfill your role in the process. The talk may go this way:

> *"I want to do everything I can to help meet our goal. As I understand your expectations, I need to devote at least X hours of uninterrupted time each day to this work. To make sure I'm investing that time on the right tasks, would you like to meet briefly to go over what I plan to accomplish during that period?"*

With a response like this, you establish that you're on board with the boss's agenda and you assume an implied agreement that he or she believes that your work should be uninterrupted. But by asking for the boss's advice on your approach, you soften your declaration and offer an opportunity for the boss to reaffirm your need for uninterrupted time.

The verbal delegator

The verbal-delegator type of manager can really gum up productivity and performance. In my experience with skilled staff members, delegating small projects, small tasks, and deadlines works better through writing. The verbal delegator often delegates because something popped into his head and he wants to move it off his plate because he doesn't want to think about it again. He moves into some subordinate's world at that moment, regardless of schedule.

Your best solution is to try to turn the verbal delegator to a nonverbal delegator. To do so, urge your boss to put any work request in writing. This ensures that you get the directions straight and avoids the risk that the boss will double-assign a task. The icing on *this* cake is that you reduce the number of interruptions. If your supervisor has to put the order in writing, he's sitting at the computer writing up an e-mail rather than buzzing you on the phone or stopping in your cubicle. If you're working with a boss who's still in the information cul-de-sac trying to find his way to the information highway, then use written request forms instead. You can use something as simple as the example in Figure 9-1.

Request Form

Date: _____

Request:

_____
_____
_____
_____
_____
_____
_____
_____
_____
_____

Figure 9-1:
Written
request
forms clarify
details and
reduce
interrup-
tions.

Requested By: _____
Date To Be Completed By: _____
Completed By: _____
Date Completed: _____

Working with Intrusive Clients

Most businesses have customers of some sort — and most embrace a philosophy of placing a high level of value on their customers. From department stores to fast-food drive-throughs, most companies follow some iteration of "the customer is always right."

That said, you know that to provide the best service to each customer, you have to seek some balance. If the squeaky-wheel clients take up more than their share of your time and resources, you won't be able to give the attention to other deserving customers. Although all customers and clients are important to a growing and thriving business, some *believe* they're more important than others — even if they aren't. Some customers just require more attention, and they often manifest those feelings by being more disruptive. Their interruptions are simply cries for attention — they want to be valued and appreciated.

The truth is that some customers and clients really do have more value than others to the company. Their revenue to the company is larger. They buy products and services that have higher profit margins. They're more influential in the marketplace as your advocates in sending you more business through referrals. To assume that all customers and clients are alike is a naïve approach.

When dealing with intrusive clients and investing large amounts of time, make sure they're worth it. If they're high maintenance, they must be also high revenue and high reward. In the following sections, I tell you how to handle customers who want attention.

Giving a bit of attention that goes a long way

I'm amazed at how taken for granted customers and clients are in today's business world. Expressing appreciation packs a powerful professional punch. When was the last time you were thanked or told, "I appreciate your business," by your attorney, doctor, dentist, accountant, realtor, dry cleaner, gas station attendant, grocery clerk, barista, or food server? Just that simple act stands out significantly as a positive interruption for clients.

A preemptive strike can reduce the interruptions you may entertain from some of your more high-maintenance clientele. Here are a few strategies for making your customers feel appreciated and — at the same time — reducing interruptions from them:

- ✔ **Send a handwritten thank-you note for their business.** Then send one again any time they upgrade, add to their order, or increase their business with you.

- ✔ **Remember their birthdays.** Send a handwritten card or small token.

  A terrific service for mailing cards is Send Out Cards (`www.dirk zeller.com/SOC`). You can program a business follow-up plan for key clients or even your nephew's birthdays for years in advance with a few clicks of the mouse.

- ✔ **Call them on a regular basis.** How frequently you should call depends on the business, the client, and other particulars. But a check-in for no other reason than to make sure everything is going okay racks up a lot of points.

- ✔ **Deliver added value.** Forward articles of personal or professional interest. Alert customers to resources, products, and services that may or may not be related to your business interests. This gesture conveys that you value the relationship beyond business motives. (See Chapter 6 for tips on keeping client information with a customer relationship management [CRM] program.)

Another technique is calling customers back and telling them that they're so important that you squeezed them into your schedule or that you called them first. This technique is extremely effective when you return a call before the appointed time. If you informed them on voice mail that you'll be calling them back at 11a.m. and you manage to get your priorities done early and can start calling the high-interruption clients back at 10:30 a.m., they'll think you walk on water.

Setting clients' expectations

Educating customers about your availability is important. Let new customers know your schedule and the best times to reach you as well as how to leave a message when you can't be reached. As part of this education, you also want to establish how quickly they can expect a response from you after they leave a message: Within 24 hours? The same business day?

What you're trying to avoid is the person who calls you back five times that day because you were in meetings. With every call, the client gets more frustrated you haven't called her back. Or worse yet, she reaches you on the fifth call before you're walking into your most important meeting of the day, creating the worst interruption of your life because she unloads on you and ruins your focus.

Creating reasonable expectations is key in good customer relations. Taking 24 hours to return a client's call may be reasonable — but it won't seem that way if the client expects to hear from you within an hour.

As for existing clients and customers, be sure to update them whenever your availability circumstances change. If, for example, your work hours are changing — maybe you're switching to part time or a four-day workweek — notify customers of the schedule revisions and your new availability. Depending on the importance of the client and the immediacy of the situations you deal with, you may even want to let customers know when you're on vacation or on a business trip in which you can't be reached.

You can also reinforce wait times through your voice mail message. By leaving your availability and response details as part of your message, callers are more likely to recall and retain. Here's an example:

> *"You've reached Dirk Zeller. I am out of the office today, Tuesday, September second. Please leave a message and I will return your call by end-of-day Wednesday, September third. If you need immediate assistance, please call so-and-so. Until then, make it a great day!"*

I've set the scenario: The caller shouldn't expect a return call from me today. And in fact, because I'll be returning to an inbox filled with calls, e-mail, and correspondence, I may not be able to get back until as late as the end of the day. I've offered, however, a back-up plan if the situation is more urgent. This should satisfy virtually anyone who calls.

Don't be tempted to include "If it's an emergency, call me on my cellphone" unless you're prepared for lots of interruptions. After all, isn't *interruption* exactly what you're trying to avoid?

Chapter 10

Overcoming Procrastination, a Notorious Time Thief

*M*uch of my work today — writing, developing far-reaching sales programs for clients, and putting together and presenting training workshops — involves long-term, complex, multi-staged projects that require great investments of research, development, and time. And with business booming, I can't afford to get behind.

And I don't have to — not when I can conquer those tendencies to put things off. In this chapter, I show you what procrastination is and how to recognize it. Not all procrastination is bad, however, so I help you see the difference between good reasons to postpone action and mere excuses to put something off.

But most importantly, I provide tools and tactics to help you overcome that debilitating paralysis that keeps you from getting started or the attacks that slow you down or stop you mid-project. One of the most important principles in overcoming procrastination is to take the first step — so go ahead and get started.

Staring Down the Source: How Procrastination Takes Hold

Although many people believe that they postpone the unpleasant when they indulge in procrastination, fact is, putting things off carries a lot of emotional unpleasantness. Boiled down to its purest form, *procrastination* is simply deferring or delaying action. But of course, it's not nearly that simple. Understanding what provokes procrastination and how it affects you is the first step in overcoming the impulses that keep you from moving forward.

Recognizing procrastination isn't always easy, especially when your time of reckoning is a few weeks or months away. You may simply believe you're waiting until the right time to get started. Here are some indications that you may be putting off what you shouldn't.

Calling on short-sighted logic: "I have plenty of time"

It's easy to justify the idea that you don't have to start on a project when its completion date isn't for some time off. Perhaps your tax returns don't have to be submitted until April 15, and it's the middle of January. True, you still have time, so you don't need to put "file taxes" at the top of your priority list at this point. But you should pull your documents together at least 30 days before the deadline. If you use an accountant, you may need even more time to have meetings and research a few deductions to get the proper documentation. Procrastinators, on the other hand, tend to cling to this logic way past the point of manageability. Nine times out of ten, the procrastinator who says "later" in January is scrambling to get in the extension form at 11 p.m. on April 14.

Avoiding the unpleasant: "I don't want to think about it now"

If you just discovered that you hold the winning lottery ticket, you wouldn't delay calling in for your reward. Who feels conflicted about winning money? But putting off tasks that are unpleasant, that are difficult to accomplish, or that you feel conflicted about is human nature. Consider these examples:

- You delay turning in the expense report for your recent business trip. Tallying up receipts is such a bore.
- You put off having the birds-and-bees talk with your preteen.

✔ You've ignored keeping up with your quarterly statistics for weeks.

✔ You rearrange your office and clean your desk instead of picking up the phone and starting on your sales calls for the day.

When someone faces a situation that requires confrontation with others, the tendency is also to procrastinate. Most humans — talk show hosts excluded — seem hard-wired to avoid disagreements with others. Sometimes, however, what may have been a small confrontation turns into a major confrontation because it builds over time. Say, for instance, Boy meets Girl. Boy and Girl go out. Boy decides he wants to go out with someone else. Boy keeps putting off "the talk" with Girl because he knows it'll be uncomfortable. But every time Boy postpones until the next date, he has a miserable time with Girl and adds even more guilt and discomfort.

Or take the case of delaying a disciplinary action with an employee. When you avoid that conversation, the employee's behavior may continue or become even worse. In some cases, it can lead to cause for dismissal. But most companies require that certain steps be taken to resolve issues before termination, and documenting disciplinary actions is one of those steps. Because you haven't followed the process, you're in the middle of an unavoidable and ugly conflict that you can't quickly resolve.

The longer you postpone confrontations, the worse the situation can get. And by the time you're forced to address it, all the reasons you hate confrontation are sure to be magnified.

Triggering your fears: "What if I screw up? And what if I don't?"

Sometimes putting something off stems from more than poor planning or overcommitment. Many procrastinators are unsure of themselves and their abilities. They wait until the last minute to complete projects because that way, if their work isn't well received, they can tell themselves it was because they didn't have enough time to finish the project to their satisfaction.

I know of one woman who was thrilled to have finally gotten her first book deal with a well-known publisher. She had a reasonable schedule for a nonfiction title — six months — but three months passed and she hadn't produced more than the book's introduction. After some soul-searching, she recognized that she was delaying her work because she feared that if the book were published and no one bought it or she got a bad review, that would mean she'd failed.

You can just as easily procrastinate because of fear of success as fear of failure. Fearing success and how it may change your relationships and friends is real. Many people don't reach outside their comfort zones because of what their parents, siblings, and Uncle Ned will say. In some circles, becoming too successful may cause you to leave some people behind.

Success also can affect your spouse or significant other. I have a sister-in-law who felt that all wealthy people did something wrong or unethical to acquire their wealth. With our success, Joan was more affected by her views than I, but it did make family events uncomfortable.

Paralyzed by perfection: "I'll wait till the time is right"

Sure, you want to do the best job you can. But procrastinators often use their quest for perfection as an excuse to delay. As a close cousin to fear of failure (see the preceding section), the desire for perfection can paralyze you. If you spend too much time checking facts, trying to select the perfect words or phrases, or rewriting a paragraph numerous times, you're probably doing so at the expense of other more important things. Frequently, procrastinators try to avoid and delay challenges, like projects that are mentally taxing or big-picture tasks. They rationalize that they're not in the right frame of mind, are too distracted to give it their best, or are waiting for inspiration to strike. The danger here, of course, is that by procrastinating, you push yourself into a corner and, without adequate time, do a job that's far less than perfect.

A bit of perspective may lead you to the root of the problem, because procrastination is often a symptom of something that's troubling you on a subconscious level. Perhaps consider why you feel the need for things to be perfect. Have always felt the need for perfection, even as a child? Could you have learned this behavior from circumstances in your childhood? Is your current or previous boss a perfectionist?

I'm not saying you shouldn't try to do an outstanding job. You should absolutely strive to make every task and project a masterpiece — whatever it is. But be careful not to use it as an excuse to postpone taking that first step. Doing your best with the resources you have is truly the goal in life. Use your time, skills, mental capabilities, and actions to help you avoid being paralyzed by perfection. Also, keeping the 80/20 rule in mind can help you move on to the next project or goal (turn to Chapter 4 for more on the 80/20 rule).

Sabotaging at mid-process: "I've earned a break"

Although most people are stricken by procrastination before they take their initial steps, the urge to put off completing a project occurs frequently, too. The more complex and lengthy the task, the greater the odds are of losing momentum, getting distracted, and giving up before you reach the end.

I admit that my procrastinitis hits me mid-project. Starting something new revs me up. I love launching a training course or working on a new project with a client, and I tend to dive in with enthusiasm. That's always why writing the first half of a book is significantly easier than the last half.

For information on how you can keep moving forward, see the later sections "Motivating yourself with the carrot-or-stick approach" and "Maintaining Your Motivation as You Press Ahead"

Looking for thrills: "I work best under pressure"

Many people who claim to work best under pressure are merely procrastinators in disguise. The first thing to do is to figure out whether you really work well under the pressure of tight deadlines. I know personally that most high-dominant behavioral style individuals do work best under pressure. That's only 18 percent of the population, so the chance you fit that category is about 1 in 5.

You can get a rush from having to work in a state of high productivity and hitting the deadline. You feel a sense of accomplishment in knowing that most of your colleagues couldn't have pulled it off. The problem with forcing yourself into those situations is that once in a while, you get burned by not hitting the deadline or by crashing as soon as you cross the finish line.

My best advice is to do some of the planning for your projects when you get them. Invest the time in planning out the steps even if you don't have the time to complete them. One of the benefits is that you'll be sure of the time, resources, materials, and help you'll need to pull off your project. This planning enables you to accurately gauge what you need so you get fewer surprises when you put your whole effort in motion.

And if you still feel you need more deadline-driven excitement in your job, perhaps your boss will reward you with more responsibility — and a raise to go with it.

Knowing Whether to Put It Off

Postponing action isn't productive when it holds you back, costs you time and money, and results in a negative outcome. But sometimes, putting something off is the best course of action. The challenge is knowing when it's right to procrastinate. This section helps you sort that out.

Poor procrastination: Considering the costs

With procrastination, the bottom-line loss of time, money, and productivity is enormous — enormous to you, to your company, to your country, and to the world. A global tally of the cost of procrastination is more than a little overwhelming to take in, but the negative impact is clear in closer-to-home examples, too. Here's what poor procrastination costs you:

- **Money:** Consider the impact when you pay your bills late: You get dinged with a late fee, which can be as much as $25 or more. If you do that half the time, you rack up $150 per year. And that's not factoring in the increased interest (compounded daily) you pay.

  Now crank it up a bit. When you routinely pay your bills late, your credit rating isn't so hot. So when you apply for a mortgage or home equity loan, you don't get the best interest rate. You may not even realize how much that fraction of an interest point can make over your 30-year mortgage. Your habit of procrastinating can cost you as much as $50,000 over the loan's lifetime!

- **Quality:** Putting things off until the last minute means you have less time to do the job than it probably warrants. Some of you can boast pulling an A out of such an experience. But most people, if they're honest, confess that the eleventh-hour cram session doesn't bring them their best grades — or a meaningful understanding of the material. So as you try to cram ten days into five doing a job you're not comfortable with in the first place, you lose even more sleep, work even more fatigued, and — surprise — your paper is returned to you for major rework.

- **Time:** When you put off a task, you spend a limited amount of time actively choosing not to start your project. And then there's the time that the thing you should've been doing but weren't takes up residence in your mind, even though you're doing other things. It still counts as time invested in the task you're putting off because it's affecting the quality of whatever else you're doing in the moment.

- **Your well-being:** The responsibility doesn't go away simply because you put off doing the job, and you end up carrying the guilt of not doing what you know you should. The stress of the work ahead and the not-doing it causes both emotional anxiety and physical stress, from loss of sleep to stomach problems to depression. In short, procrastination feels lousy.

Wise procrastination: Knowing when to hold 'em

The secret to successful procrastination is to do it deliberately, based on the time that you have and the status of the tasks. Take a look at what's on your plate and choose the tasks that are least time-sensitive and least at-risk, and then postpone them for a bit. In other words, allow yourself to procrastinate — but give yourself a deadline by which to complete those tasks. This section covers tasks you can afford to — and probably should — procrastinate on.

When haste could cause harm

Many tasks or decisions that require action are critical and must be accomplished in a timely manner. But when making the right decision is important, opt for procrastination if haste could result in a damaging outcome. When you feel pressured to make a choice or are forced to take an action you're uncertain of, in most cases, putting it off until you're clear-headed and can think through your decision is a good use of procrastination.

Here's an example: The salesperson offers you a hefty discount on those super-insulating windows — but it's only good at the time of the offer. Defer until tomorrow, and the price goes back up by 20 percent. You're torn. The salesperson assures you that the company is highly rated and the product is the best quality. You know you need new windows, but you hadn't planned to buy them until the salesperson knocked on your door.

In this case, your instinct to hold off is a good one. The windows and the deal are probably legitimate. But you haven't had a chance to investigate this opportunity as carefully as you should to ensure that you make a wise move. Trust me: This is probably not your last opportunity to buy those windows at a special price.

When the timing isn't right

Sometimes, the key to success is timing. You may have an important objective on your to-do list: It may be something that's critical in helping you achieve your goals. But your instinct to put on the brakes may be because the timing isn't right — the time and energy you'd put out is far greater than what you'd get in return.

Maybe you delay putting your house on the market — it's a bad time to sell, so why invest the time and energy when the likelihood of selling at the price you need to is minimal? Or perhaps you need to put in some time in the evening to prepare for a meeting in the morning. But the baby is sick, and even if you ignore his distress or leave your spouse to handle it, you're distracted and worried.

The point is that you can't possibly be as productive or accomplish as much when the timing isn't right. You may end up investing a lot more time and energy — and not get the return you hoped for. So do the best that you can; you need to invest the time necessary so that you're prepared enough for the meeting but also give the necessary assistance to your family. Learn to recognize those times that you're swimming against the current, and then stop and re-evaluate your priorities and change direction if needed.

When the task isn't critical

You're loaded down with projects and commitments, all of them important and none of them offloadable. Heck, you're not procrastinating — you're *drowning.* In situations like this, procrastinating can be a survival strategy. You just need to decide which items to put off.

If you have to put off doing something because of time limitations, make it one of the routine day-to-day tasks. These are the low-value, low-reward actions that produce limited results, something you can most likely delegate to someone else. Be cautious about postponing the growth and big-picture aspects: Even though they tend to be more long-term in scope, if you don't stay on top of these issues, the consequences can be significant.

You can put off less-important to-do items in your personal life, too. For instance, say you have to accomplish the following tasks: Do your taxes by next week, finish an important presentation for work in a week-and-a-half, paint the guest room before your in-laws come next week, and talk with your travel agent about your trip to Bali this summer. You may choose to put off painting the guest room because it's not critical to your in-laws' visit (they'll be just as happy with smoky-blue walls as moss-green ones). Or you can postpone the meeting with the travel agent because you have more time to accomplish that than you have for the taxes and the presentation.

Laying the Groundwork: Altering Your Mindset and Instituting Discipline

Everyone has three weapons in the arsenal for fighting procrastination. Call upon these formidable forces, unleash their power, and reclaim control of your time:

✔ **Decision:** First, it's important to recognize procrastination when you see it and admit that you're guilty. At that point, you can take action to squelch the urge. Decide to begin the steps to stay on course with your obligation. In short, make a commitment and hold fast.

> ✔ **Determination:** Determination is the push that gets you through the late hours, the long days, and the uncomfortable places that make you want to put off your obligation. It's the commitment to see the task through to completion and on time. Although determination is often an innate sense of responsibility, it's also a habit that you can learn, and constant practice keeps it working.

> ✔ **Discipline:** Just as you use discipline to train yourself in other areas — picking up a sport or taking a class; sticking to a time-management plan and schedule-planning system; going on a diet or undertaking an exercise plan — your vigilant effort to keep on course with your commitments can serve as a major motivator. Approach your procrastination with the same focus: Discipline yourself to get started and stay on course.

The following sections name a few alternate routes to keep you on track so you arrive at your destination — on time.

Motivating yourself with the carrot-or-stick approach

The nature of human beings is to move away from pain and toward pleasure. In setting up a prioritization plan, you can use the carrot-or-stick approach to drive yourself toward accomplishment. When you feel the urge to procrastinate, maybe what you need is a carrot dangling in front of your face — an incentive to keep pressing on. Hey, it worked when you were a kid: "If you clean your room now, you can stay up tonight and watch monster movies." On the other hand, some folks respond better to reminders of consequences — the threat of the stick. For them, the promise of a reward gets no reaction, but avoiding negative consequences scares them into action.

Here's an example: You hate working out — it means you have to get up earlier to get to the gym, work up a sweat when you could be getting another hour of sleep or enjoying a latte and the newspaper. But keep in mind the end result of your choice: the awful feeling of being overweight or out of shape, ill-fitting clothing, high blood pressure, and low stamina. On the flip side is the pleasure of a fit physique; boundless energy; and a stab at a longer, healthier life.

A work-life example is the salesperson who drives herself to put in two hours of prospecting calls each day (instead of just one) by reminding herself that a higher commission check, management recognition, and a grander family vacation are the rewards for the effort. If she neglects this effort, consequences await her: a poor performance evaluation, lower income, more effort to make up for sales shortfall, and perhaps even termination.

Seeking reward

If anticipating the pleasurable consequences of tackling an action you don't really enjoy motivates you to perform it, then focus on those positives. And if rewards help, shower yourself with them. If the vision of a latte and your favorite scone gives you the get-up-and-go to take care of your task, go for it (after you finish the job, of course!). Or if a vacation moves you toward finishing an onerous freelance project, set a date for when you'll book the trip, and follow through when you wrap up the project.

Whenever motivation lags, pause to remind yourself of your incentive upon achieving success. Consider tacking up an enticing photo near your most tempting place of hesitation. The photo can be any number of things: A place you want to go, a person you want to spend time with, someone with qualities you'd like to attain, and so on. If your reward for a freelance writing project is a Caribbean vacation, for example, tack up a photo of a tropical setting or beach along a sparkling blue ocean right by your computer.

Avoiding consequences

If you're more leery of the results of neglect than excited about a reward upon completion, ask yourself about the consequences you'll face if you fail to complete certain steps toward your goal, and remind yourself of them as often as you need to.

If you find that consequences are your surest motivators, make sure you focus on the immediate ones. Unfortunately, when consequences are delayed, the human response is to delay positive action. Skipping your workout today won't give you a heart attack tomorrow — so why not sleep in a little longer? Putting off your prospecting calls today won't reduce your paycheck this week. Because skipping these steps toward your ultimate goal doesn't immediately produce pain, it's easy to (wrongly) convince yourself that there are no consequences.

You can set up new, unpleasant consequences if you have trouble focusing on the long term. Several years ago, two of my clients struggled with procrastination. They'd fill out every last page of paperwork, sharpen their pencils, and arrange their paper clips before they'd begin their important work. Striving to be recognized as employee-of-the-month didn't motivate them, so I tried something a little unorthodox: I had each of them write a $500 check and send it to me. One client made the check out to a political party that he absolutely abhorred and would never contribute to; the other salesperson made out the check to a competitor. If they didn't break through their procrastination, I'd have permission to address and mail those checks. As expected, I never sent those checks. Their desire to avoid violating their political beliefs or giving money to their biggest competitor ensured their daily move through the valley of procrastination. If you opt for this plan, you can have a boss, friend, or even your spouse hold the money.

Recognizing excuses and shoving them aside

Procrastination is definitely in your control, but some influences in your life certainly seem to affect your inclination to procrastinate. And when that happens, the tendency is to make excuses, to blame someone or something else.

Resisting peer pressure

It's a fact of life: Co-workers, friends, acquaintances, and family all seem to conspire to tempt you away from what you *should* be doing. But on some level, when you want to avoid an obligation, you're looking for those opportunities to postpone, and it's great to have someone else or some situation to blame.

Say, for example, that your friend tries to talk you into taking the day off to go to the beach. You have a big presentation coming up the next week and you need every minute to prepare beforehand. But it's a painfully tedious process, you're dreading the presentation, and the last thing you want to be doing is writing yourself a speech. Sounds like a great opportunity to procrastinate. But here's where discipline comes in.

When another person encourages you to forsake your work, before you submit to the pressure, acknowledge that you're likely using this person as an excuse. Then remind yourself what you need to do to meet your priorities now. Here's the real question: Is taking time off with your friend bringing you closer to or further away from your goals?

Seeing whether outside forces really do prevent work

Sometimes, you may feel like you're forced to procrastinate due to some external factor beyond your control — weather, traffic jam, power failure. Trust me — I know the feeling.

Recently, I was working on a chapter of this book at home. The weather was beautiful and I longed to join my family outside. Suddenly, the power went out. Although my laptop was still working fine, I didn't have access to the Internet, which I needed for some fact-checking. What a perfect excuse to stop work and call it a day! Okay, fact is, I didn't *need* Internet access to continue working on my chapter. I knew I could make good progress, even if I couldn't tie everything up. I just wanted a reason to justify putting off the chapter until later.

In situations like this one, step back and assess the situation. Ask yourself the following:

- ✔ Is there another way you can accomplish this task?
- ✔ Would the quality of your work be compromised if you were to complete the task under these circumstances?
- ✔ Can you at least take some action to stay on track?

In my case, I had to confess that I could indeed continue to work on my chapter — and that I really did want to finish it that day. Although the quality of my work wouldn't be affected, I wouldn't be able to finish the chapter without online confirmation of a few things. I also knew that rain was in the forecast for the next day. So I determined to make myself forge ahead, writing as much as I could for another hour. Then I planned a break to get together the fixings for a family cookout, followed by another hour of work before I fired up the grill.

Granted, in certain situations, you have no choice but to put off your task. If you're poised to cut the grass and a sudden downpour soaks the lawn, you have to postpone the chore. But be sure that you're not manipulating the situation so that you have an honorable excuse to do what you wanted to do, anyway.

You have some options when you really can't make progress on the task at hand:

- ✔ Move to the next most-important task on your list and come back to the most-important one later.
- ✔ Trade time off. Take a break this afternoon but plan to work later this week during your previously scheduled afternoon off. Or choose to get up earlier later in the week to make up for it.

Give me a break: Putting off procrastination

Sounds counterintuitive, I know, but sometimes putting off procrastination is the proverbial hair of the dog that bit you. That is, a little planned procrastination can solve a larger procrastination problem. As soon as you become aware that you're procrastinating, don't beat yourself up; instead, allow yourself to procrastinate — but just not yet.

Here's how it works: Identify the ways you're likely to put off working on your project. Then, instead of fighting a losing battle with your willpower, tell yourself it's okay to do those activities — after you put in a set amount of work on your project.

Suppose you're trying to get a good head start on a paper for a class, but you've been putting it off for almost anything else that comes along: a lunch date, a shopping errand, even a TV show. You can plan to run that errand — *after* you spend a half-hour getting your notes in order and reviewing your outline. Chances are, by the time you look up at the clock, you'll have spent an hour or longer and have made a lot more progress than you anticipated. You may decide to keep on working, now that you're engrossed in the task. But even if you do break at this point, you'll have gotten more done than had you simply quit earlier. The psychological edge is likely to help motivate you to make even further progress.

When postponing your procrastination, give yourself fairly short time commitments. Tell yourself you'll just spend a half hour or an hour on the project before you allow yourself a break. This is more likely to keep you on task than if you commit yourself to three hours of work. With that time commitment, you may end up procrastinating on your procrastination of procrastinating — uh, I think.

Conquering Dreaded Tasks with Sandwich Tactics

Sometimes what's on your plate seems so big that you can't sink your teeth into any of it. In these cases, taking things apart may be the best way to make progress, stay on track, and put away that project. Here's the breakdown.

The eat-the-crust-first approach: Starting with the tough job

One extremely successful technique to move beyond procrastination is to tackle the toughest job first. Or if you're working on a single, big task, take on the most difficult aspect of it before the rest.

I advise coordinating this tough-stuff-first effort so that you start it first thing in the morning, a time when most people are at their peak in terms of energy, intensity, and focus. If you conquer the most difficult task first, your day will be a lot more productive.

To ratchet up your results further, start the prep work for the toughest tasks the night before. In Chapter 4, I share how you can set the stage and make quick work of even your most challenging projects. When you prepare well for your effort, you won't spend 30 minutes just getting ready to go.

If you get stuck on the big task, you can regain momentum with the salami approach or Swiss-cheese approach, which I outline next.

The Swiss-cheese approach: Poking little holes in the task

When biting into a major or complicated task seems overwhelming, start with the easier pieces — the aspects that you know you can complete quickly and with little effort. In this way, you poke holes in the project, making lighter work of the steps that remain after you polish off the manageable aspects.

For example, suppose you're facing your kitchen after a dinner party: dishes piled to the tops of the cupboards, leftovers cooling in their serving dishes, the sink clogged with kitchen scraps, and the roaster pan caked with burned food and tenacious grease. The job is more than you can fathom at midnight. You're tempted to turn around, go to bed, and hope the kitchen fairies come in the night to transform your kitchen into its former spotless self.

Or you can tell yourself you'll do one simple thing before you turn out the lights: maybe put away all the food and scrape the scraps into the compost bin or garbage disposal. And then when you make short work of that, you tell yourself that filling up the dishwasher with at least one load won't take that long. When that's done, you decide you can at least rinse and stack the other dishes. By the time you poke these holes into the project, not too much is left. Even if you give up at this point, the task that awaits you in the morning isn't nearly so formidable.

The salami approach: Finishing it one slice at a time

The salami approach is a great tactic for those long-term projects in which the deadline seems so far away that you convince yourself you don't need to start yet. So you don't resort to cramming at the eleventh hour, take the time immediately to cut up the project into bite-sized pieces. These slices should be small enough that you can schedule them day-by-day or at least week-by-week.

The number of ways you can slice and dice a large task are many, but here's one option for breaking it down:

1. **Set time aside to plan the project completely so you can begin working on it and cut it down to size.**

2. **Create an action order of what needs to be done and when.**

   Creating a time line helps you segment the task into pieces.

3. Figure out what materials you need for the task.

Collect all the materials and make them ready and available.

When I begin my book projects, the publisher gives me a certain amount of time, usually several months, to complete the manuscript. I know from experience that I can't look at the project as a single huge step; it's too daunting. So I break it up. For example, if I have six months to write the book and it's 24 chapters long, I break down the project into chapter slices. So instead of "write book in six months," it's "write chapter this week." Or it may be "write ten pages a day this week" or some other breakdown that's meaningful to me.

The discard-the-garnish approach: Getting it off your plate

Often when you order an entree at a restaurant, the dish may include some sprigs of parsley or an orange slice in addition to a side or two and a drizzle of some fancy sauce. It makes for a pretty presentation, and it's edible, too. But unless you're really hungry, those items are often still on your plate when the bus person clears off the table.

Just as with a restaurant meal, you probably have a few commitments on your plate that aren't really a key part of your responsibilities. Take a look at your schedule and see whether some of these tasks are mere garnishes. You then have choices:

✔ Remove them from your plate.

✔ Give them to someone else.

✔ Save them until you finish everything else.

Maintaining Your Motivation as You Press Ahead

Everyone has struggled with procrastination, and many still do. I have yet to meet a person who doesn't battle with the temptations of putting off those obligations that seem too big, too hard, or just plain no fun. Recognizing your tendencies is the first step toward recovery. By following the strategies I outline in this chapter, you can make remarkable progress in overcoming the procrastination.

Staying on the right course, however, is a never-ending vigil. Use these maintenance tactics to do so:

- **Keep your expectations realistic.** Before you beat yourself up for your woeful procrastinating ways once again, take a look at your schedule and first figure out whether what you're attempting to accomplish is realistic. Have you accepted an assignment you're not qualified to take on, or is too much expected of you? Have you committed to an absurd deadline?

  Again, when you begin to feel overwhelmed by your workload, this may be an indicator that you'll slip into postponement mode. So do whatever you can to get over being overwhelmed. It may require some adjustment in expectations — your co-workers', your boss's, or yours.

- **Handle the big stuff and delegate the rest.** When you find that too many obligations and projects are demanding your attention to the point that you're putting off making headway on any of them, it's time to lighten your load.

  After you examine your workload and identify what's really important to your job or your career goals, you know what to attend to first. But instead of putting those smaller or less-important tasks on the back burner, see whether someone else can take over for you.

- **Prevent clutter overload.** Another sign that your procrastinating proclivities may soon raise their ugly head — or already have: Your office or home is cluttered with a confusion of papers and files, your e-mail inbox contains more than a week's worth of unread mail, and you've lost control of your schedule.

  You can't maintain control of your time or stay on top of your obligations if your life has become so disorganized that you can't keep on top of your work and home. It's no wonder you're procrastinating — if you have a project in all that mess, you don't even know where to start.

  You may be on overload. You may have too many projects at once. At any rate, it's time to clear your head and your desk. Take a day once a month or a few hours to purge, file, respond, and clean up. (See Chapter 5 for tips on clearing your workspace.)

- **Focus on maintaining a healthy balance.** Both your work life and your personal life are important to your well-being. Keep an eye on the scale to be sure that these different areas are in balance. If you get weighted down at the office, you lose energy and perspective, and procrastination — both at home and at work — creeps in. If family issues take over, you risk your performance at work. When one aspect of your life gets out of whack, do everything you can to regain balance.

Chapter 11

Making Wise Yet Quick Decisions

. . . .

In This Chapter

▶ Avoiding roadblocks to decision-making

▶ Following a six-step system to better decisions

▶ Getting unstuck

. . . .

*L*ife is always serving up decisions, and making choices — even wrong ones — is how you grow, mature, and accomplish the things that make life meaningful. If you're stymied by small decisions, you never have the time and energy to seek out choices that lead to a more enriching and success-ful life. In other words, decisiveness is more than a useful tool; it's a way of living. Indecision, on the other hand, is a way of drifting, simply surrendering to fate.

It's all too easy to get bogged down weighing and reweighing options in a pur-gatory of analysis paralysis, but endless second-guessing and falling prey to the tyranny of what-if only bleeds you of energy. Sitting on the fence is ineffi-cient, not to mention uncomfortable. And *not* deciding? Well, that's a decision itself — with its own consequences.

Like many important life skills, effective decision-making isn't taught in school. Most people learn by trial and error and through the experiences of other people. Unfortunately, this approach can leave you floundering in a sea of changing choices. So in this chapter, I help you tap into your inner wisdom, enabling you to make better decisions because of your level of dis-cernment and to take action more quickly because of your ability to under-stand, evaluate, and consider all possible outcomes.

When you begin to feel more confident about making smaller decisions, you find it easier to apply what you've discovered to larger challenges. You see that you can break down what seems confusing, or even overwhelming, into a series of smaller steps. Eventually, you'll be comfortable enough with making decisions that you *invite* them, because being able to quickly and confidently make decisions gives you power and control over your life.

Looking at the Source of Most Decision-Related Struggles

Why is making a decision so hard? It usually comes down to fear. Fear of making the wrong choice. Fear of regret. The more afraid you are of tripping up, the more you torture yourself by evaluating, debating, analyzing, and obsessing over every decision.

Before you begin to work on your decision-making skills, you need to see where the problem lies. Take a moment to ask yourself these big-picture questions:

- ✔ What's one area of your life you'd like to change but have avoided taking action?
- ✔ What's really holding you back?
- ✔ What's the worst thing that can happen if you decide to take action?
- ✔ What are the odds that the worst really will happen?
- ✔ Would you be likely to live through — and even learn valuable lessons from — making a mistake?

Armed with the answers to these questions, realize that the fear is probably unfounded — that the worst that can happen is very unlikely. Then decide to take action on your finding today.

Whittling Major Decisions Down to a Manageable Size

Lucky people make good decisions once in a while. Successful people have a system they consistently use to approach situations that require decisions: a plan of action that works no matter what the circumstances or stress level.

Here's why: Individual decisions rarely exist in a vacuum. Daily decisions, ranging from how and when you discipline your children to whether to stick to a regular savings plan, have consequences that may reveal themselves only years down the road. The key is to make clear-headed choices *today* and build on good results instead of haphazardly cleaning mistakes as you go. Use the following six steps to whittle the formidable task of making a decision down to manageable size.

Step 1: Evaluate the gravity of the decision

Can't decide between the lobster and the steak? Don't lose your appetite over it. Even if you make the wrong choice, chances are you'll be over your regret by your next meal. (Or you *could* choose the surf-and-turf.) Many other life decisions — changing your job or career, buying a home, or undergoing surgery — have lasting (sometimes even life-or-death) consequences that can significantly affect your family or employees. Obviously, these decisions deserve much more attention, time, and care.

The key is to approach situations in every facet of your life with a cool head so you can accurately assess the size and gravity of the situation you're up against. Following is a list of the larger, more important areas of your life that really deserve some time and effort; decisions in other areas of your life need not require much time or thought.

- ✔ **Taking care of business:** If you're a business owner, your daily decisions guide the fortunes of your family as well as those of all the employees who rely on you for a regular paycheck and benefits. You have to balance seemingly small decisions (whether to refund a customer's money) with bigger-picture choices (redirecting the business to take advantage of a potentially lucrative niche market).

  Assessing the size of a business decision isn't always a straightforward process, so look beyond the obvious to possible repercussions. For example, failing to provide a refund to a dissatisfied customer may prompt that person to post a scathing review of your customer service policy on a widely read blog; you may spend months undoing the damage. Redirecting resources to a new niche market, on the other hand, may affect the morale — and productivity — of employees in core business areas.

- ✔ **Furthering your career:** Should you decide to take a higher paying job with a longer commute? Hang up your sales hat and study to become a nurse? If you're changing your job, assess the impact of added travel expenses and less time with your family. A major career change can shake up everything from your budget to your self-image.

- ✔ **Keeping it in the family:** Some of life's major decisions involve your family: who you choose to marry, when to have children, where to live. Along with these big decisions come plenty of smaller day-to-day decisions. Who takes the kids to school? Should you take a vacation or renovate your kitchen? Even decisions that don't seem significant in the moment, such as giving your kids unsupervised use of the computer, can have unexpected repercussions. To further complicate things, you may have to step in to provide assistance or physically care for your aging parents.

✔ **Making sense of your finances:** Money isn't the most important thing in life, yet it's the lifeblood of so many important goals. Unfortunately (but perhaps not surprisingly), most marital conflict is linked to finances. The choices you make about spending, saving, and investing — individually or as a couple — can spark daily arguments and have serious long-range implications.

✔ **Staying healthy:** The good news in this area is that the simplest decisions can have the most profound effects. Deciding to eat a healthy, balanced diet, exercise daily, and take regular breaks from the stress of work can prolong and improve the quality of your life. This alone is good preparation for the more serious, sometimes life-or-death decisions you may have to make if you develop a condition such as diabetes, need surgery, or require tests.

✔ **Building strong relationships:** Happy relationships are the foundation of a happy life. If you're married, in a committed relationship, or devoted to a circle of close friends, the time and care you invest pay you back a thousandfold. If you're still looking for a spouse or life partner, the decisions you make about the qualities you want and need in someone else and the qualities and commitment you're willing to bring to a relationship shape your future for better or worse.

Step 2: Assess the time frame you have to make the decision

When you're on a time crunch for making a decision, your struggle in making that decision increases. Sometimes, you *have* to make a decision immediately because it's a life-or-death situation. For example, more than ten years ago, doctors found four blocked arteries in my father's heart, which meant a heart attack was imminent. His time frame for deciding to have bypass surgery was *now*. He was immediately admitted to the hospital and his surgery was performed first thing the following morning.

Thankfully, few decisions must be made this quickly and under life-or-death duress. That's probably why most people are so skilled at procrastinating. The key: Give yourself a reasonable deadline, allowing a comfortable but finite amount of time to research and consider your options. In decision making, you may need to slow down your process, time frame, and expectations in terms of time and results. You have to be willing to take a few breaths to pause and then decide.

Here are some questions to ask when you're assessing a reasonable time frame for making a decision — let your answers to these questions guide your next steps:

✔ Is there a shelf date on this decision?

✔ Will something good happen if you make the decision by a certain date? Will something bad happen if you don't?

✔ What's likely to happen if you make the wrong decision within this time frame?

✔ What are the consequences of postponing the decision? Can you (and your family) live with that?

Step 3: Narrow your options down to two

When faced with a multiple-choice dilemma, it helps to narrow your options. If I open my 2-year-old daughter's closet and say, "Okay, Annabelle, what do you want to wear?" she wears me out changing outfits and changing her mind. My wife, Joan, has a better strategy: She gives Annabelle only two choices.

It's a technique I call *alternative choice*, and I've used it in my sales coaching practice for 20 years. I narrow each prospect's choice down to just two options. Why? Because having too many choices is confusing. The more options you have, the harder it is to commit to just one. Research indicates that you'll be happier with your decision if you choose from a smaller number of options.

The fastest and best decision-makers are people who align their decisions with their personal or business goals; having this foundation simplifies things by narrowing your focus. Identifying your goals, vision, core values, and core purpose in life is an important first step (I help you get them on paper in Chapter 2). Then check to see which of your options don't align with your goals and cross them off the list.

To do a preliminary evaluation of your options, you need to do a limited amount of research. Give yourself a time limit for researching possibilities (perhaps only an hour online, a half-hour making phone calls, or a half day to visit stores). Then, based on your cursory research, decide which two options best align with those goals, priorities, and values. Matching options to priorities can be a bit tricky if each option addresses more than one goal — you have to decide which options meet your most important goals. I often find it helpful to apply the following filters:

✔ Impose a price range to narrow down the choices.

✔ Establish some basic criteria to whittle down the possibilities (open-toed or sling-back shoes; Asian restaurants on the east side of town; job opportunities in major West Coast cities).

If you find that limited resources are prematurely narrowing down your choices, go back to your goals and reassess your resources. List and categorize all the things you lack, and then brainstorm or research ways to overcome these holes in your plan — I help you accomplish this self-evaluation in Chapter 2.

Step 4: Check in with the reliable wisdom of your gut

Your body is a very powerful partner in decision-making, whether or not you act on what it tells you. So before you invest lots of time researching a particular course of action, stop thinking and take note of what you feel deep inside — what does intuition tell you?

Somewhere in the vicinity of their stomachs, many people detect a distinct discomfort about certain decisions they're considering — hence the term *gut feeling.* You don't have to have full-blown indigestion to know you're not feeling good about a decision. And believe me, all the positive data in the world probably won't change your gut feeling about the outcome. The best decisions both make sense logically and feel good in your gut.

Step 5: Research your top options

The more data you collect to support your decision, the more confident you feel in the face of uncertainty. Here are some great ways to gather the information that can help you decide between your top two choices:

- ✔ Read a book written by an expert.

- ✔ Arrange an information interview with someone who's already made the choice you're considering.

- ✔ Gather input from family members and friends who will be affected by your decision.

- ✔ Post a question on a message board related to your situation.

- ✔ Read trade magazines, Web sites, and blogs targeted to the market or area you're researching.

The usefulness of data in your quest to make wise choices comes with a caveat: Nowadays, you can literally drown in a sea of data. And when that happens, analysis paralysis sets in. So as you do your research, make sure that the data is valuable, credible, and usable. Remember that data is there to *support* your decision, not *make* your decision.

Step 6: Determine the most efficient way to get your desired result

Take a close look at what you're trying to achieve, quantifying (where possible) what your decision will cost in terms of time, effort, and resources — both short-term and long-term. Then look at your desired end result to see which path is the best way for you to get there.

Success is subjective. What I may deem important or how I measure the cost of a result is unique to *me*. You have to do what's right for you. Here are a few questions to get you thinking:

- ✔ How will you know when you've achieved a level of success that satisfies you?

- ✔ How much time will this take? Is the amount of time and money you'll have to invest worth the result?

- ✔ What would a satisfactory outcome be? What would an outstanding result be for you?

- ✔ What are you willing to do to achieve the satisfactory level?

- ✔ Can you tangibly or quantifiably measure the results? How would you accomplish that?

You can certainly use a pros and cons list to help refine the direct route to your desired result. As you make your list, rate your priorities on a scale of 1 to 10 to give each response some weight.

Evaluating the Results and Making Adjustments

After you implement your decision, be sure to evaluate the results. Most people make time errors in not evaluating the decisions they make soon enough. Some of the skill in making decisions is changing courses when you're sure that you're heading the wrong directions with your recent decision. Evaluating results on regular intervals helps you decide when it's time to change course. It's like in golf: The marginal shots won't kill your round, but the poor shots cost you big strokes. The shot that follows the poor shot matters significantly. Make sure you give your project enough time to have a chance to succeed, though — try making minor adjustments before scrapping your decision altogether.

Here are some questions to ask in the short term to see whether a change is warranted:

- ✔ How is the result measuring up to your expectations?
- ✔ Are you achieving the objectives you outlined in advance?
- ✔ How could you improve the results that you're trying to achieve?
- ✔ If you knew at the beginning what you know now, would you have still selected this course of action?
- ✔ If you were to make a change, what would that be?
- ✔ What result would be worth making a change? What are the odds that change will lead to the desired result?

Refining Your Approach According to Your Behavioral Profile

Everyone reacts differently in situations that require important decisions. Some people are naturally more comfortable taking risks and don't need a lot of data to back up their decisions. Others need a much more detailed analysis of the facts before acting. There's no right or wrong way to be. But knowing your *DISC behavioral profile* — a report on your behavioral styles and preferences — can help you understand your own natural tendencies.

DISC is an acronym for *Dominance, Influence, Steadiness,* and *Compliance.* Most people who take the DISC assessment score high in two or three areas, which point you to the common weaknesses people with similar behavior patterns often have. Your DISC score provides a realistic picture of how you tend to react to stressful situations, how much data you need to make a decision, and the pace you like to work at.

Whether or not you realize it, your DISC style — and the styles of others you live and work with — comes out full-force in complex situations, when the pressure is on and the decisions you make carry a lot of weight. When you're behind on bills, overwhelmed by a project, or have problems at home, your natural tendencies can lead you into some poor decisions. Understanding your DISC style helps you recognize mistakes and adjust your behavior before it's too late. You can establish rules to keep yourself on track and refine your decision-making skills.

On the Web site for my company, Sales Champions, I offer a free DISC assessment that you're welcome to use. Go to www.saleschampions.com/freedisc and answer the 12 questions — it takes less than ten minutes. This gives you basic knowledge of your core behavioral style. No matter what career field you're in, knowing your behavioral style can help you perform better.

This section helps you understand those four main DISC scores and guides you in understanding your own natural tendencies. You also gain insight into how people with different styles are likely to react to the same set of circumstances.

I'm a Dominant Influencer, which means I'm inclined to seek out risk. But I've learned I need someone to slow me down. Thankfully, my wife, Joan, is a Steady, gifted at researching the details that I once thought of as minutiae but are extremely valuable to making sound decisions. I would've made far fewer mistakes in life and business if I'd understood this earlier in our marriage.

The high Dominant

Dominance measures how you respond to problems and challenges. People who score high on this aspect tend to be assertive, direct, focused, and driven. They're more inclined to go with their gut than the advice of other people, and they make decisions quickly based on the results or the net bottom line.

The high Dominant person is also commonly referred to as the *driver* or *director.* The Dominance factor causes these people to make decisions that are bold and risk-oriented. These people are confident, decisive, competitive, aggressive, and at times demanding. They desire a challenge, so they're well stimulated and can look back and exclaim, "Look what I accomplished."

Their focus is the bottom line, the result, the achievement of their goal. If the actions or decisions don't lead to the result, Dominants usually try to omit them. Dominants are bottom-line organizers, so what they do needs less paperwork, and unnecessary steps get cut out from the process.

Dominants are self-motivated. They get to the office early, stay later, and pay almost any price necessary to achieve the success that they desire. They'll work long and hard to make it happen.

The natural tendencies of a Dominant are to be direct, aggressive, and pointed in their decision-making and fast-paced both in speech and decisions. Dominant people have short decision cycles, little fear if a problem or unforeseen challenge arises, high ego strength, and desire to achieve bottom-line results.

As a high Dominant, you need to use the strength of conviction and good instincts but slow down enough to get the facts to support your gut. If you score high in the Dominance category, take extra care to thoroughly assess the data about your options and consider potential downsides of each of them before making a decision.

The trajectory of DISC

DISC is a universal language of people observation, measuring how humans act and react in certain situations. The four-point behavioral profile has evolved from roots that stretch as far back as Empedocles' discoveries in 444 BCE. Hippocrates refined DISC in 440 BCE to four humors, or temperaments: sanguine, melancholic, choleric, and phlegmatic. In 1928, Harvard doctoral graduate Dr. William Marston published his landmark book, *The Emotions of Normal People*, to establish the more modern version that DISC theory uses today. Today, hundreds of thousands of companies use DISC in their biggest hiring decisions.

The high Influencer

Influence measures how you respond to people. A high score on Influence often reveals people who are fun, engaging, talkative, and optimistic about the outcome of the decisions they make. They base their decisions on emotion (some call it *intuition*) and are swayed by how they feel about a certain situation or problem.

The high Influencer is also considered expressive, sanguine, enthusiastic, gregarious, persuasive, optimistic, personable, and popular. Influencers want to make whatever they engage in fun. Decisions need to present fun options and fun opportunities.

High Influencers exude optimism and enthusiasm for life and their jobs. When the road becomes challenging or the decision is especially complex, the optimism for a positive outcome carries them through. High influencers are also highly emotional. This means that their feelings and emotions can influence their actions heavily.

High Influencers need to interact and verbalize. They need to talk out a decision with themselves or with others. When they're talking it out with others, they're looking for agreement, excitement, and optimism out of the other party.

High Influencers crave public recognition. They want to be liked by others. They connect and build a high level of trust in others quickly and easily. They also transfer trust (often indiscriminately) to others, so they can be taken advantage of as well. A smooth talker with a great presentation can talk them into decisions. The trust level goes up, their guard goes down, and they just decided to join a monastery in Tibet overnight.

The natural tendencies of an Influencer are to be outgoing, highly relational, social, verbally persuasive, and fast-paced but friendly. The lack of research for an influencer is legendary. "If it feels good, do it" is their motto.

If you're a high Influencer, establish boundaries to protect yourself. Build rules, such as allowing yourself to make a large purchase only after a 24-hour waiting period or discussing it with someone else. Or have someone check your ideas and thoughts before you take action, preferably a Steady (see the next section). The truth is that Influencers need a system to slow them down.

The high Steady

Steadiness measures how you respond to the pace of things going on around you. People who score high in steadiness tend to be very methodical and cautious in their approach to any goal. They have a process that works well for them, and they don't want to be hurried into deciding or taking action. When allowed to operate at their own pace, they're relaxed and extremely patient.

The high Steady is often called a *relater* or *amiable*. These people make their decisions through patience, persistence, and sincerity. They possess good listening skills because of their high desire to serve people around them. They want to get opinions not to raise their status because they really desire the input. They're more laid back and low stress when making most decisions. But when the stress of making a decision becomes extreme, Steadies retreat into their shells and won't come out even if a nuclear holocaust is upon them.

Steadies are more behind-the-scenes people. They're there to do what's best for their family, clients, co-workers, and company before themselves. They put themselves last in any decision — that is, until they reach their limit. When that happens, it's like Mount Vesuvius erupting.

After Steadies make a decision, they're unbending. High Steadies desire completion. They want to finish what they start. They want to see their decision to the end. They may cling to a bad decision for too long before they enact change.

Steadies tend to be structured, take few risks, and are predictable in their process to making decisions. They're persistent, organized, unemotional, slow to adjust, slow-paced, and conflict-avoidant in gathering and evaluating facts. In the decision process, these people get neither too high nor too low as they work toward the final decision.

These people are outstanding researchers. They often get the task of gathering information so another person or team can make the decision. However, Steadies may feel pressured to act. They may do solid research but be out of connection with the team because the team is ready to go and the Steadies are still uncomfortable. Steadies are still people-oriented, so working with others can mean the deliberation process is extreme.

If you're a high Steady, recognize that if other people are involved in the decision, you may have problems convincing them of the validity of your conclusions because of your lack of excitement. This is especially true if you're in a new position without a track record.

If you have a high score in Steadiness, remember that sometimes change is necessary, so you may need to change the course you're on from time to time. Whenever you're feeling stressed, be careful to step back and evaluate your circumstances and decide whether the best approach to continue with is a different one.

The high Compliant

Compliance measures how you respond to rules and procedures set by others. High scorers in compliance are often precise, detail-oriented, and committed to accuracy. Their fear of being wrong is extreme, and it often sends them back to gather more data. The decision-making procedure is slow and methodical. They use their level of accuracy, diplomacy, systemization, and high personal standards to make the exact right decision.

They meticulously plan their decision process, questions, auxiliary information, evaluations, and spreadsheets, odds of success, risk, and organization before they make the final choice. For a high Compliant, a 95 percent score leaves too many variables to begin. The risk of a negative outcome is too high.

Compliants are polite and courteous in their approach. These people are guarded, accurate, careful, thoughtful questioners, reliant on lots of support materials, patient, objective, and thorough. They're naturally introverted, so they're more task-oriented rather than relationship-driven.

If you're a high Compliant, you'll need to force yourself to define exactly what information, data, evaluations, and input you need in order to feel confident that you've made the right decision. As you come closer to decision-making time, be careful not to become obsessive in your search for information, which is often a subconscious ploy to avoid making the decision. To avoid this trap, you must establish in advance the who, what, when, how, and how long, so you get only the information that you need and then make your call.

Seeking Counsel When You're Stuck

Consequences are real, so depending on the size and scope of the decision you're facing, your fear of facing the consequences of a wrong choice is only natural. You may realize you don't have or know how to get all the information you need to make an informed decision. Or maybe life has thrown a wrench into your best-laid plan and now you're uncertain of your next move. For whatever reason, you're stuck.

Before you get off track or into a tight spot, try to identify a number of people who have faced the kind of challenges you're facing. You can call on any one of them when you need a reality check, expert advice, or simply a sounding board.

Learning from others' successes — or failures

Sometimes the most valuable role another person can play in your success is as an example of what works — or doesn't. You can discover an enormous amount by studying the lessons other people have learned, often through much trial and error.

Trial and error is the most expensive way to learn, in terms of time, money, effort, and emotion. So why reinvent the wheel? Chances are excellent that someone else has already paved the way to the solution you need. Study the decisions of successful people you admire and discover a wealth of guidance in all areas of life — from business to personal well-being — that you can easily apply to your own life. Most people who write an autobiography share their successes and failures, leaving a pathway for you to follow or warnings to be heeded.

Frequently, you can discover more from defeat than from victory. If you watch others closely, you can see what not to do, which is often more valuable than knowing what to do.

Just because other people failed doesn't automatically mean that an idea, strategy, or system doesn't work. Consider the following four factors to make sure failure is still the most likely outcome:

- **Timing:** Sometimes the timing is off on a decision or project. The timing was too early or too late, so they didn't achieve results due to timing problems.

- **Implementation:** The decision to act was right but the planning of the action was lacking. Maybe they didn't think out the details of the plan enough to achieve success, or perhaps the plan was out of order. Maybe the individual steps were out of order, so the decision was destined to fail.

- **The person applying the plan:** You can have the right decision, the right timing, the right plan, and the right steps, and still see someone fail. The failure may occur in that the person who's leading the execution is the wrong person with the wrong skills.

- **Duration:** Persistence to a plan is a prerequisite to success. Often, people quit before they really know whether their decision will work as planned or whether they need an adjustment. This wastes unbelievable amounts of time. Most people in business quit before they've made slight adjustments to the plan and execution of their decision. In business with a new strategy, marketing, sales, management, personnel, and customer service, you need a handful of months to really know if something works. It takes that long to collect the data to be sure of your decision. When you're observing other people's failures, ask whether they gave their decision or plan sufficient time to triumph.

Getting a different perspective on similar situations

New ideas are fundamental to growth. You don't always have the best ones alone. Sometimes you're too close to the situation to have the right solution for your challenges and decisions. You're unable to see all the moving parts. You can be emotionally attached to the outcome and let what you want to see influence your judgment of what you're likely to see.

It's very easy to get so close to a situation that you literally can't see it anymore. In that case, a fresh perspective can be just the ticket you need to get back on track. Cultivate the ability to think outside the box by becoming a student of other people's ideas. Often, one good idea linked with a decision to take action is all you need to create a fortune in life. Resolve to read more, listen to more motivational and business CDs, attend more seminars, and brainstorm with other people. Here are a few of my favorite books:

- *Think and Grow Rich* by Napoleon Hill
- *Focal Point* by Brian Tracy
- *The Power of Positive Thinking* by Dr. Norman Vincent Peale

Turning to a mentor or coach for strategizing help

Many of the world's most successful people have benefited from having a mentor. Why not ask a more experienced friend or teacher to share his or her experience with you? Some schools and professions have mentoring programs, pairing newcomers with more experienced colleagues who guide you along the road to advancement.

Hiring a personal or business coach is another option. In addition to helping you clarify your personal, business, or relationship goals, your coach can guide you in developing strategies for reaching each milestone and (perhaps most importantly) hold you accountable through the implementation process. Business coaches often specialize in different practice areas, such as executive coaching, corporate coaching, and leadership coaching.

Part IV
Maintaining Efficiency When Working with Others

The 5th Wave By Rich Tennant

RICHTENNANT

"Ted and I spent over 120 man-hours together analyzing the survey data, and here's what we discovered: Ted borrows pens and never returns them, he intentionally squeaks his chair to annoy me, and, evidently, I talk in my sleep."

In this part . . .

In the world of business, there's no hall monitor to tell your co-worker to stop disturbing you and go back to her cubicle. There's no bell that declares the meeting is over. There's no tardy notice when a client fails to show up for an appointment. But when you're expected to perform at a certain level on your job, there are no excuses for less-than-acceptable work. That's why a few new lessons on how to manage meetings, appointments, presentations, and other activities spent with colleagues, clients, and business associates are certain to advance your time management skills. Chapter 12 helps you keep your boss on track, and Chapter 13 gets down to the business of meetings with co-workers — a how-to on setting and conducting a productive and expedient meeting. And finally, Chapter 14 examines how to make appointments with clients, present your ideas, and move the process along to get to yes faster.

Chapter 12

Coping with a Time-Wasting Boss

. . . .

In This Chapter

▶ Helping your boss meet deadlines

▶ Protecting your personal time

▶ Working with and reforming a procrastinating or workaholic boss

. . . .

I entered the work world prepared to be impressed by those running the show. Surely everyone out there knew more than I did, worked as hard as or harder than I did, and provided employees with everything they needed to perform superbly and eventually be promoted themselves. After all, that's why the boss is the *boss*, right? However, I've since discovered that although many good bosses are out there, not every manager or supervisor is an employee's dream, and even decent bosses can be poor time managers.

A boss who manages time beautifully can help make your career. But if you report to an inefficient Hindenburg of hot air or even a boss with only average time-management skills, you have three choices:

✔ **Deal with it, knowing that your opportunities for advancement are likely to drop because other teams and departments can outproduce you.** No matter how hard you work to overcome it, this situation reflects poorly on your skills and abilities. In addition, stress takes its toll on both your potential advancement and your mental and physical health.

✔ **Move on, either to another department or position within your company or to another company altogether.** If you switch companies, though, you may also leave behind benefits, vacation and personal time, and possibly a company that's a good place to work.

✔ **Gently and unobtrusively help your boss provide the tools you need to do your job in the timeframe that you need them.** Accomplishing these goals lowers your stress, improves your work life, multiplies your advancement opportunities, and enhances your value to the company. That's why this chapter helps you examine the impact your boss's work style has on your productivity and ability to manage your time. It also tells you how to outline and implement an action plan to improve that work style if unnecessary.

Fulfilling Your Objectives to Help Your Boss Meet Hers

Whether you like it or not, your boss's time is more valuable than yours. Delegating activities to the lowest-paid competent person — someone who can complete assignments as well as the boss while freeing the boss to focus on higher-level tasks with more expensive price tags — is a basic business practice. Your goal is to supply your boss with more time. The more you take on, the better it is for your boss and for you. Ideally, your pay increases and your opportunities for advancement are directly tied to how valuable you are to your boss, how well you support her, and how much you contribute to the department.

I coach salespeople around the globe, and I have a lot of sales clients who are in real estate, insurance, and financial planning. Top performers in these fields have assistants who work for them, and I tell the assistants that one of their primary jobs is to keep their bosses on task — that is, prospecting — daily. Many salespeople put off prospecting and try to stay busy with other tasks. I tell the sales assistants that the best way they can spend their time is to help their bosses prospect with greater consistency.

The best bosses have already assessed themselves and their staff and are using the information to minimize team weaknesses by maximizing everyone's strengths. You, of course, may not have a "best boss" — or you may simply have a good boss who lacks this ability or hasn't yet figured out how to use it to full advantage.

Workers often expect perfection from their bosses, and vice versa. Begin by understanding that you and your boss are both human and that you both have weaknesses. That said, determining how your boss operates makes life easier for both of you and is essential to your success.

Sit down and look at your boss as objectively as possible. Start with some of the same general questions your boss answers when she completes your performance appraisal, and listen for conversational clues whenever you speak with her:

- ✔ What are your boss's long-term goals? It's usually safe to assume that most people are looking for more: more money, more prestige, more challenge.

- ✔ What are your boss's strengths?

- ✔ What are your boss's weaknesses?

- ✔ What is your boss's greatest frustration?

- ✔ What's the best use of your boss's time?

After you assess your boss's situation, try to pinpoint ways you can better support your boss. Doing so leads to a well-oiled working relationship with your boss and greater productivity for you both. (And assessing someone's performance is a good skill to have on your résumé — you'll use it when *you're* the boss!) Ask yourself these questions:

- How can you help alleviate your boss's frustration?
- How can you help your boss spend more time on tasks that only she can do?

Maintaining Personal Boundaries

Part of being a responsible employee includes setting boundaries for yourself, both in regard to the allocation of your work responsibilities as well as in your work-life balance. That's not to say, however, that you should be on the defensive with your employer. The objective is to maintain a positive working relationship for all — you need a healthy balance between work and personal time in order to function most effectively, and at the same time, you need to make sure you're a valuable, dependable, hard-working resource for your employer.

Sometimes, you may find yourself in a situation where your employer fails to acknowledge your need for work-life balance — this is often the case when you're working for a workaholic. Most workaholics think everyone else operates the same way they do. If you don't, they may feel your level of commitment doesn't match theirs because your hours at the office aren't at the (sometimes unbelievable) levels theirs are.

You can expect to work longer hours once in a while, depending on deadlines, but don't let yourself become the office whipping boy and regularly work longer hours just because your boss does. Here are some solutions:

- **Communicate reasonable expectations.** Figuring out how to defend your boundaries is about communicating reasonable expectations so you don't get burned out. At the same time, you want to convey support and a willingness to go the extra mile. But your goal is to make working overtime the exception rather than the rule. Here are some ways to tactfully discuss schedule concerns:

  - *"I have X projects to finish by the date you've given me. Is there something you want me to drop or put off so I can take on this project?"*

  - *"I appreciate your confidence in me, but I know if I take on this project, my other responsibilities and commitments will suffer."*

- *"I can do that, but I'm afraid I can't finish it until middle of next week. Is that all right?"*

- *"I have a number of key projects in the queue right now. Can we talk about what's most important in the next two or three weeks and balance that with what I can realistically do in that time?"*

✔ **Clearly establish boundaries around your personal time.** Most workaholics continue to impose unless you actively defend your off time by having something planned. Treat family events as you would any work appointment (see Chapter 3). T-ball games, ballet classes, church activities, and even family dinners are appointments not to be missed. The workaholic boss doesn't need to know more than that you're booked — and unavailable.

You may not be able to avoid being on call, at least once in awhile, for a workaholic boss. You can't always be booked because your boss will see your unavailability as lack of commitment. To offset this perception, you may want to share details of your prior commitment, such as, "Bobby's soccer team is playing the most important game of the season, and he'd be crushed if I weren't there." Other times, a simple "I already have plans" or "I'm committed" suffices.

✔ **Know when to say no (gracefully, of course).** You don't need to take a Miss Manners class to discover how to say no. All you need are a few tried-and-true phrases. Here are a few of my favorites:

- *"I'm committed to going to (such-and-such athletic event, birthday, or recital), and I can't miss it. I promised my (son, daughter, wife, grandson, granddaughter, third cousin twice removed)."*

- *"I wish you'd brought this up a few days ago. I've committed to going to the symphony, and we've already paid for tickets."* Or *"I'm sorry. Our family is taking an underwater basket-weaving class. We've looked forward to it for months."*

- *"Let me get back to you tomorrow — I need to check with the family to see what's planned."*

Preparing to Discuss Your Concerns with Your Boss

If all else fails (or if your job is rapidly becoming intolerable), you may want to have a serious conversation with your boss. If you're frustrated and getting more exasperated daily, approach your boss soon. Waiting until you're ready to explode with rage won't help your cause. Prepare by writing notes, if it helps, and then just do it.

Identifying concerns and gathering supporting evidence

Assignments usually come from the top down, and how your boss hands off those responsibilities can have big effects on your schedule. One of the most frustrating situations in business is working for a boss who procrastinates, dumping several to-do items on your lap at once, or one who's a workaholic, expecting everyone else to push the work through. If your boss's procrastination, disorganization, or overdeveloped drive for advancement (which may have landed your boss in his position in the first place!) is affecting your work or putting your career in jeopardy, try applying the following techniques:

1. **Identify the problem, figuring out the who, what, where, when, how, and why of the issue.**

   Look at where you're losing the most time, and list specific examples that illustrate your points. Where do you notice the biggest problems? In planning? Advance notice? Overcommitment? Poor organization?

   Also make sure that *you* aren't part of the problem: Are you taking responsibility for solving some of the problems yourself? Or are you waiting for someone to tell you in detail how to complete every step of the project?

2. **Gather supporting facts.**

   If your workload is unmanageable, try keeping a time sheet for a few weeks. Perhaps your boss is a performance bottleneck because he's unrealistic about what can be done in a given time frame or because he can't say no to new projects. Document hours you work on various projects and include the time you spend on generic administrative tasks, such as project-related telephone calls and e-mail. Then, instead of saying, "Boss, I don't have time for this new project," you can point to your time sheet and say, "Look, Boss. There are 40 hours in a work week; to complete my current assignments, I'd have to work 80 hours per week for the next four months. The numbers have spoken, Boss. Something's got to give!"

3. **Describe how these problems inhibit your job performance and efficiency.**

   Bring up how putting things off causes you and others in the department to deviate from the company's mission statement and core values. Or explain how disorganization forces you to waste time with more frequent stops and starts to the project, along with more interruptions of your boss's time because you have more questions throughout the project.

4. **Devise a few viable solutions.**

Regardless of your boss's strengths and weaknesses, he appreciates successful solutions. Staff members who point out that the company or department is underserving customers, losing sales to competitors, or wasting company dollars are a dime a dozen, but true problem-solvers are rare. If you have a favorite among solutions you propose, make sure to let your boss in on it — and be enthusiastic. If you're right, it could earn you a few feathers in your cap and set you on the road to more responsibility and a tidy salary increase.

Consider the following solutions:

- **Can system and procedural changes improve existing processes?** Talk about time frames and work flow, supporting your ideas with industry figures and statistics if you can find them. Show proof of typical turnaround times.

    Use specific examples. Cite examples of past projects when work flow, deadlines, and quality expectations were well-defined, and show how the work produced was excellent. Focusing on policies, procedures, and time lines is less personal and therefore less confrontational.

- **Would you benefit from brief, fairly frequent meetings with your boss?** Consider recommending that you touch base more often. Meetings don't have to last 60 or even 30 minutes. Ask your boss to meet more often so you can "better align your work with his priorities." Then use the meetings to keep ahead of the land mines that lie ahead.

Your enthusiasm may also boost your boss's confidence enough to act on your suggestions. Over time, as your boss gains confidence in your ability to make mid-range decisions, those decisions (and lower-level ones) will be delegated to you. You win twice: Your boss has fewer decisions to put off making, and you have more responsibility!

Keep your expectations realistic. Don't expect your boss to change. Do expect to be hit, at least occasionally, with fallout from his work style, and do what you can to work with it so you can meet your own objectives.

Reflecting on your boss's behavior style

Before broaching project and schedule concerns with your boss, think through the discussion thoroughly and plan your focus. Your boss has a particular behavioral style that dictates how she reacts to events and situations. If you're knowledgeable about your boss's behavior, you can open the lines of communication and discuss how and why she makes decisions. Then, and only then, can you prepare for the roadblocks and one-step-backs that come up in any project and deal productively and positively with your boss throughout the process. Essentially, your boss's behavior patterns revolve around the dimensions I cover in the subsections that follow.

You can use what you know about your boss's values and behavior to frame the conversation in a way that gets your point across. For instance, if your boss is task-focused, position problems in terms of task accomplishment ("Boss, in order for this project to surpass customer expectations by *X* date, I need the following specific information: A, B, and C."). If you report to a people-focused supervisor, couch your questions in softer terms ("Boss, I'm feeling frustrated by the way this project is going. Can we talk?").

In addition to getting an overall perspective of your boss's behavioral pattern through the sections that follow, one formal way to get a clearer picture of yourself and your boss's basic tendencies is to take a validated behavioral assessment. I've made an assessment available at my Web site (`www.sales champions.com/DISC`), and you and your boss can take it for free; Chapter 8 tells you all about this DISC profile.

Focusing first on people or tasks

Is your boss people-oriented — warm, persuasive, engaged with people, and relying on feelings and connections with others to get things done? Or is your boss more oriented to facts, figures, and task lists? Here's how these types compare:

- ✔ **Task-focused managers:** These people may take time to talk to subordinates about issues and challenges *only* if the problems are seriously blocking progress. This can be frustrating because without direction or corrections, you and your co-workers may feel you're spinning your wheels, doing the wrong things the wrong way (only to have to redo them later). The communication you have with a facts-and-figures boss is usually labored, infrequent, and impersonal. On the pro side: Task-focused managers don't often interrupt. If you know your boss is task-oriented, understand that she's driven by deadlines, results, and accomplishments. That doesn't mean your boss doesn't *like* people; it means that she focuses first on tasks and then on people.

- ✔ **People-focused supervisors:** These bosses spend more time communicating and cultivating a feeling of teamwork, and deadlines are often fairly fluid. Although you may feel good about your relationship with these bosses, the amount of work getting done is often compromised: Highly interactive managers can be walking, breathing interruptions.

Following rules and procedures

Does your boss bend the rules or follow them absolutely? If your boss is strictly rules-oriented, expect quick changes to be limited.

Some bosses follow rules so closely and consistently that, in reality, the rules are ruts. Rigidity in today's rapidly changing business world sounds a professional death knell. A boss who lacks responsiveness to change won't be your boss for very long in the future. That rigidity can also put your job and career in jeopardy.

On the other hand, if your boss tends not to follow rules, follows them only sporadically, or allows employees to bend the rules to achieve desired results, you have other issues. If this approach has set you and your fellow employees up for a fall, you may be able to help your boss understand that some rules were made for good reasons and that sometimes following the rules gives you and other employees better control of your time and energy, allowing you to work more efficiently.

Facing problems and challenges

Is your boss risk-seeking or risk-averse? Does your boss solve problems aggressively, approaching them fearlessly and expecting success? Or is she cautious and deliberate?

Expect more changes, interruptions, short deadlines, and performance demands from a risk-seeking boss. How well you work with a risk-seeker depends on your own work style and preferences. Does this type of up-and-down, stop-and-go make you crazy or cause you to shut down? Are you willing and able to handle lots of projects going at once? With the risk-taking boss, that's what you get.

The risk-seeker's opposite is the risk-averse boss, with whom problems and challenges usually come at a slower, more controlled pace. If your boss is risk-averse, you probably won't get hit with ten things today that have deadlines of yesterday. However, the challenge is that a risk-adverse boss is more inclined to fight change and protect the status quo. When change is imminent, then the time left to make the change will be shorter because so much energy was invested in the-way-we've-always-done-it.

Planning and tackling new projects

How does your boss respond to new projects? Does she chunk them into smaller, more manageable tasks, plan and delegate well, consult a calendar, and assign interim deadlines? Or does she leap ahead without planning, get stressed out, and then move from planning to implementation and back to planning again? Maybe your boss is a combination or is a complete maverick in how she approaches new assignments.

Handling pressure

How does your boss handle pressing deadlines or work overload — with grace or blow-ups? When pressure increases, is she paralyzed, frustrated, curt, lethargic, and unproductive? Or is she energized, challenged, positive, encouraging, and determined to meet deadlines and exceed expectations?

Pacing work

How does your boss pace her work? Does your boss work at a steady and predictable pace, one project at a time? Or is your boss more of a binge worker, varying the tasks themselves as well as the speed and intensity of work, laboring without break for days or weeks, then slowing down, and then gearing up again?

Not surprisingly, the volume of work you get from a steady worker is easy to manage and plan for, but the volume of work from a binge boss arrives in bunches. Binge bosses often commit to too many projects because they have unrealistic expectations of what can be accomplished in a given time.

Taking responsibility and responding to missed goals

If goals, quotas, and standards of performance are set aggressively, then people in the company won't hit them all. Your boss can affect how many are achieved by deciding how lofty the goals, quotas, and performance standards will be. That's where there can be a disconnect. When goals aren't met, what does your boss do? Does she make excuses or look for scapegoats? Blame the marketplace, other departments, employees, the competition, or unfair pricing? Or does she work alongside employees to figure out solutions by trying new ideas, approaches, and strategies? Does your boss engage everyone to solve problems and overcome challenges, or is her preferred style more autocratic?

You've probably already stumbled across your boss's ego. Can you tell your boss that she's wrong (or even suggest it) without bringing down a hailstorm? If you can, your boss's ego is probably healthy and intact but not out of control.

Initiating and Fostering a Win-Win Discussion

Envision the conversation about your boss's time management from start to finish. Imagine the meeting as a calm, productive, successful exchange of information in which neither you nor your boss is unduly upset. Practicing the meeting in your head helps the actual meeting come closer to what you've envisioned. You may still face some bumps, but you may be surprised at how smoothly the meeting goes. Athletes use this technique to prepare for competitions, and it works equally well in difficult interpersonal situations.

As you enter the conversation, think positive, but be prepared for a negative reaction. No one likes to be told, even gently or indirectly, that he or she lacks skills or is causing problems. Here are some tips for a productive conversation:

- ✔ **Approach your boss in private.** Your boss won't hear a word you say if he's losing face in front of others, regardless of whether they're peers, superiors, or subordinates. I suggest setting an appointment with your boss to discuss a large issue like this. Don't do it in the course of your normal daily or weekly meeting; your boss already has an agenda set for that meeting, at least mentally.

- ✔ **Explain your concerns in a cool, calm, encouraging manner.** Keep the dialogue work-centered. Tell your boss how delaying affects your job performance and outline what you could accomplish if lead times and decisions were more timely — or whatever the case may be.

  Frame your discussion in a positive *I* mode, using I-statements rather than you-statements, to make the discussion go more smoothly ("I could get more work done if . . ." or "I could help you so much more if . . ."). Avoid telling your boss how you feel, and stay away from personal attacks ("If only you'd . . ." or "You should be more/less . . ." or "I hate it when you . . ."). Though your feelings are involved, you're discussing a performance issue.

  If your boss hates to be wrong — and worse, hates being told he's wrong, especially by subordinates — swaddle that baby in soft flannel: "Boss? Jimmy Jones said he already gave you those sales charts you were looking for last week. But maybe he's mistaken."

  Avoid nagging your boss. Remaining encouraging for extended periods of time without becoming impatient or critical can be difficult, but try. Nagging can put your job at risk.

- ✔ **Present possible solutions and solicit some from your boss, even if you think you have the solution nailed.** People buy into solutions more fully if they've helped develop them. Ask what you can do to help. Offer to take some items off your boss's plate so he can devote more time to decision-making.

- ✔ **Close the discussion by assuring your boss that you're a team player and that you want to do the best job for him, as well as for the company and its customers.** Be clear that you want to support your boss's goals and objectives, not undermine them. Tell your boss that you realize your advancement is linked to his and that your job is to make your boss look good. Ask your boss to help you do that to the best of your ability.

Watch other employees in your department. Does anyone seem to handle your boss's ego more capably than anyone else? Study that person's technique and try it yourself.

Irreconcilable Differences: Knowing When to Move On

If you find that your work style is drastically different from that of your boss and it's impossible for you (or your boss) to adjust, you may have to bite the bullet and look for another job and a boss whose time-management style is more in tune with yours. If you've checked yourself and can honestly say you're doing everything in your power to make the situation better, accept that your job may require you to take on more responsibility than your job title, skills, and even your experience warrant.

A few years ago, I hired Clara as my assistant. Although I explained my work style to Clara before she came on board, she spent the first six weeks on the job trying to change me. (I fall into the risk-taker category: I have lots of projects, ideas, and deadlines going at all times). Finally, after weeks of frustration, Clara told me she needed materials four weeks in advance of a speaking event or she couldn't guarantee that my workbooks and presentation slides would be finished. I tried to adjust my work style to meet Clara's request for additional time, but in the end, we agreed that our work styles were incompatible, and Clara left to find employment elsewhere.

Chapter 13

Mastering Meetings with Co-Workers

*I*f you regard meetings as a massive waste of time, then read on. You're in good company if meeting invitations cause your stomach to tie up in knots and your blood to pressure to climb a little higher. That feeling may arise because you know you'll walk out with more projects on your already overflowing plate. Or because your day is so packed with to-dos that squeezing in one more commitment is certain to push you over the edge. Or because you know from experience that you'll find yourself a prisoner of the Meeting That Wouldn't Die.

Sadly, meetings with colleagues, co-workers, and corporate minions — as well as appointments with clients, customers, vendors, and so on — are an important part of business life. Meetings aid in the communication of critical issues, stimulate needed action, and help measure and maintain progress. But far too often, the meeting is overused, confused, and abused, leading to gross inefficiencies and wastes of time. I can't help you make meetings go away, but I can offer strategies to tame them from wild time-predators into a manageable and even productive part of your job.

Your meetings may be ones that you set and manage, or they may be appointments that someone else is eager to arrange with you. The initiator starts out with a little more control of the situation simply because he or she is setting the appointment, but just because you're the invitee doesn't mean you have to relinquish control or time. Regardless of whether you're leading the meeting or simply participating in it, this chapter gives you valuable strategies and tactics that you can use before, during, and after meetings to make them more valuable and less time-consuming.

Devising Objectives, Listing Attendees, and Crafting an Agenda

When I'm the one calling a meeting, I adhere to a strategy, supported by research, of investing twice the time in preparation as the length of the meeting. If the meeting is scheduled for an hour, I put in approximately two hours. This section explains how you can best fill that prep time.

Clarifying the purpose of the meeting

Before you schedule a meeting, get your arms around the big picture and consider all the specifics. Begin your preparations by starting with the goal and working backward. What outcome do you desire for this meeting? How are you most likely to arrive at that outcome?

At first consideration, you may think that if you're the one asking for the meeting, you automatically have a good handle on why you need to meet. Sure, you may know that you want to get to the bottom of the service problems you're having with your office supplies vendor, but chances are you have a ways to go before you've crystallized the situation and how you can to resolve it.

So give the purpose of the meeting careful thought. Start with the motivating factor for the action. Is it to get to the bottom of the service problems with your vendor? Really? Do you just want to understand the problems, or would you rather clear up the problem at the conclusion of the meeting?

Be clear with yourself about what you want to walk away with. Put it into as precise a framework as possible, identifying the action you seek and when you want it accomplished. The questions you ask yourself before the meeting really increase its effectiveness and efficiency. Here's the need-to-know info:

- ✔ What's the problem or goal?
- ✔ How do you want it resolved or accomplished?
- ✔ What do the parties involved have to do to make that happen?
- ✔ When should this action be accomplished?

Look at the difference between the following two statements of purpose; the second includes the proper amount of detail:

> *"Hi, Mary. I'd like to meet with you to discuss the problems we've been having with your service department."*

> *"Hi, Mary. We've been having some issues with prompt service calls from your company for the past three months. I'd like to meet with you so we*

can clear up any barriers that may be causing this problem and get back on track with on-time response within the next two weeks."

Often, while working through the process of clarifying the purpose of the meeting, you may discover other ways to address the issue you want to meet about. This exercise may help you realize that a phone call or other action can resolve the situation — without holding a meeting at all.

Creating a guest list

For the most effective meetings, keep the size to as few people as necessary to accomplish the goal of the gathering. Numerous studies show that five to eight is the ideal number of participants for a productive meeting. Of course, the subject matter often dictates the number of people who attend a meeting, but I agree that as soon as the number of attendees climbs above eight or ten, the return on time investment begins to decline rapidly. In addition to taking more people away from their primary duties, the larger number increases unproductive discussion.

The individuals invited should be able to represent others and assume the responsibility of communicating the results of the meeting to those people. Don't invite someone just because he or she would be offended not to be included.

Given a limited number of meeting participants, you want to make sure that everyone who *must* be at the meeting is invited. Depending on the purpose and topic of your meeting, consider these criteria when making out the guest list:

- Have you included people who have the information or answers to critical questions?

- Did you invite those in a position to authorize decisions required to move ahead?

- Have you considered representatives from each of the departments or areas that will be affected or play a role in the outcome of the meeting?

- Did you include someone who can take notes and communicate the details of the meeting to attendees and others who aren't part of the meeting?

    Official *minutes* — a detailed chronological record of everything that happened during the meeting — may not be necessary, especially if meetings involve few participants. But at the very least, you should invite someone you can assign to take notes. I suggest giving that responsibility to someone else so the host can focus on shepherding the meeting to its productive conclusion. Here's what the notes should capture:

    - Key discussion points

    - Significant concerns or unresolved questions

    - The action items and all details surrounding them

Meeting overload in the United States

Is the United States a nation on a fast track to meeting meltdown? Have meetings overtaken the world of business like some invasive corporate kudzu? Consider these findings:

✔ The average professional employee spends approximately 1.7 hours per day in meetings, according to 3M Meetings Management Institute.

✔ Executive employees spend close to 50 percent of their time in meetings.

✔ In any given day, more than 17 million meetings are underway in the United States.

✔ The most productive meetings take less than one hour, but the average meeting length is two hours.

✔ In a survey by Microsoft, participants felt that 71 percent of the meetings they attended were unproductive.

✔ In a survey conducted by MCI Conferencing, 91 percent of the participants admitted to daydreaming in meetings, and 39 percent had actually dozed off during a meeting.

✔ The same survey showed that 73 percent had brought other work to a meeting.

While considering the right people to invite, give some thought to the *wrong* people as well. Don't weigh down the invite list with *redundants* — people representing the same area or interest. When you have a choice of two people, consider their communication styles and which candidate may be more compatible to the meeting environment: the co-worker who likes to hold forth with filibuster-length pronouncements or the colleague whose contributions add value to the discussion?

Holding informal, preliminary mini-meetings

Setting up a meeting to discuss a meeting? Okay, before you declare me certifiably insane from meeting overload, hear me out: Prep work is all about keeping the meeting as short and focused as possible. The better you prepare, the more you accomplish in less time. So yes, if a quick mini-meeting improves the outcome of the big meeting (such as if the project you're working on is complex or if you'll have multiple presenters at the meeting), it's worth the effort.

Here's how it works: Say you've set a meeting with eight co-workers to talk about a project that involves multiple departments. You anticipate some of the attendees may resist the proposals you plan to present. Instead of walking into the meeting and spending some or all of it defending your program or deflecting criticism, meet informally with just a couple of the participants at a time; getting feedback from people you trust is a helpful way to fine-tune your planning. Share with them a preview of your intent for the meeting and ask for their feedback — even proactively ask them to play devil's advocate and point out what they think some of the challenges may be. That 15 minutes or so that you spend with each key person helps you identify the curveballs that would've been thrown your way during the meeting — you can now prepare a response to them. And believe it or not, you've gained support from those attendees. Because you sought them out for their input, they're more likely to support your plan, particularly if you take their concerns into account.

Mini-meetings are best set for a week in advance. This allows you to adjust the agenda, revise your presentation, and be better prepared for reactions. Face-to-face meetings are advisable when possible, though they aren't always practical, so use your best judgment. You don't have to schedule a formal meeting; stand-up conversations or quick sit-downs in your office or theirs work well. (Chapter 8 provides insight on choosing the best medium for your message.)

Putting together the agenda

A tailor-made agenda allows you to proceed in the most direct path with the fewest distractions. Here's the process you follow to ensure that your agenda provides all the pertinent details:

1. **Create a detailed outline for the meeting.**

   Although the purpose of the meeting determines the agenda, all agendas contain some consistent elements:

   - An agenda begins with greeting and introducing all the participants as well as reviewing housekeeping issues, such as the length of the meeting and who's taking notes.

   - It reviews the goals, ensuring that everyone understands the purpose of the meeting and what the expected outcome is.

   - At the conclusion of the meeting, the *action items* cover any follow-up activity expected of the participants.

Components of the agenda need to be specific. Don't just have an agenda that has "old business" and "new business." List the projects and discussion points as well as any interim decisions that need to be made. Be sure to use a format that identifies main topics, subtopics, and then action points in outline format. Providing detail helps spark ideas and conveys to the attendees that to get through everything, the conversation has to keep moving.

Try to keep the agenda to a single page. Like a résumé, you want to communicate that there's substance but not overwhelm the readers with so much detail that their eyes glaze over.

2. **Clarify which items on the agenda are reports or presentations and which are discussions.**

   Make these notes in the margin of the document for all to see.

3. **Assign a time limit for each agenda item.**

   Printing it on the agenda helps participants adhere to the times. Again, you can place this info in the margin so all attendees know the expected time you're granting to this issue.

Say you're discussing the launch of a company-wide environmental initiative. A solid agenda may look like the example in Figure 13-1.

Send out the agenda a few days before the meeting, giving invitees at least a day to review it. This allows them to request that you add to or change the agenda based on information you may not have had. It also gives you a heads-up if any items have sparked a bit of controversy — you're better prepared to head off problems if you're aware ahead of time.

Sample Meeting Agenda

I) Greeting and Introduction (5 minutes)

II) Overview of meeting (5 minutes)
    a. Length of meeting
    b. Roles of participants

III) Summary of what is to be covered and review of the goals (10 minutes)

IV) First Item (15 minutes)
    a. The problem or goal
    b. Possible solutions
    c. Who needs to be involved?
    d. What do they need to do to make that happen?
    e. When should it be accomplished?

V) Second Item (15 minutes)
    a. The problem or goal
    b. Possible solutions
    c. Who needs to be involved?
    d. What do they need to do to make that happen?
    e. When should it be accomplished?

VI) Closing/Q & A/Action Plans (10 minutes)

Figure 13-1:
A meeting agenda outline to follow (adapt time slots according to your needs).

Scheduling the Time and Place

Smart scheduling can go a long way toward maximizing time effectiveness when setting up business meetings. Issues such as *where* and *when* to meet can determine whether a meeting takes a huge chomp or a small nibble out of your day.

How far in advance of the meeting you send out the invitations depends on the type of meeting that you're holding. If this is a once-per-year, all-company meeting, then 6 months in advance may be necessary. If this is a 2-person check-up meeting, 24 hours to 2 days may be enough. If other people are presenting and you need to allow more lead time so they can prepare, you may need a week. As with all decisions, use your best judgment.

Choosing a teleconferencing company

As business is increasingly conducted on a global basis, face-to-face meetings are rapidly becoming the exception rather than the rule. And that's a good thing. It reduces the expense and time of travel, not to mention the heavy carbon footprint on the environment.

Although nothing can replicate a face-to-face encounter, video, telephone, and Internet conferencing technology continue to improve so that a meeting with colleagues scattered around the world is literally as easy as pressing a button.

A number of teleconferencing companies, such as Sparks Communications and Excel Conferencing, facilitate such global exchanges. Services vary from company to company in quality, security, recording, and a host of other features. When choosing a teleconferencing service, think about features such as these:

✔ Digital recording, so you can capture the conversation and share it with others; some services offer that service for a nominal fee

✔ Multiple codes, so you can conduct more than one conference at a time using a universally known company-wide phone number

✔ A security feature to announce all attendees before they're placed in conference, keeping out uninvited guests and preventing eavesdropping on proprietary calls

Another way to expand your capabilities is with an online conference service such as GoToMeeting (www.gotomeeting.com) or WebEx (webex.com). These services enable you to operate a PowerPoint presentation from a centralized location and control a slide show on hundreds of computers around the world. You still need to be on a conference line and have audio with a WebEx-type platform, but you simply mute the call, and only the people who dial in with the host code or codes can be heard. That allows you to be interactive without the risk of having someone ruin the call for others, alleviating the problem of background noise from 500 people. It also allows you to screen questions because you're the only one who sees them. Each participant can log in, interact, ask questions, and make comments without uttering a word.

Finding a good time slot

For internal meetings, the best time to schedule them is before lunch or before the end of the day; with lunch or home on the horizon, people tend to be a bit more efficient and less likely to drag down a meeting with wandering discussions, lengthy oratories, and micro-debate. Be careful, though, *how far* before or after lunch you hold the meeting. Here's some advice:

- ✔ **Schedule meetings for mid-morning or close to lunch, not first thing in the morning.** The most productive time for most people is early in the morning. That's when most people have the highest level of energy and focus. My view is that most internal meetings in a company don't require that level of focus. Employees need that time to tackle the priorities for the day.

- ✔ **Schedule meetings mid-afternoon or near the end of the workday, not right after lunch.** Many people suffer from a little lethargy in the early afternoon after the midday meal. After the body is fed, the brain is more focused on digestion than discussion. Better your attendees spend this slow time answering e-mail or dealing with paperwork than dozing off in the middle of your meeting.

For meetings, don't make the mistake of doing a pitch-in — pitch-ins tend to drift into recipe discussions. I'd even advise against having lunch brought in. Why? Somehow in these situations, the food seems to take over. There's always someone who didn't get what they requested, and others' orders are mixed up.

If your guest list is small, you're meeting with an outside vendor or a client with a service problem, or you need to be off-site with other managers or employees of your company, you may find that a business lunch is best. Lunch meetings can be very productive. The meeting leader can introduce the topics, present reports, or provide updates while the rest of the attendees are attending to their pastrami and potato salad. No one's distracted by hunger, and the eating part is usually fairly short before the lunch stuff is cleared away and everyone gives the meeting undivided attention. Also, being off-site has its advantages in lowering the distraction factor — office emergencies tend not to find you as easily. One caveat of lunch meetings: The more relaxed environment may lead to a longer meeting, so be sure to weigh your priorities before scheduling.

Considering the location

If all the attendees are in one place, your choice about location is simple: Meet wherever you have the space and resources you need. Most companies have a few conference rooms of varying sizes, so meeting space is rarely a problem. Choose a location that's large enough for your group, and make sure any equipment you need is available.

You don't have to hold a meeting in a traditional location if other options are available. For instance, if you're meeting about problems on the production line, you may meet in the plant for a walk-through before sequestering yourselves in a quieter spot. Do choose such a location with care, though — the location you choose needs to foster a good environment for achieving the objectives of the meeting. Your goal is to schedule and run a meeting that's as efficient and short as possible. If the logistics get complicated, you defeat your purpose.

If you're the invitee, ask whether you can have an agenda in advance so you can better prepare. Review the agenda in advance, and based on the topics and subtopics of the meeting, determine what relates directly to your job, customers, and department.

If you're not leading the meeting, you still have responsibilities before, during, and after the meeting. If everyone comes prepared, the value of the meeting increases while the time you spend at the meeting decreases. Here are some general questions to review and even craft responses for:

- ✔ What are the most important agenda items as they relate to your job?

- ✔ Have you found specific solutions to the issues that'll be presented?

- ✔ What do you have to share to help the department, your company, and your co-workers for each agenda item?

- ✔ Are you or your department having problems that relate to the issues on the agenda?

- ✔ Can you take on projects that'll help out and advance your career? Which projects?

The Day Of: Running the Meeting Well

The secret to holding a productive meeting that eats up the least amount of time is half in the planning and half in the organization and facilitation. If you're the meeting initiator, it's up to you to grab the old bull by the horns and stay in the saddle. If you're not the one holding the reins, help the meeting stay on track by only bringing up issues that align with the agenda. If an open dialogue time is part of the meeting, save your off-the-agenda problem for then. You may even go to the meeting initiator in advance to see whether your item can be placed on the agenda.

Being on time, prepared, and engaged is the best help that any attendee can give to the meeting leader. If the meeting has openings for discussion on issues, then chime in with something of value. My best advice is to be brief, bright, and concise. You win more points and respect if you're prepared and on point rather than rambling. If someone else uses the meeting to talk about nothing, help the leader guide that person back in the fold, perhaps by pointing out that time is short and that the meeting is running over. The more you can support the leader, the better the meeting will flow and the less time it'll take.

Arriving early for set-up

Everyone's suffered through this scenario: The meeting host starts his presentation and the PowerPoint won't work. There's a problem with the laptop connection. The videoconferencing equipment is down. So you wait while someone runs to get the tech people to fix it. The minutes tick off and you're ticked off at the host for wasting your valuable time.

Here are some ways to make sure your meeting's ready to go:

- ✔ **Get to the meeting room early to test out all the equipment.** If something's not working, you still have time to get the tech people in to work out the bugs. You may be able to delegate this testing, but that depends on the competency level of the staff. I generally arrive between 60 to 90 minutes early so I can test all the audio-visual equipment personally.

  If the meeting is off-site, are people available to help you set up? If you've used the venue before, did the staff previously handle the logistics capably?

- ✔ **Be sure to have the needed charts, graphs, handouts, and any other material critical to your presentation.** Bring extra copies of handouts or other items that attendees may forget.

- ✔ **You may want to check the heating or air-conditioning system.** That way, you can be sure participants won't be leaving the room for their sweaters or opening the door to get a breeze.

Launching the meeting

No matter the meeting's length or formality, the most important rule to launching your meeting off right is to start on time. Even if some of the folks haven't yet arrived. Even if your boss hasn't arrived. If your office environment is one in which start times aren't respected and attendees walk in 10, 15 minutes late, resolve to do your part to reeducate your people.

How you launch the meeting has a lot to do with your success in maintaining control. If the meeting is with a customer, client, or prospect, you may want to allow for a little more small talk, but otherwise dispense with the chitchat before the meeting begins. Suggest that if people want to catch up, they should come early.

Dealing with habitual latecomers

If attendees typically arrive at meetings late, deal with the problem head-on: Talk with the culprits individually. Visit habitual latecomers before the meeting to make sure they arrive on time, or chat with them after the meeting and ask for their cooperation in arranging their schedule so they can arrive on time in the future. If that doesn't work, you may have to resort to stronger action:

✔ Reward early attendees. Give the on-time people single gifts of company logo wear, coffee cups, movie tickets, or coffee shop gift cards.

✔ Hand out the most desirable projects or assignments in the first five minutes, leaving the tougher or less desirable assignments to the tardy people.

✔ Create a late-meeting fund. Latecomers have to kick in some cash to the kitty. I suggest making the late fee enough to cause a bit of pain but not a financial hardship. Depending on your work environment, this may be $5 or $100. Asking people to pay up can be touchy, but if you have a relatively informal environment, you can establish that late funds go to the company's charity of choice or have the money go toward coffee and doughnuts for the department.

✔ When the appointed time for the meeting arrives, lock the door. This suggestion isn't for the faint at heart — you're sending the message loud and clear, preventing latecomers from slipping in under the radar. Latecomers either have to knock and ask to be let in or must return to their offices and miss the meeting.

Begin by taking five minutes to establish the ground rules:

✔ Define the main purpose and objectives quickly.

✔ Make sure an agenda is visible to all attendees. When attendees can follow the flow, you have fewer distractions and interruptions.

✔ Tell the group what you want to have accomplished by the time you end the meeting at the appointed time.

✔ Explain whether attendees should hold questions until a certain point on the agenda.

✔ If you have a large number of attendees and are concerned that some members will hold the floor, advise the group of discussion guidelines. For example, you may want to explain that everyone will have an opportunity to speak, but each person can hold the floor for only three minutes at a time before someone else gets to speak.

✔ If your meeting is scheduled for longer than an hour, plan for a break and let the attendees know about it. If everyone knows they'll get a bio-break at a given point on the agenda, it'll help reduce walkouts that disrupt the meeting as people leave one by one. Be sure to tell them how long it'll be. (Five minutes? Ten minutes?) Then reconvene when you say you will.

✔ **Ban cellphones and Blackberries!** Allow me to climb up on my soapbox: I thought it was bad enough when meeting attendees kept their cellphones on ring and then actually carried on hushed conversations as the meeting was conducted around them. Now it's worse: They're busy checking messages on their Blackberries and text-messaging — who knows whether it's business or personal?

As part of your meeting preamble, tell the folks to turn off their cellphones and PDAs or whatever electronic devices and put them away. You may even tell them that if a phone rings during the meeting, discussion will halt until the phone is turned off and the interruption is concluded. This usually shames people enough so that they're willing to adhere to the rules.

Keeping the meeting moving

As for smooth-running meetings, the agenda is your best friend. There's a reason you come up with one: to make sure you accomplish what you set out to do when you scheduled the meeting. Sticking to the time parameters also establishes you as a person of your word and sets a positive precedent for future meetings, so follow the plan.

Your skill as a facilitator can also influence the movement of a meeting. Here are some tips for staying on track:

✔ **Get input from participants as you go along.** Your ability to ask questions and involve each participant keeps everyone engaged and the momentum going forward. You shouldn't have to backtrack, because attendees contribute to the conversation before you move on to the next major topic.

✔ **Don't adjust the time given to each topic as you work through the agenda.** This virtually guarantees that you'll get behind and either meet longer than scheduled or simply not get through all the items. And you know what that means: another meeting!

If something doesn't look like it'll be resolved in time, you may want to create a smaller group to meet and discuss solutions so you can come back to the larger group at an appointed time. Put that separate meeting on your action list and set it up at the end of the current meeting.

✔ **Remind attendees of the agenda.** The agenda serves as your enforcer when someone gets off-track or goes on a little too long. For instance, you can say something like the following:

"Joe, you make some good points, but I promised we'd end the meeting at 2 p.m., and if we're going to get everything done, we have to

> *stick to the agenda. I'll make a note of your concerns to follow up after the meeting."*
>
> *"That's an important point — can we add it to the end of the agenda and discuss it if we have time left?"*

✔ **Never rehash, backtrack, or review to catch up late arrivals.** Set the standard that they need to bring themselves up to speed after the conclusion of the meeting. It's a monumental waste of everyone's time to rehash the last ten minutes because of someone else's lack of regard.

✔ **Give attendees a ten-minute warning before the end of the meeting.** Just as the last two minutes are critical in a football game, the last ten minutes of a meeting carry that level of importance. If attendees have been out of the game mentally, you can now grab their attention. If they've been with you the whole time, they're alerted that it's time to wrap up and focus on the conclusion.

Assigning action items

As the meeting leader, your job is to make sure that action items are agreed upon and assigned with specific instructions. Failing to assign action items can turn a meeting from a productive collaboration into a colossal waste of time. Especially when the situation is time-sensitive, you can put a project at great risk if no one puts the action items into action.

After you identify an action item, record it and either assign it then and there, or wait until the discussion has concluded and assign all the action items at once. Be sure to clarify the following:

✔ Who's responsible for seeing that the action is fulfilled

✔ What, exactly, needs to be done

✔ When the action item must be started and completed

✔ Where the chokepoints of the project are

✔ The interim timelines for each phase of the project

✔ Who is to be notified of progress and at what points of the process

✔ The expected outcome

Don't neglect this critical step in the meeting process. Without it, you may find yourself in yet another meeting revisiting the same issue — and discovering that because of delay, the project is at risk.

If you want career advancement and an increase in income, make sure that as a meeting participant, you're stepping up to volunteer for action items that benefit the company and group. The people who are engaged are the people who earn more income.

Making plans without a little fire behind them

When we were first married, Joan and I would talk about upcoming plans or errands we had to accomplish. We might discuss that we needed to buy charcoal for our weekend cookout, for example. Joan and I were always in complete accord in these discussions. But more often than not, when it came time for the cookout — and we were without charcoal — we'd look at each other and say the same thing: "I thought we agreed that you were going to get the charcoal." Well, we had agreed — that we needed charcoal. We just didn't pin down the action item and to whom it belonged.

Summarizing and concluding the meeting

Work in time at the end of the agenda — at least five minutes — to review the meeting. Your job as the meeting leader is to make sure that all attendees understand and accept the outcome and follow-up action from the meeting. In your summation, be sure to touch on these points:

- ✔ Key highlights of presentations and discussions
- ✔ All action items and to whom they're assigned
- ✔ Unresolved issues and how they'll be addressed
- ✔ Any follow-up activity, including setting the next meeting

Take this opportunity to ask whether anyone has questions, concerns, or issues he or she feels are unresolved. Your primary objective is to make sure everyone understands what's been decided upon and to ensure that anyone with action items on his or her plate is aware and has taken ownership of that responsibility.

TIP

If the questions are very specific and do not pertain to the whole group, or if they're more complex and require more time than is left in the meeting, simply make note of any comments and commit to addressing them after the meeting — this isn't the time for continued or protracted discussion. You don't want to waste the group's time if you need a protracted discussion with one person. A quick judgment at this stage allows you to avoid boring others and wasting their time.

REMEMBER

Don't extend the meeting, even if you didn't complete everything you'd hoped. Agree to set another meeting, or if a couple of people can address and resolve the other agenda items, suggest that those folks stay after to tie things up.

Following Up for Maximum Productivity

Most people forget a large chunk of what happened at a meeting. They leave the meeting and walk back into their office with tasks that have piled up in the last hour. Their minds move to those quickly even before you've left the meeting room. That's why you should usually plan to spend at least an hour following up on your meeting to ensure an effective outcome. Follow-ups should be twofold: communicate the results of the meeting and periodically review the status of action items:

1. **Within 24 hours, distribute the meeting notes to all attendees.**

   Send out an e-mail that summarizes the same points you made at the end of the meeting regarding decisions you agreed to and responsibility for action. By putting your understanding in writing — and requesting confirmation from the recipients — you further clarify what happens next. This way, no one can drop the ball and later on claim that that's not the way he or she understood it. Be sure to give notes to any other employees who weren't invited but may be affected or involved in the action items.

2. **Keep an eye on the list of action items covered in the meeting and check in with each associated individual regularly to see how he or she is progressing.**

   Also make sure that you continue to remind that person of the time line of completion that was arranged at the meeting. Then make sure that you hold him or her to the time line.

   No, you're not responsible if an employee doesn't follow through. And no, it shouldn't be your job to hover over all the meeting attendees who were assigned action items. But in terms of protecting the time you've invested in the project, it's well worth a few minutes to shoot off a reminder or a quick status request by e-mail.

   To help you stay on track with the check-ins, keep the notes visible so you're reminded of them throughout the day. Or add notes to your day-planner to remind you to check on an employee's status. For example, if one attendee was asked to send out an announcement in the company newsletter by Friday, list on your to-do notes to check in with the individual on Wednesday.

Chapter 14

Optimizing Collaboration with Business Associates

*T*he goal for any businessperson should be to set appointments with prospects and clients. This is true whether your job is based in service or sales. You're not in sales, you say? Believe it or not, you sell every day, no matter what your profession: You're successful when others buy into your ideas. And as a salesperson, one of your key functions is to both qualify and conduct appointments with prospects, whether on the phone or face to face. When you *qualify* a person or an appointment, you're determining the parameters and odds of doing business with this person or company, evaluating how much, how soon, and at what cost.

Achieving high levels of customer satisfaction and loyalty is easier if you have regular appointments with your clients. Educating, training, and helping your clients book appointments with you shows them your commitment and caring for them. It makes them feel special and allows you to deal with problems and challenges before they become large and out of control. In most cases, these appointments center on solving problems.

In Chapter 8, I help you decide which communication medium is best for whatever situation you're facing. In this chapter, I help you make the most of your appointments with business associates. These appointments require planning and careful listening because they're two-way discussions that involve more than simply delivering information. Even if you don't buy into the fact that you're in sales, I guarantee that treating your decision-makers as customers will make it much easier to bring them around to your way of thinking.

Determining Whether an Appointment Is Worth Your While

In any capacity where you're trying to influence change through your powers of persuasion, the biggest factor you need to consider is the opportunity cost of that person's input or business. When you invest time and effort into a prospect who doesn't buy, the *opportunity cost* is what you would have gained by investing your time in a prospect who would've responded favorably.

Having spent more than 20 years of my life in 100-percent commission sales with no salary base, company car, expense account, and so forth, I'm fanatical about knowing the opportunity cost of a prospect. When you get paid only for results, you do everything you can to zero in on the people most likely to offer a high return on your investment of time and energy. I assess associates in two ways:

- ✔ By the time investment they'll require (that is, whether they're high or low maintenance)
- ✔ In light of their probable return

High-maintenance personalities usually come with inflated egos and are difficult to satisfy. These personalities expect a lot, don't give in, and keep charging forward until they get what they want. With low-maintenance personalities, on the other hand, the time you invest is usually minimal, and the individual's satisfaction level is higher than that of high-maintenance personalities.

The higher maintenance the customer is, the higher the return needs to be for an appointment to be worth your while. The best approach is to cut your losses and avoid investing in time-draining, high-maintenance, low-return opportunities. You experience far less frustration by investing in low-maintenance folks, and even when those low-maintenance associates give you a lower return, they enable you to have the energy and time to find low-maintenance opportunities that do yield high returns. My experience with low-maintenance, low-return personalities is that their appreciation of you grows over time. The constant value you provide increases their trust, which in turn increases the quantity of business they do with you, reducing the time you invest to get that business.

Obviously, the ideal associate is of the low-maintenance, high-return variety because these people let you trade small quantities of time for profitable business opportunities. Unfortunately, these people don't grow on trees. You have to work to earn their loyalty; after you earn it, make sure you hold onto them for life.

No matter what sort of business role you're in, you have to evaluate the ratio of the time investment to the return of a business relationship. So how do you gauge the probable return, the likelihood that your appointment with someone will pay off? I use the DNA^2 model, which evaluates four qualities: *desire, need, ability,* and *authority.*

Desire

People do things for a reason. The reason, or *desire,* must be there at some level for you to even book an appointment. Does the other party want to enter into a strategic partnership or marketing alliance? Does this person have the desire to continue the service relationships after you solve the problem you're meeting on?

If you take all the time you need to really pinpoint the desire, you may find it challenging to book an appointment because you questioned the person to death. At this point, you're simply trying to gauge whether the desire is there at all.

 One of the best ways to gauge desire in a prospect or business relationship is to ask for an appointment. The last place a sales prospect who lacks desire wants to be is in front of a salesperson pushing to meet quota. As soon as you have an indication that a face-to-face meeting would help move the relationship, sale, or business alliance along, go for the appointment.

 The desire of a human being directly connects to time frame. The time frame to action is shorter when the person has a higher desire to meet, acquire your product or service, solve a problem between your two companies, or forge a new strategic alliance. The higher the desire, the higher — and quicker — your potential return.

Need

Before you book an appointment, making sure that the other person has a *need* is paramount. Is your colleague, strategic partner, or prospect experiencing a quantifiable void that you can help fill or bridge? In sales, the need is a specific and identifiable problem that your service can help a prospect overcome and resolve.

Spotting needs in most people as well as in most companies is relatively easy. Both people and companies usually know where some of their problems and challenges exist. However, they may not know the scope, size, or true source of those problems or challenges; they often focus on the symptoms rather than the disease.

Essentially, what you're assessing here is whether the client, prospect of strategic alliance, or partner is experiencing any sort of pain that points to an underlying need, whether he or she realizes what that need is. The greater the pain, the greater the need and urgency to alleviate the pain. Of course, you plan to be the one to relieve that pain with your product or service.

Ability

The *ability* of a company or person is connected to financial capacity. Nothing is a bigger waste of time than to meet with someone who doesn't have the money to act. Are dollars in the budget for what you're proposing? If not, can the other person shift dollars from another area to this project? Would he be willing to? Ask the prospect, "If we can solve this issue, do you have room left in this years budget to make the investment?"

Can he request a budget increase in this area? When is his next budgetary cycle so you can potentially be in the budget for next year? Some people and companies leave more flexibility in their discretionary dollars; for others, it's etched in stone. Try to gauge the other party's flexibility and access to financial resources.

If you ask questions about money before you book an appointment, some people may feel you're trying to screen them out or get at their soft underbelly, so try booking the appointment first. As soon as you have the appointment in hand, you've been granted permission to ask questions because they now assume you're preparing for the appointment. If their responses aren't right, graciously tell them that after further discussion, you've realized you won't be able to help them and you don't want to waste their valuable time by having them meet with you.

Authority

Authority is related to someone's power to be the ultimate decision-maker. Does the buck stop here? Many people in business portray that position, but in reality, they don't have the authority to change suppliers or vendors. They lack the power to alter specifications or delivery schedules. They can't sign off on a strategic marketing alliance between your company and theirs.

If others will be involved in the final decisions, you want to include them in the appointment at the outset. By not including them, you guarantee at least another meeting. You may be creating an adversary rather than an ally. The decision-maker who's left out feels slighted and blindsided and may lose status by not being part of the solution. She may try to bring in competition, making your task harder.

If not everyone can attend the appointment you're trying to book, try to defer the appointment until later to allow all decision-makers to be present. When that's not possible, you have to make a judgment call about whether to meet without everyone there or press the issue and risk turning off the person who feels she has the power but doesn't.

Without all the decision-makers present, you're relying on who you do meet with to convey your message well. If you're in sales, this is an especially ineffective strategy. Rarely will anyone do a better job selling your position, views, and benefits in alignment with the size and cost of the problems more effectively than you.

Preparing for the Appointment

Too often, people wing-and-a-prayer appointments, which can waste time and turn off the other attendees. The best insurance policy to having a productive appointment is preparation. Determine the objectives, problems, discussion points, information, decision process, and framework for the appointment in advance. Ask questions about timing, problems and challenges, expectations, new opportunities, the current service level of your firm, and a host of other issues that are service and sales oriented. You're really *qualifying* the appointment, determining the odds of a positive outcome if you invest your time in this appointment (in the preceding section, I show you how to qualify the *prospect*).

Identifying and qualifying the problem

In qualifying the problem at hand, you're trying to determine the *who, what, when, where,* and *why* of how to continue an existing business relationship or forge a new business relationship. If you're in sales or servicing, you ask these questions outright. If you're preparing an unsolicited proposal, you ask yourself these questions and use the answers in the preparation and design of your presentation.

Asking questions is at the root of good customer service or good sales. In the following subsections, I discuss questions that help you explore the other party's view of the problem, their time line, their experience with previous service providers, and your competition.

Understanding their understanding of the problem

Your presentation should clearly show what's in it for the other party, so ask questions that help you understand their view of the problem — how it happened, what you can do, how they'd like to see it solved, and the like:

- ✔ *"What is the problem or challenge currently? How do you feel about this problem?*
- ✔ *"How large is this problem? What do you think this problem is costing you?"*

✔ *"When did you first discover this problem? How long have you had it? When did it begin to become significant?"*

✔ *"Where is the root cause of this issue? How did it happen from your view?"*

✔ *"Do you think we could help you with part of the problem? What part would that be? In an ideal situation, what would you like us to do?"*

✔ *"How do you think we should solve the problem? What have you tried in the past?"*

✔ *"Where do we go from this point? Where do you want us to be a month, 6 months, or a year from now?"*

Getting a feel for the time line

Knowing exactly when your associate wants a project done rather than *as soon as possible* can enable you to better manage your time and the results. The term *ASAP* has little value to anyone in the business world because it's so open to interpretation. You can increase performance and decrease stress by throwing out the term ASAP and going to specific time frames, deadlines such as "before close of business tomorrow" or "by the end of the week" or "by noon today."

A flexible time frame is often linked to lower motivation, lower desire, and less flexibility in the terms, conditions, and price parameters. You can use questions like these to ferret out a more precise time frame:

✔ *"How soon do you need this?"*

✔ *"Can you tell me about the perfect time frame?"*

✔ *"If we couldn't hit that deadline due to the work involved, is there another time that'd be acceptable?"*

✔ *"When will you make a decision?"*

Inquiring about past experiences

The past filters into future decision-making. The experiences the other person has had with your company, and with companies like yours, will be factored into the equation. To maximize the results and minimize the time you invest, you need to understand those previous experiences. If you'll be making some type of sales, product, or service presentation at the appointment, the knowledge about past experiences does the following:

✔ Influences what you emphasize in the presentation

✔ Affects how you structure the presentation

✔ Influences the reassurances you offer during the presentation

✔ Offers a glimpse of the sale objections you may encounter in selling to this prospect

Here are some effective questions about past experiences:

- ✔ *"Could you tell me about how you like to work with service providers?"*

- ✔ *"Have you ever had a time when a supplier or strategic partner didn't meet your needs? What happened? Can you give me a little more detail of that situation?"*

- ✔ *"What's your typical process for a decision like this?"*

Finding out what you're up against

Most of the time in the business world, you're in competition. You're competing not only for new relationships but also to keep the relationships you have now. Thinking that your competitors aren't trying to secure your current accounts — or that your competitors could never get those clients away from you — is naïve.

Before an important business appointment, you need to know the competition, who else the decision-makers are considering, or what other options they're considering. They may be considering putting in-house resources into the problem, so you may be competing against an internal department in the company rather then an external competitor. Questions such as the ones here can help you understand your competition:

- ✔ *"Who else are you considering for this task?"*

- ✔ *"Do you intend to outsource this problem?"*

- ✔ *"How did you select X as a possible solution source?"*

- ✔ *"Are you looking at any options besides Y?"*

Determining the objectives for the appointment

The real goals of any appointment are to create decisions, action items, and progressive movement toward a predetermined objective. To accomplish that, you need to know clearly what the goals, targets, and objectives of the appointment are — for both you and the other party. You need to know whether a decision will be made in the course of the appointment and what details need to be understood and conveyed to lead to that decision.

The determining-objectives segment of qualifying the meeting is so important. Don't rush. Too many professionals at this stage take the same standard answers — "we just want the job done" or "we just want the problem solved" or "we just want more widgets sold." The challenge with these obvious responses is that you haven't really gained anything of value. You don't have any insight into how others are thinking, what's important to them, or how they may decide. And that's a problem because they'll judge your service, solution, or product by how it resolves the unseen or unknown additional issues.

Here are some questions to help you clarify the other party's objectives:

- ✔ *"How will you gauge success in this project?"*
- ✔ *"What do you specifically want from us in service?"*
- ✔ *"What are the top three things you would like us to provide for you?"*
- ✔ *"How will you evaluate a successful long-term relationship between us?"*
- ✔ *"Is there anything else that I've missed that factors into your final decision?"*

For many of these questions, you'll likely receive the obvious reflex response. To avoid wasting your time, employ the besides-that technique of probing:

- ✔ *"Besides that, what else are you hoping to accomplish?"*
- ✔ *"Besides that, is there anything else you want?"*
- ✔ *"Besides that, what else would you ideally like for "this" to do?"*
- ✔ *"Besides the X problem, is there any other problem we need a solution for?"*

Of course, your objectives matter as well because they guide your approach to the meeting. For instance, if the goal of the meeting is to gather and evaluate information, you want to set the meeting's agenda to gather more information and to confirm the qualifying you've done thus far. You want to pinpoint terms, conditions, specifications, expectations, a time line, and the competition. You want to get to know the decision-maker so you can better tailor the final-decision presentation that comes later.

On the other hand, the meeting geared toward getting someone to make a final decision focuses on the potential road blocks and challenges (and even solves objections if it's a sales presentation). You want to know who'll be attending the meeting. You have to make sure the key people who really do make the decision are present. You also want to evaluate the landscape of people. Who are your internal advocates? Who will present the biggest challenge to convince?

Creating an agenda

Planning for the eventual outcome or planning out the pathway to the outcome is really *scripting* the results. Most professionals use some form of scripting so they can more easily replicate their successes. Attorneys use legal briefs to script out their arguments, evidence, and questions for each witness, both for the plaintiff and the complainant. They anticipate what will happen before entering the courtroom. They never ask a question that they don't already know the answer to. Similarly, a pilot follows a checklist before taking off and landing — that's also a script. (If your pilot lacks the checklist, get off the plane!)

Creating an agenda for the meeting is essentially one way to script out a meeting. The agenda allows you to proceed to the objective of the meeting in the most direct path with the least distractions. By devising a script or checklist for an appointment, you can consider the problems or roadblocks you may encounter and craft responses in advance. You anticipate questions that'll be raised and figure out your responses.

Create an agenda that follows a logical path of

- Reconfirming what you discovered in advance of the meeting
- Opening up to other discussion points and problems so you clearly understand the issues
- Guiding the other party to your solutions and why they should accept them
- Offering any guarantees for their satisfaction
- Asking them to commit to action now or with in a specific time frame

I personally like the final agenda item to indicate that a decision will be made at the meeting. By having the final item be "making the decision to move forward" or "completing the paperwork" or whatever phrase you want to use, you set the stage. You're basically foreshadowing that the other party will have enough information to take action. It's clear and concise in the agenda, so they can't miss it. And if they say they won't be making a decision today, at least you know and can ask why. The agenda item is also there so you don't wimp out in moving a decision forward.

You want to hand the agenda out and ask for approval to operate in this manner. For example, you may say

- *"I've prepared an agenda for this appointment. Would it be all right if we use it to guide us?"*
- *"Is there anything that I might've missed that's a concern of yours?"*
- *"So this format is agreeable to you?"*

The truth is that 99 times out of 100, they're almost so stunned at your preparedness and professionalism they don't know what to say but *yes!*

Beginning the Appointment on Solid Ground

Too many people are late in the business world without understanding the ramifications. For some customers, your being late smacks of saying, "My time is more important than yours." That may not be your intention, but that's the message some people receive from you.

What to do if you're early

If you're operating on the premise that you'll never be late, then you'll probably be early by ten minutes or so most of the time. Here are some things that you can do with that time:

✔ **Observe:** Take a few minutes to observe the pictures, periodicals, and paraphernalia in your appointment's office. What does the person read or subscribe to? Are there pictures that obviously reflect your appointment's hobbies or interests? Is the furniture and décor more utilitarian or showy?

✔ **Engage:** Strike up a quick conversation with the frontline staff, such as the receptionist. Don't monopolize her time and be a nuisance. Be pleasant and respectful of her and her workload. You want to connect with her so when you call on the phone, you'll be put through rather than screened out. Building a personal connection with the gatekeeper is always a wise use of time.

✔ **Review:** Review your agenda, qualifying questions, and responses. Review what you're going to say. Giving your notes a final once-over never hurts. You can never be too prepared for an appointment.

✔ **Read:** You should always carry something of value to read, whether it's a trade journal, self-improvement book title, or your tear file (a collection of articles you've torn from magazines or journals to read later). Time is too valuable not to invest in something, even in the waiting room.

Don't be late! Leave enough of a margin for travel time, traffic delays, forgotten items, or any other curveball of life. My view toward people who are tardy is not positive. If you're late to a meeting with me, the likelihood that we'll engage in business has dropped dramatically. I know of many CEOs of companies who feel the same way because of the value they place on their time. The higher you go in the organizational structure of a company, the more you'll encounter that view. These people are at the top of the organizational chart because of their time management and business skills.

If you're going to be late even by one minute, call ahead. The professional and courteous person informs his appointment of his delay so she can invest her time in something other than waiting. If you're doing a lunch appointment, call the restaurant and have the host or hostess inform your appointment of your delay.

Of course, showing up on time (and keeping the small talk to a reasonable level) is only the first step. In this section, I explain how to get your appointment off to a great start.

Confirming the objectives

The first agenda item I recommend is reconfirming the answers to the qualifying questions (see the earlier section "Preparing for the Appointment"). You want to ensure you recorded all the other party's responses correctly and make sure that nothing has changed. You also want to further impress them that you took the care not only to listen but also to record their responses.

If you've gotten all the decision-makers to the appointment, recognize that in most cases, you qualified only one of them. You have no idea whether the goals, objectives, expectations, and past experiences are the same as those of the person you actually talked with before the appointment. To build your credibility and increase their trust level of you and your firm, ask for input from the other decision-makers as you confirm the answers. Having these answers allows you to further approach the other party's needs, wants, and desires.

The more you focus on *them* at this stage, the more effective the meeting will be. Most people are permanently tuned to radio station WIIFM: *What's in it for me?* To persuade others, you have to tune your meetings and presentations to their frequency of WIIFM.

Presenting your ideas

After you confirm the answers to the qualifying questions and further uncover needs, wants, desires, and expectations, you're ready to transition to the section of the appointment I call *Why Do Business with Me?* or *Why My Solutions?* Here's where you're really making your presentation. At this point, you've built enough understanding and trust that you can focus on building value for your solutions, products, services, or anything else you're advocating.

Linking your recommendation to the other party's goals

Ford Motor Company won big with its Mustang, Explorer, and Taurus. Boeing still dominates the air with its 737 and 747, both introduced in the 1960s. Microsoft blew away the competition when it introduced Windows in the mid-1980s. Big wins don't come along every day (Ford also produced the Edsel, a huge flop in the late 1950s that cost the company $350 million), but they're every company's top goal.

If you want to speed decision-making, help people connect your proposal to big wins: their company's and their own. In fact, even smaller wins, such as significant savings, better-informed executives, and happier employees, are keys to success, both yours and other people's. Begin by helping people answer these questions:

- *"What's in it for me?"*
- *"How will this make me look good?"*
- *"What's the primary benefit if I act now?"*
- *"What other advantages do I accrue by acting sooner rather than later?"*
- *"How does this benefit my department?"*
- *"How does this help my company?"*

Helping decision-makers answer these questions allows you to sit, if only for a short time, behind the other person's desk. When you approach problems from that perspective, you align your goals with theirs and you both win big.

Detailing the value of your proposed solution

After you link your offering with your decision-makers' goals, press on. Make sure your decision-makers see all the advantages of going with your idea — and be specific. "It's really good!" or "It's better than what you have now" or "I promise you'll like it" — these statements might as well be in a foreign language for all the information they convey. Specifics draw pictures; they *convince*. For example, if you're trying to sell your company's product to a client, work with your decision-maker to discover detailed benefits in

- Price
- Terms over the competition
- More streamlined systems
- Faster turnarounds
- Better, more reliable information that's available more quickly
- Better customer relations
- Security and peace of mind

Show how buying your brand of running shoes, agreeing with your proposal for the company picnic, or selecting the paper vendor you recommend advances corporate goals and delivers specific advantages to everyone involved, and decisions will drop like ripe fruit into your lap.

In this fast-moving, high-tech world, today's up-to-the-minute information is tomorrow's old news. Those who make rapid decisions often end up with trophies, it's true, but the *quality* of decisions made is at least as important as how quickly they're made. Do your homework and deal honestly and effectively with hurdles and objections, and you'll win every time. Persuading others to give up the *right* decision for a *quick* decision damages your relationships and your credibility.

ANECDOTE

Making the sale to a discriminating 3-year-old

Selling ideas at home is sometimes as challenging as anything you face at the office. Joan and I, for example, were recently in the final stages of closing the sale of big-girl panties to our 3-year-old daughter, Annabelle. Annabelle will be the final arbiter of when that fateful day comes, but that doesn't stop Joan and me from constantly reminding Annabelle of the value, benefit, and comfort of wearing big-girl panties. Here's how we do it:

✔ *"In big-girl panties, you'll always be clean and dry. Won't that be nice?"*

✔ *"When you wear big-girl panties, you'll be able to run faster after Wesley* [her older brother].*"*

✔ *"Next year, you'll wear big-girl panties, just like the other kids at preschool."*

Laugh if you like, but these benefits and values, described in glowing details, are important to our small customer. (Notice we state our benefits in positive rather than negative terms: We help Annabelle envision her future glory; we don't tell her she *won't* be wearing diapers, *won't* be soggy and messy, and so on). The same is true of all customers: Decision-making accelerates if you continue to impress them with the numerous advantages of your proposal.

Gauging your progress

As you present your solution, you periodically want to test how you're doing. Are you on the right track to success with the other party? Have you made the right conclusions about their needs and problems, and do your solutions or proposed changes meet and exceed those needs? You also want to confirm that you haven't missed anything thus far.

These progress checks can be as simple as "Does this make sense?" "Am I heading in the right direction?" or "Can you see anything I've missed?" You may even offer to open things up to questions and answers at the end.

Tailoring the Presentation to Your Client's Decision-Making Style

For more than ten years, I've been teaching and coaching behavioral strategies based on four styles of the DISC program — Dominant, Influencer, Steady, and Compliant (to find out more about your style and that of others, see Chapter 13) During your appointment, you can rein in your expectations and bypass a lot of frustration if you recognize upfront what type of decision-maker you're dealing with. Different decision-making styles require varying amounts and types of information, which in turn dictate how quickly people make decisions. For instance, the decision cycle tends to be shorter for Dominants and Influencers. Dominants base decisions on gut feelings and convictions, and Influencers base decisions on feelings. Neither Dominants nor Influencers need as many facts, figures, and details as Steadies and Compliants do.

A good way to identify someone's behavioral style is to know what kinds of questions each type is likely to ask. In this section, I include some sample questions for each personality type. (Note that I provide more sample questions for Steadies and Compliants than I do for Influencers and Dominants. That's because Steadies and Compliants typically ask more questions.) I also explain how you can tweak your presentation so you best appeal to each personality type.

Keep in mind that people can exhibit overlapping characteristics of two or even three different styles.

Getting to the point with Dominants

Questions that Dominants deliver are direct, forceful, and sometimes designed to intimidate. If you waffle, give up control, or hesitate too long, they won't respect you and you won't get the decision you're looking for. Dominants ask

- ✔ *"Who else have you told this to?"*
- ✔ *"What's my bottom line result, advantage, or cost?"*
- ✔ *"What makes you sure this is right for us?"*

Two different styles, two different approaches

I'll never forget my first management job. Although I had five people reporting to me, two stand out in my memory: Lee and Tim.

When I delegated a project to Lee, she obligingly took notes and went off to work. She might come back to me numerous times during the project with questions she hadn't previously thought of or with anecdotes about how the work was proceeding. She tended to check back frequently during the project to make sure she was on the right track, and she quickly made adjustments if she wasn't. Lee was flexible, communicative, a fast worker, and an excellent employee.

On the other hand, when approaching Tim, I learned to dole out information in small pieces and give him time to get used to new ideas. If I barraged him with information and expected him to trot off and begin working, as Lee did, it didn't happen. If, however, I gave him time to absorb the information, ask questions upfront, work on another project for a day or two, and return to the new project I'd assigned, Tim came through for me every time — as long as I gave *him* time. And he often came up with more-innovative solutions than Lee did. Tim was also an excellent employee.

Dominants test your self-confidence and conclusions. If you don't demonstrate overwhelming belief and conviction, they refuse to move forward. To steer the Dominant toward the decision you seek, keep these tips in mind:

✔ Be brief, be bright, be gone.

✔ Don't waste time with testimonials.

✔ Use a direct business approach.

✔ Get to the point quickly and solve the problem.

Dazzling the trendsetting Influencer

Influencers typically deliver questions with warmth and even playfulness. They ask questions to uncover your emotions and determine relationships. That's how they make decisions. Here are some typical Influencer questions:

✔ *"Why do you feel we should do this?"*

✔ *"How much newer is this latest technology?"*

✔ *"How many others have it?"*

✔ *"Can you lower your price a little?"*

Influencers see themselves as trendsetting and cutting-edge. They tend to make flashy, fast, and sometimes even reckless decisions. An Influencer waits in line all day for the release of the latest telecommunications gadget so he or she can be one of the first to own one.

To appeal to an Influencer, follow these recommendations:

✔ Allow time to warm up and socialize.

✔ Focus, make it fun, and use stories.

✔ Hit the high points; don't be too detailed.

✔ Present showy new services, ideas, and products with sizzle.

Reassuring the Steady

A Steady's questioning is typically nonconfrontational, service-oriented, and information-seeking. Steadies look for a high level of security before they're willing to make decisions, even those involving small changes. Examples of Steady questions include the following:

- ✔ *"Have there been times this didn't work? Tell me about those."*
- ✔ *"I receive good service. Why should I change?"*
- ✔ *"How long have you been in business?"*
- ✔ *"What happens if this doesn't work?"*
- ✔ *"Can you call me in a week? I want to think it over."*

Steadies want to be certain that if they proceed, they won't be surprised by problems or negative outcomes. They tend to put off decisions as long as possible. Here's how to help expedite the process:

- ✔ Win the decision with a deliberate approach.
- ✔ Use plenty of proof and statistics to make your point.
- ✔ Earn trust and friendship first; talk about family and hobbies.
- ✔ Answer all questions and confirm their agreement with your responses.

Be careful with Steadies; they'd rather say *maybe* until hell freezes over than have to face you with a *no*. They can waste a lot of time because they know how to appear interested when they really aren't. And if they aren't interested, they privately hope you won't call back — ever. (For more info on *maybes,* see the later section "Handling Indecision.")

Providing facts and figures for the Compliant

A Compliant's typical questioning process is just that: a process. Compliants do nothing without an organized plan. They want all the facts, figures, data, and studies you can give them, and then they evaluate the data by pound of paper. For Compliants, a 99-percent probability of success is, in many cases, too low. Examples of Compliant questions include the following:

- ✔ *"What warranty do you offer?"*
- ✔ *"What are your qualifications?"*
- ✔ *"How long has this product been out?"*
- ✔ *"What's the return or refund rate on it?"*
- ✔ *"What other facts can you share with me?"*

Here's how to move a Compliant closer to a decision:

✔ Provide time to absorb details and facts before you expect the next step.

✔ Use other Compliants' and Steadies' testimonials.

✔ Go slowly and avoid small talk; get to the point with truckloads of support data in hand.

✔ Suggest only established or tried-and-true solutions; Compliants are suspicious of anything new or unproven.

Handling Indecision

Time lost in meetings is consolidated and obvious — everyone yawns through those minutes and hours together. But think how many decisions — from which shirt to wear to work to which pajamas to wear to bed — people make daily. Time spent dawdling about *any* decision, big or small, adds up. Additionally, the longer a decision takes, the greater the probability of a *no*. As eminent Harvard theologian Harvey Cox put it, "Not to decide is to decide."

The good news is that no matter how many closed-end questions you ask, there are only three possible answers: *yes, no,* and *maybe*. If you can bring your decision-maker to the crossroads of yes/no/maybe, he or she has to choose, usually sooner rather than later. The biggest time waster at this stage is taking too long to get to the crossroads.

Yes-and-no answers are typically easy to recognize, and the appropriate response is more straightforward. But then you face the biggest, blackest hole of wasted time ever: the dreaded *maybe*. The Maybe Zone, like the Bermuda Triangle, is an awful place: You're alone, fogged in, and disconnected. Your dials and gauges go blank, and time and space — not to mention progress — stand still.

In this section, I explain how to understand the reason for that indecision, ask questions to break through the Maybe Zone barriers, and build your case. I also explain a few alternate sources of rescue — getting past choke points and turning to other decision-makers.

Assessing the reason behind a "maybe"

I'm guilty of drifting into the Maybe Zone myself. I say *maybe* when I'm tired, I'm not ready to deal with the issue, or I don't feel like a battle. Or I hope that ignoring the question will make it go away (fat chance). Eventually, I have to respond.

When faced with a *maybe*, your best response is to determine whether you've thoroughly researched your decision-maker's

- ✔ Motivation
- ✔ Need
- ✔ Authority
- ✔ Ability
- ✔ Time line
- ✔ Possible obstacles
- ✔ Possible stalls

Make sure you've covered these bases. If you have and you're still stuck, try to figure out whether your decision-maker is saying *maybe* because he or she is

- ✔ Reluctant to disappoint you and hoping you forget
- ✔ Too tired to make a decision right now
- ✔ Missing information
- ✔ Needing a third party's counsel or approval before making the final decision

The reason for the *maybe* lets you know what you're up against. It helps you identify when the *maybe* is a really a veiled *no* because the other party is too tired or too nice to tell you the truth. If you let *maybes* go unchallenged, decision time stretches on, and the odds of a resounding *yes!* diminish with each passing day.

Asking questions

Opened-ended questions are king in terms of moving past a *maybe*. They functionally pass the baton, or dialogue, to the other person. They require thoughtful and more-detailed responses than a simple *yes* or *no*. As the asker, you guide and maintain control of the conversation, discovering a wealth of information because you're listening rather than speaking.

Here are some questions to help boost you out of the Maybe Zone:

- ✔ *"How do you typically make these types of decisions?"*
- ✔ *"Tell me about your decision-making process. What information do you need, and when do you need it?"*
- ✔ *"Who else is part of the final decision?"*
- ✔ *"Is this a change you believe you have to or would like to make?"*

✔ *"Is there anything you can see now that may delay your decision?"*

✔ *"Under what circumstance would you consider agreeing to my proposal?"*

✔ *"Do you ever see yourself using a service such as ours?"*

✔ *"Are there conditions that we could include that would allow us to move ahead? What would those circumstances, services, guarantees, or conditions be?"*

If your time in the Maybe Zone expands, or worse, begins transforming itself into a No Zone, call on another line of defense: the invaluable and underrated *why*. The question word *why* is a longtime friend of mine. With its help, I've broken through barriers I thought were insurmountable. See what happens when you ask the following:

✔ *"Why do you feel the way you do about my proposal?"*

✔ *"Why do you believe you need to wait?"*

✔ *"Why are you more comfortable making this decision next week?"*

✔ *"Why do you need to get Joe's opinion on this?"*

✔ *"Why do you feel you need to think it over?"*

One winter, we were in Palm Desert for a family vacation. Wesley, at 5, decided to open a lemonade stand in front of the golf course. We went to the store and bought lemonade, cookies, paper cups, construction paper, and felt-tip pens to make a sign. As soon as Wesley's lemonade stand opened, I could barely get him to wait until the golfers putted before he went down to the green to make his sale presentation for lemonade. He walked up to the first group and asked them if they wanted lemonade. I heard them say *no* and thought, "I hope he doesn't get discouraged." But I heard Wesley say, "Why? It's really good lemonade. It's refreshing, and I made it myself." These adults were no match for Wesley and his *why*. They were the first of many people to buy from him. He sold more than $22 worth of lemonade and would have sold more if he hadn't run out. You can learn a lot from a 5-year-old who isn't scared to ask *why*.

Outlining pros and cons

Countless how-to books advise readers to list pros and cons when making decisions. If your client is drifting in the decision-making doldrums — that dreaded Maybe Zone — encourage him or her to make a written for-and-against-list. This technique works best in person, but you can do it over the phone if necessary. (You can also make a list yourself and share it with the decision-maker, but it's better if that person comes up with the list because then he or she owns the ideas.)

If you're fortunate enough to meet with your decision-maker in person, ask him or her to make two columns on the paper and write *For* or *Positive* at the top of the left column and *Against* or *Negative* at the top of the right column. Suggest that your decision-maker start with the Positive column. Let him or her begin working alone. Usually, people start strong and then lose steam. It's okay to ask, "What about *X?* Do you see that as a positive?" Pose your advantage as a question so it becomes your decision-maker's idea. Provide encouragement as the list lengthens. Aim for a Positive list of at least 15 to 20 items.

Then shift to the Negative side. *Here you are mute.* Your job is to sit quietly and let the other person struggle to fill the page. If your proposal is valid, your decision-maker should sweat to come up with a list of negatives. When the exercise is finished, the two sides should be starkly different. Ideally, your pros list is packed with excellent reasons to act and act now.

Building urgency by addressing the decision-maker's time line

A frequent cause of delays in decision-making is undefined time lines and expectations. A common stall tactic is "send me more information." (You've just sent more than 200 pages of documentation — who could need more?) To find out more and help prompt a decision, ask the following:

- *"How much more information do you need?"* (Try not to sound incredulous when you say this!)

- *"What specifically do you need? Is there anything in addition to this material that you'll need to make a decision?"*

- *"Does anyone else need this information?"*

- *"Provided I get all this to you by X date, when do you think you might arrive at a decision?"*

- *"What issues do you feel this additional information will help you resolve?"*

- *"Would you like to discuss your concerns directly with me?"*

- *"Should we set another time to talk one week from now?"*

These questions help you figure out the following:

- What, exactly, your customer needs

- What that person plans to do with the information and when he or she plans to do it

- How soon you can expect action after providing it

Shrinking perceived risks

Of course, it's always possible that you've screeched to a halt because your decision-maker has valid questions and concerns. Wouldn't it be wonderful if you could clear away these stumbling blocks? You can — by addressing the risks the decision-maker is wary of, and then dismantling them. The step-by-step process outlined here dramatically raises the odds of moving your decision-maker to a choice, whether hesitation stems from logic or caution:

1. **Identify concrete concerns and determine how important they are.**

   If someone's unsure, he or she tends to blow up risks to mythical proportions, and the longer you let the risk rattle around in someone's brain, the less likely it is that the decision will end up in your favor. Ask the following:

   - *"What's the biggest concern you have with my recommendation? What do you believe the odds of that happening are?"*

   - *"What downsides do you see, now and in the future?"*

2. **Quantify the risks.**

   Deal with risks in a straightforward fashion. Help the decision-maker whittle them down to a level he or she can tolerate. As when detailing benefits, specific numbers and percentages go further than generalities such as *big, small, quite a lot, too much,* and the like. Ask questions such as these:

   - *"On a scale of one to ten, what amount of risk is acceptable?"*

   - *"If you had to give me a percentage, what percentage of risk can you tolerate?"*

    When someone says, "That's too much risk," you may have to pluck numbers out of your head to prime the pump: Is a 30-percent chance of failure too great? Yes? How about a 10-percent chance?

3. **After laying the groundwork, ask about solutions.**

   Try some of these questions:

   - *"What can we change or adjust to bring the risk down to the 10-percent level that's acceptable to you?"*

   - *"Are others offering something that makes you feel working with us may entail more risk than working with them?"*

   - *"Is there something you need that we haven't offered? Something that reduces your feeling of risk and increases your comfort?"*

4. **Make others comfortable with your proposal and assure them they can achieve the results they want.**

   Decisions come fast and furious if risks seem manageable and acceptable for those making up their minds.

As you persuade people to make up their minds, remember that some decision-makers hesitate because they're afraid to make mistakes. If you aim to get customers, colleagues, bosses, employees, and even your children to make good decisions in reasonable time, be aware of — and address, whether directly or more subtly — the fear that makes them hesitate.

Making last-ditch efforts to get out of the Maybe Zone

You say you've done everything in the preceding sections, and your decision-maker still hasn't budged from the Maybe Zone? Be bold! It never hurts to give it one more shot before giving up. Here are some good tactics:

- **Revisit your qualifying questions.** Re-evaluate the other person's authority to act, and ask whether the person's budget has become an issue. Has the budget changed since you began the process? Has someone with greater authority frozen spending from the cost center that would pay for your purchase? (See the earlier section "Determining Whether an Appointment Is Worth Your While" for more on qualifying prospects.)

- **Allow the decision-maker to review the numbers or consult with someone else.** Even the company president may need the board of directors' approval before acting. Outside business, if the decision is significant, one spouse often defers a decision until he or she can talk with the other spouse. Ask decision-makers whether they need to consult anything or anyone else.

- **Enlist the help of internal advocates.** If a stalemate draws on (and on), step back. Who in the corporation wants the job done and done now? *Someone* stands to gain some benefit — whether it's recognition, income, prestige, or advancement — by moving forward. These people are your internal advocates. You may never have met them, and they may not be directly involved in the decision-making. In fact, they probably aren't involved, or the decision would've already been made. If that's the case, draw these folks into the loop so they can champion your solution from inside. Advise them of the progress (or lack of progress) you're making and ask for their help. Once again, align your interests with theirs so you're pulling together.

- **Ferret out the choke point.** A decision may slow or stall because there's a designated blocker, also known as a *choke point*. My company, Sales Champions, has a designated blocker. We send people to this person to vet all issues and problems, and our designated blocker deliberately, cautiously, and painstakingly evaluates all details before presenting recommendations to the senior management team.

Moving beyond the choke point is easier and faster if you win over the blocker. Get to know this person and define his or her needs, power, influence, and decision style (see the earlier section "Tailoring the Presentation to Your Client's Decision-Making Style"); then deal with the blocker as you would with any other decision-maker. If you find the blocker doesn't have real power, go around him or her to your internal advocates or to someone who has the power to make the decision.

Knowing when to give up

I often tell my salespeople that if a decision-maker implies repeatedly that he or she *wants* to make a decision and then does nothing after a handful of inquiries to move forward, continued efforts to convince that person can be like watering a dead plant: Although the activity my make you feel busy, you won't revive the plant.

It's a long journey from the impasse of mild interest or indifference to the desire and need of someone who's ready to decide. Chances are, if your decision-maker is tiptoeing around an answer, he or she has already made a decision: the decision to wait. Here are questions to help you assess your investment of time:

✔ On a scale of 1 to 10, what are the odds this person will move forward now?

✔ On a scale of 1 to 10, what are the odds this person will *ever* move forward?

✔ How much time must you invest to dramatically improve those odds?

For those in sales, a fourth question may be whether you really want this customer now and for the long run. Obviously, if you're trying to sell an idea to your boss or spouse, jettisoning the relationship isn't an option. But in other cases, weigh the time you're putting in and examine what you're gaining; in business parlance, *analyze the return* on your investment.

Addressing Straggling Concerns and Inviting Action

In all appointments comes a moment in which you want to create agreement or action items. You want total buy-in to move forward with the whole recommendation (or some of it if you can't gain it all). At some point in the meeting, you have to *ask for* what you want to have happen next. At this point, someone needs to

✔ Make a definitive statement concerning what he or she believes needs to happen in the next steps

✔ Ask others to participate

If you're trying to get a company to participate in a charity fundraiser, someone has to list the benefits to the charity, the company, and the employees and say, "Let's go do it." In a sales presentation, you need to make a definitive statement about the value of your products and services and ask the prospect to do business with you.

In the end, if you don't ask, you don't get. There's no receiving without asking. In this section, I explain how to address decision-makers' straggling concerns, present a solution, and invite everyone to take action.

Step 1: Pause

After your decision-maker has raised an argument or concern, pause. A pause works magic and invests the pauser (that's you) with control of the conversation. It forces your decision-maker to think (and it may even cause the temperature in the room to go up a few degrees).

If you pause, you avoid seeming defensive by jumping to answer the decision-maker's concerns before he or she has finished voicing them. A pause lets you *hear* what your decision-maker is saying and lets him or her finish the thought. It also gives you a moment to collect your thoughts. If you're trying to formulate a response while your prospect is speaking, you may miss out on your decision-maker's real issues. Pauses also prevent you from interrupting the other person when he or she is expressing concerns, which can make you seem hurried or, worse, uncaring and inconsiderate.

Step 2: Acknowledge

After you pause, acknowledge your decision-maker's concern. Even if the concern seems ridiculous to you, acknowledge that the decision-maker's view carries weight, that you heard it, and that you understand. Acknowledging also buys you additional time to solve problems.

Acknowledgement is not the same as agreement. You needn't agree with your decision-maker's concern; you merely need to recognize that it's valid to him or her. To bridge the gap between you and your decision-maker, you have three options:

✔ You can change your thinking to agree with your decision-maker's.

✔ You can tactfully convince your decision-maker that your approach accomplishes the desired results more effectively.

✔ You and your decision-maker can meet somewhere in the middle.

You can even thank your decision-maker without agreeing. Here are some effective statements for neutral acknowledgment:

✔ _"I can see why that might be a concern."_

✔ _"That's a terrific question. I'm glad you asked it."_

✔ _"Thank you for bringing that up. I want to be sure to address that for you."_

✔ _"I understand your concern."_

Another effective technique is to link a probing question to the end of your acknowledgment. It increases your decision-maker's trust in you and shows that you care how he or she feels. Here are some of my favorites:

✔ _"I understand your concern in this area. Tell me, why do you feel that way?"_

✔ _"I see where that might cause concern. Can you tell me more, please?"_

✔ _"I appreciate your hesitation. Have you had a previous bad experience with A?"_

An acknowledgment followed by a probing question provides a bridge to the next step in the process: exploration.

When acknowledging, avoid the word _but_. _But_ negates every word that follows it and makes you appear defensive. What's more, it casts a negative pall over the entire statement. Sometimes _and_ makes a good substitute. Listen to the difference:

✔ _"You did a great job, but you made a few mistakes."_ (Compare: _"You did a great job, and I know you'll be able to correct these few mistakes in no time."_)

✔ _"I understand why you want a snake, but your mother won't like it."_ (Compare: _"I understand why you want a snake. Have you thought about what your mother will say?"_)

Step 3: Explore

Exploring (another word for _probing_) clarifies your decision-maker's concern. What's causing the concern? Did a previous supplier drop the ball? Does the decision-maker distrust you and your company? Has he or she heard a horror story from a friend or colleague?

If you explore well, you gain a better understanding of the size, intensity, and emotional context of your decision-maker's concern. Here are some exploration questions:

✔ _"Can we talk about your views on this in depth?"_

✔ _"What is the primary influence that is causing you to view my proposal this way?"_

> ✔ *"Is there a reason you feel I'm not qualified to be considered for this promotion?"*

Step 4: Isolate

Your goal is to move beyond the smoke and mirrors and get to the real problem. You can't help someone make the right decision unless you know everything that's blocking the decision. Using scripts to isolate reasons for concern dramatically increases persuasiveness. Here are some questions that help you pin down the problem:

> ✔ *"Suppose we could find a satisfactory solution to this concern of yours. Would you give me the go-ahead?"*
> ✔ *"Is this the only reason holding you back from finalizing this decision?"*
> ✔ *"Other than X, is there any other reason you can think of that would cause you not to move forward?"*
> ✔ *"If this problem didn't exist, would you be ready to proceed right now?"*

These techniques get the decision-maker to consider your proposal from a *what-if* standpoint. What would your decision-maker do if you had the power to solve the problem right now?

Sometimes you may isolate the cause for hesitation only to discover that you can't meet your decision-maker's demands in terms of price, service, delivery, and so on. Nonetheless, the insight you gain allows you to cement your relationship with the decision-maker and possibly develop a chance to serve him or her in the future.

Step 5: Answer

After you isolate the exact problem or problems, you move to the answer stage. As you offer your answer, strive for conviction, strong belief in your view, and real solutions; instill confidence that you can help your decision-maker achieve his or her objectives. Make your delivery enthusiastic. If you're not excited about these terrific opportunities, how can you expect your decision-maker to be?

Here are some examples of answers that acknowledge the decision-maker's concerns and offer a solution that addresses those issues:

> ✔ *"Although I understand your concern about my experience, I'm not new to serving customers. I had a 96 percent customer service satisfaction rating at my last job. I really believe my view and application of customer service would be well-suited for this new position."*

> ✔ *"I can see that you're trying to balance the price with quality. Although our price is more, our quality is better. Because you're going to be using this widget for ten years, your reduced maintenance costs, fewer disruptions, and lower frustration with your staff will make ours a better value and pay for the difference by the third year."*

Finishing Up and Confirming Commitment

The final item on your agenda should indicate that the other party will make a decision at the meeting. In a *summation-close,* all you're doing is confirming the details and gaining some level of commitment for that action. The commitment for action can be joint or one-sided.

In your summation-close, list the agreed-upon action items, services, or points with a commitment statement to confirm that you understand or that they're committing to take action, providing you follow through on the listed items. This technique can also work internally with superiors and subordinates or at home.

Here are some examples of summation-closes:

> ✔ *"So if we provide X and Y and Z, would we have a basis of doing business together?"*

> ✔ *"So what you're saying is if someone solves X problem and Y problem, you'll make the decision to work with that company, correct?"*

> ✔ *"I'm hearing you want us to X and Y and Z. Is that right? Terrific! What will you do then?"*

Confirming commitment is the final step: the natural ending to a good decision. It reconfirms that your decision-maker is ready to act *now,* re-emphasizes your belief in yourself and your proposal, and helps assure that the decision-maker takes action. Here are some excellent ways to confirm commitment:

> ✔ *"There's no doubt in my mind that the solutions we've discussed are exactly what you need. Let's go ahead and get started now."*

> ✔ *"You've made me so happy by agreeing to marry me. I promise to spend the rest of my life making sure you never regret your decision. Now, let's go tell our parents."*

> ✔ *"I'm confident that you'll be elated with this X. It will perform exactly as we discussed today. Let's get this paperwork taken care of so it can start working for you right away."*

Following Up Post-Mortem as One Final Effort

Sometimes when you fail to reach your objective at the appointment, the follow-up you do after the appointment can be more valuable than the appointment itself. Most people forget a large chunk of what you say at an appointment. They leave the meeting and walk back into their offices with backed-up items to address that have piled up in the last hour.

The best follow-up strategy is one that's agreed upon and scheduled by both or all meeting participants. If you need another face-to-face or phone meeting, schedule it before the meeting adjourns. Following up always becomes harder if you leave it loose or to chance. "Sometime next week" is too vague — set a date.

You can make a great post-appointment impression with handwritten thank-you notes. After every significant face-to-face meeting, I write them even today. These notes cut through a busy, overcommitted professional life.

Part V

Advanced Time Management for Specific Folks

The 5th Wave   By Rich Tennant

In this part . . .

*I*f you have the basics of time management down,
you're ready to kick into high gear. Part V offers advice
targeted to specific job levels and functions. If you're an
administrative assistant, for instance, you may have little
control over your day-to-day responsibilities, but you're
expected to keep the boss's schedule running as smoothly
as a Swiss train. Chapter 15 can put you on the right track.
If you're in sales, you've hitched your time management
wagon to prospects, so Chapter 16 helps you balance
your time so you devote enough time to actually making
the sale. Of course, business owners and executives,
as well as corporate management, have to direct the
activities of other employees — which means that as the
boss, you're only as time-efficient as your least-efficient
staffer. Chapters 17 and 18 carry advice most critical to
the management set.

Chapter 15

Time Management for Administrative Staff

*T*he absent-minded boss and the capable secretary (the power behind the office) are all-too-familiar stereotypes in TV and movies. You know, the bumbling department head who oversleeps on the day of the big presentation to the company's biggest client? The administrative assistant comes to the rescue and whips up a presentation with minutes to spare, succeeds in winning over the CEO, and persuades the client to double their business — finally stepping back to give full credit to the ever-clueless boss.

I sure hope that most of international megacorporations aren't operating under these circumstances! But I can say this with certainty: No matter how organized and capable the head of the department or company is, the administrative staff plays a key role in the smooth operations and ultimate success of any business. An organized and efficient assistant helps keep the boss and others in the department on track, often managing multiple appointment schedules, arranging meetings, facilitating communication, anticipating the needs of the organization, and responding to them in a proactive manner. A good assistant supports the department and business objectives and takes on duties that free up others at the management or executive level so the bigwigs can use their expertise to do what they do best: lead, sell, create, produce, or facilitate.

Virtually all the information in this book is of value to administrative staff. In this chapter, however, I zero in on the unique circumstances of the administrative person and how to use time management to further success — for the individual, the department, the boss, and the business.

Recognizing Common Pitfalls

For the administrative person, some responsibilities that come with the territory are prone to begetting *busy-ness* — meetings and phone calls, for example. In and of themselves, they're benign, but an inefficient participant may misuse, confuse, and abuse them. As an administrative assistant, answering the phone and taking notes in meetings may be part of your job description, which can put you at the mercy of others.

Getting a handle on busy-ness generators is important to your productivity, both on a daily and long-term basis. Administrative staff members are especially vulnerable to the following time-zappers:

- **Regular meetings:** In many meetings, a lot is discussed, little is shared, and even less is acted upon. Chapter 13 tells you how to take control of meetings efficiency — even when you're not the one leading the meeting.

- **One-on-one meetings:** You may be trapped with a long-winded supervisor or employee who frequently veers off topic. Chapter 9 helps you deal with talkative co-workers, and Chapter 12 includes tips on dealing with your boss.

- **Phone calls:** Calls may come from customers who have difficulty communicating what help they're looking for. I tell you how to handle phone calls quickly and productively in Chapter 9.

- **Piles of paper:** Papers may seem to get moved from point to point on your desk — but never get filed, acted upon, delegated, or even recycled. Check out Chapter 5 to discover how to handle paper *just once*.

- **Stalled projects:** You may get stuck waiting for direction from a supervisor or co-worker who's either unavailable or unwilling to offer a decision. In Chapter 11, I offer some strategies for decision-making that help a stalled project move forward.

Keeping Your Eyes on the Goal: Your Boss's Lead

First and foremost, it's critical for you to know your boss's goals — from big-picture vision (where does your boss see the company in five years?) to weekly or even daily to-do priorities. Without that understanding, you may put all your energy into creating an ultra-sophisticated, cross-referenced computerized filing system that puts the Library of Congress to shame — when what's really important to the boss and the company is high-touch customer service and time spent attending to clients. So get a hold of these goals and consider them your Ten Commandments from 9 to 5.

Over the course of my career, I've worked with some outstanding support staff — and others who, well, may have been better suited for another career. I can tell you that the one defining skill that the best assistants shared was this: They understood what made me tick. They made an effort to discover my goals and business priorities. They observed how I operated and liked to communicate. They found out my strengths as well as areas in which I relied on them for help.

Those assistants who caught on to my business approach were then able to complement my strengths with theirs — they were better able to be proactive and work independently. They were more productive and made efficient use of the eight-plus hours each day that we worked together. They became a critical member of the team. In this section, you find out how you can do the same.

Getting face time with the boss

Regular meetings with your supervisor are critical to making sure you're in synch with his or her priorities and that you're investing your time and energies into the appropriate tasks. You may run across owners of entrepreneurial startups, corporate department heads, and CEOs of Fortune 100 companies. But as for meetings, there are only two types of bosses in the world: those who love meetings and those who hate them.

Boosting your admin image: Ask and you shall receive

The administrative assistant who builds a communicative relationship with the boss or department, contains busy-work to a minimum, and recognizes and focuses on the critical goals is bound to be perceived as a valuable member of the team. Using your well-honed time-management skills to coax order and more productivity from the staff helps the business and positions you as an indispensable player. I hope your boss recognizes this and rewards you well.

If not, it's perfectly okay to remind the boss of what you contribute to the bottom line. When it's time for performance evaluation, try to quantify your efforts as they pertain to sales: For example, by supporting a sales staff of three, you're freeing up X amount of their time to devote to revenue-generating, which may translate to Y more sales for the company. Then do the math: Your efforts add Z dollars to the company's bottom line. That ought to get the boss's attention!

Dealing with a meeting-phobe

I admit it: I hate meetings. I'm a driven, get-it-done guy who assumes that because *I* know what needs to be done, everyone else does, too. Besides, I don't have time for meetings — there's too much to do!

I know, I know — shame on me. But in the real world of business, meeting-phobic managers are certainly not the exception. If you find yourself reporting to someone who'd rather have a root canal than sit in a meeting, it's your challenge to wrangle regular face-to-face meetings in as painless a manner possible.

The key to convincing your boss to meet with you is to show her the benefit of regular meetings. Explain that by meeting regularly, she'll get more done, reduce interruptions, and improve her chances for advancement and raises. Tell her that meeting for 10 minutes a day or 30 minutes a week will save her from having you come in to ask questions to clarify projects.

After you establish the value of these meetings, you'll be more likely to convince your boss that more time or greater frequency would benefit both of you. Start small and work up to that more-frequent or longer meeting. Also, be sure not to overstay your welcome. If the meeting is for 15 minutes, then be ready to leave at that point. Give your boss, not you, the power to extend the meeting. You'll leave the boss wanting more, which is a good strategy.

If you can't convince your boss to hold regular one-on-one meetings, try these other tactics to get more time with your boss:

- ✓ **Make it informal.** Instead of asking for a sit-down meeting, grab the boss for a stand-up conversation at the water cooler. Stop in — when you know things are slow — and ask whether it's okay to interrupt with a few questions.

- ✓ **Make it short.** Whether scheduled or impromptu, keep the encounter brief — perhaps no longer than a half hour. Make sure that the boss understands from the outset that you'll be quick. Perhaps begin with a statement like "I have three quick issues I want to run by you."

- ✓ **Make it productive.** That means you should know exactly what you want to accomplish or find out from this exchange. Ask specifics rather than generalities: "Does the *X* project take priority over the *Y* project?" rather than "What are our priorities this week?"

Working for a meeting-phile

If you find yourself working for a meeting advocate, you shouldn't have a problem with face-to-face communications. A boss who is partial to formal meetings may schedule a standing weekly meeting or even a daily status review.

On the downside, a meeting-driven manager may be prone to *micromanaging* — getting involved in what you and other employees are doing and perhaps creating friction and inefficiencies. Having too many meetings diverts energy and resources from more-productive activities for you and the boss. And the excess can be a sign that your boss is avoiding decision-making and action.

If you find yourself meeting to death, you may need to step up and guide the meeting through specific questions that lead to action:

✔ *"What is our agenda for this meeting?"*

✔ *"What are we hoping to accomplish by the end of the meeting?"*

✔ *"What action point do you want me to record?"*

✔ *"Who do I assign this to?"*

✔ *"What time frame should we attach to this?"*

Asking the right questions

Now for a little reality check: Odds are your boss's goals don't exist in list form. In fact, your boss may not even be able to *articulate* these visions. In reality, many supervisors aren't necessarily good communicators, effective time managers, or very well-organized. (So how did they ever get promoted? You'll have to read another book to find that answer.)

You won't always work for an individual who can communicate, is organized, manages time well, or even has leadership qualities. But that doesn't let you off the hook for pursuing an understanding of your boss's goals and objectives. It's your job to seek out this understanding through observing, interacting, and questioning.

If your boss is unable to communicate well, you can ask questions to draw out the guiding goals and objectives. Try some of these to elicit information regarding big-picture goals:

✔ *"Does the company have a corporate mission or vision?"*

✔ *"Where do you see this department in three years?"*

✔ *"What do you think is more important in the long-run: X or Y?"*

✔ *"How do you measure your own success in your job?"*

A supervisor who's ineffective at communicating big goals may also struggle to convey what's important on a day-to-day basis. Your interviewing skills come in handy in this situation, as well. First, start with direct questions about what the boss wants:

✔ *"What do we have to accomplish?"*

✔ *"What are your priorities for me?"*

✔ *"How can I best support your efforts?"*

✔ *"How should I accomplish this task?"*

✔ *"What's the standard in terms of quality?"*

✔ *"Who else do I need to involve? Who can provide me with more information?"*

✔ *"Can I check back to make sure that I'm heading in the right direction?"*

✔ *"Do we have any immediate problems to address before we can proceed?"*

To flesh out further detail, employ what I call an *add-on technique,* attaching a time frame to your question to power up focus, production, and better time management. Here are some examples:

✔ *"What do we have to accomplish this week/today/before lunch?"*

✔ *"What are your priorities for me for this quarter/this month/this week/in the next hour?"*

Another technique I recommend is to follow up any of the boss's responses with this question: Besides that, is there anything else? Here's why: First, it helps identify anything else that needs your attention in the time frame given. Second, it forces your supervisor to pay attention to what he or she is saying. When people are busy, they have a tendency to switch to auto-pilot and not really think deeply about what they're doing. By following up with the anything-else question, you give the boss an opportunity to stop and think through what he or she has just charged you with and determine whether everything has been covered.

Adopting Strategies to Stay On Track

Good news: Just because you leave work every day with a stack of papers on your desk or e-mail still sitting in your inbox doesn't mean you're doing a bad job. On the contrary, if you end each day with everything accomplished on your to-do list and ready to face the next day with a clean slate, you probably *aren't* doing your job (that or your company may be in trouble).

Fact is, when a company finds itself scrambling to keep up with business, it's usually a sign of robust health. And employees who are weighed down with the heaviest workloads are those who management considers indispensable. You've heard the old saw "If you want something done, give it to a busy person."

So when your boss hands you yet *another* top-priority project, consider it a compliment! What determines your success is how you protect your workspace and focus from invasion and how you prioritize your work, tackling the tasks that are most important first.

Starting with a few simple steps

Sometimes you need to slow down in order to speed up, to put a halt to *busyness* so you can get down to business. It's easy to get sucked into a vortex of activity at the office, drowning in a whirlpool of tasks and to-dos so that you can't even stop long enough to ask for help. Have you ever said to someone who offered to help you with a project, "I'm too busy; I don't have time to show you how to help me"?

Too frequently, that frenzy of activity is obscuring the fact that, well, you're not accomplishing very much. When you find yourself swimming in circles, it may be time to stop the frantic flailing and come up for air. By doing so, you may just discover you're not as far from shore as you feared. Here are some steps you can take:

- ✔ **Get to work a bit early so you can review, reload, and get ready for a productive day.** Employees with refined time management skills arrive regularly from 5 to 15 minutes before their work shift. This is especially true for administrative staff — individuals who support supervisors or a group of people. As soon as the others arrive, they may commandeer your schedule. A quiet time to prepare for the onslaught helps minimize inevitable diversions.

- ✔ **Work routine rest stops into your daily schedule to review and evaluate your progress.** I suggest scheduling at least 15 minutes at the end of the workday to take measure. Keep track of how you spend your time by assessing the tasks according to four main categories: revenue supporting, service supporting, meetings, and project supporting. (Figure 15-1 provides a snippet from a time-tracking sheet you may want to use.) Did you accomplish what you'd intended? What went well? What went poorly? Who and what interrupted your efforts? What changes would improve the situation? What do you need to accomplish tomorrow? What adjustments to your schedule can you make?

- ✔ **Take a work break in the middle of the day.** You may be tempted to work through lunch, but working an eight-hour-plus day without a break to clear your head and step away will *not* help you accomplish more. If you don't want to take an hour, fine. Get away for a *half* hour. Leave your desk behind and meet a friend for a quick bite or a walk. At least head for the company break room.

Time	Activity	RS	SS	M	PS
		RS	SS	M	PS
7:00-7:30		RS	SS	M	PS
7:30-8:00		RS	SS	M	PS
8:00-8:30		RS	SS	M	PS
8:30-9:00		RS	SS	M	PS
9:00-9:30		RS	SS	M	PS
9:30-10:00		RS	SS	M	PS
10:00-10:30		RS	SS	M	PS
10:30-11:00		RS	SS	M	PS
11:00-11:30		RS	SS	M	PS
11:30-12:00		RS	SS	M	PS
12:00-12:30		RS	SS	M	PS
etc.					

Figure 15-1:
What a time-tracking sheet for an admin assistant might look like.

_____ Total Revenue Supporting Hours (**RS**)
_____ Total Service Supporting Hours (**SS**)
_____ Total Meeting Hours (**M**)
_____ Total Project Supporting Hours (**PS**)

Do not — I repeat — do *not* take lunch at your desk! You end up taking business calls, answering co-workers' questions, and jumping up if your boss calls your name. You need at least 30 minutes to clear your mind, exercise your body, or enjoy a change of scenery so you can use your time more effectively the rest of the day.

Protecting peak productivity periods

Most people are at their peak in the morning hours. But whatever time you're most productive, do your best to set aside that period for tasks that require greater attention and focus. If you can, relegate meetings, filing, simple administrative tasks, and other no-brainer activities to other times of day; devote your concentrated energies to challenging projects.

Safeguarding your peak time may be tough. Administrative folks are typically extremely exposed to interruption. Often, their desks are set in an open area, accessible to everyone in the office. And these people are frequently responsible for answering incoming calls for several people.

Here are a few tips for protecting your periods of peak productivity:

- ✔ Use the time-block system (see Chapter 4) to schedule your most productive hours.

- ✔ Say no to *multitasking,* which involves juggling several tasks at one time. (See Chapter 1 for more on the perils of multitasking.)

- ✔ Post a sign or implement some sort of signal to alert other employees to hold off interruptions until a given time. You may not be able to completely block disruption, but you can reduce it.

- ✔ Enlist your boss's support in guarding your time blocks. Ask whether you can get phone relief during this time (maybe someone else can man the phones for an hour). If you can't get help on a routine basis, at least ask about getting it as needed.

- ✔ When given a project with a deadline, make sure your supervisor understands the time resources the task requires. (Bosses are notorious for underestimating the amount of effort required to complete a project.) He or she may then be more supportive of your need for distraction-free time blocks.

Getting your priorities in order

The first thing you need to do is make sure your priorities are straight. Whether you get that information from the boss or in a departmental meeting or you're following your gut, you want to be clear on what's most important — what projects command your attention *first.*

Typically, the money-generating activities (or in the case of an administrative assistant, the supporting activities that lead to money-generating activities) are what should come first. Having been in sales for more than half my life, I'm highly attuned to the importance of bottom-line activities. But the fact is that *all* companies are in sales to some degree. And all employees — even those who don't sell or direct sales — are connected to the sales efforts of the firm. There's really nothing more important in any company than increasing sales and therefore increasing profit.

You may be an administrative assistant in the IT department or in finance, but if the sales team fails, everyone in the company is at risk. So if you need to type a sales proposal, book a sales appointment for your boss, or send information that was requested by a new potential customer, these activities take precedence over the day-to-day paper pushing that most administrative staff members engage in. In a very real sense, your job and the future of the company rely on the sales department. Anything you can do to support and enhance sales efforts increases your value.

Seeking clarification about your objectives

Regarding activities whose priorities aren't clear, there's a wrong way and a right way to get clarification. Instead of posing an open-ended question (which is a *good* thing to do when you want to get people to talk), giving your boss a multiple-choice option can help narrow the focus and make it easier to get an answer to one:

> Wrong: *"Okay, what exactly is my priority here?"*

> Right: *"I'm currently working on A, B, and C. In order to know how to best schedule my time, which one — A, B, or C — is the most critical?"*

Now, let me throw you a trickier situation: Suppose you support several people in the department and two people are insisting that their project is priority. Your first step is to try to talk to the two of them together. By acknowledging the importance of both projects and linking the prioritization to a common goal, you're more likely to get the two of them to mutually agree on the priority:

> *"I'll do my best to get both of these projects completed as quickly as possible. But which project do you believe is the most critical to our department's bottom line?"*

If they don't agree? Well, you'll have to rely on the boss to be the tie-breaker.

Creating and qualifying a comprehensive task list

As soon as you've established your objectives, it's time to make a list of everything you have to do. Administrative assistants tend to be good list-makers — a skill that everyone should acquire. But there's more to making a good list than meets the eye.

The key to constructing a good task list — whether on computer or with note-pad and pencil — is to focus on the *what*. Getting diverted by the *how* and *why* drains the efficiency out of this important step in prioritizing. As you jot down those projects, don't question, judge, or analyze a single item — just get them all down. By taking this productive step, you'll find you have time later to dissect the particulars of each project.

Use the list-making tools that come with your software to keep track of tasks and projects. Microsoft Outlook, for example, has a Tasks feature. You can reorder, add, and eliminate items as much and as often as necessary without wearing out erasers and using up your notepad.

As soon as you have your full list, you're ready to establish the order of attack. Instead of creating a numerical order from 1 to whatever, group the items based on when they must be completed (*Note:* This task follows the process I outline in Chapter 4, but because administrative assistants often don't have the *delegate* and *eliminate* options, I've reduced the number of categories and broke them out according to the urgency of the task):

1. Critical to complete today

2. Preferable to complete today

3. Important to finish in the next few days

4. Can be completed within a week or longer

A common tendency for those who love lists is to finish the items that can be crossed off quickly. It's so satisfying to see those checkmarks by the completed tasks — the more, the better. The smarter strategy, however, is to do the most important items first — not the ones that take the least amount of time to finish. That doesn't mean, however, that you put your efforts *only* on that reorganization proposal, deferring everything else until it's completed. It means you have to break down the big job into many smaller but critical steps. Thus, number one on your list for tomorrow is *not* "finish reorganization proposal" but rather "review staff suggestions for reorganization proposal."

Did you cross off all your critical-to-complete-today tasks before you went home? That, in my book, is the measure of a successful day. A productive and efficient administrative person probably finishes the preferable-to-complete-today items, and maybe a few others, before going home, ready to tackle the constantly adjusting list again the next morning.

Chapter 16

Time Management for Salespeople

A salesperson does so much more than simply sell. A salesperson prospects, qualifies, cold-calls, warm-calls, networks, follows up, generates leads, serves customers, asks for referrals, develops marketing plans, prepares proposals, handles objections, role-plays and rehearses, researches, troubleshoots, files, mails, and asks for the close.

Yet all this boils down to that most fundamental function: making the sale. Boosting the bottom line. Generating revenue. Producing income. The efforts and energies of the salesperson all have to flow in the direction of selling. And the more time the salesperson can devote to making the sale, the more successful the salesperson becomes.

Top performers use their time more effectively to create leads at a higher rate per hour and invest less time convincing people to buy, to buy through them, and to take action now. In the world of sales, time management is a critical skill.

Through decades of experience as a sales leader, sales coach, motivational speaker, and consultant, I discovered that few sales professionals understand exactly how to effectively invest their time when faced with the many tasks required of the job. Early in my career, I developed a system for time management that has served me and thousands of my clients well. By sticking with this program, I achieved and exceeded any sales goal I ever set for myself. And you can, too. In this chapter, I share these not-so-secret secrets with you.

Breaking Your Time-Investment Portfolio into Three Categories

Just as a good financial planner chooses diverse investments to balance a portfolio, a professional of any sort balances the way he or she invests time in the many job-related tasks required on a daily or weekly basis. And just as the well-balanced investment portfolio differs for individuals at various life stages, time investment varies according to profession.

For the salesperson, that time-investment portfolio divides naturally into three categories of activities that make up a salesperson's job:

- ✔ Direct income-producing activities (DIPA)
- ✔ Indirect income-producing activities (IIPA)
- ✔ Production-supporting activities (PSA)

Figure 16-1 shows an ideal breakdown of your time into DIPA, IIPA, and PSA. When I take on a new client in my practice as a sales coach, the first thing I look at is where the salesperson invests his or her time. In the vast majority of cases, I discover the time allocation between DIPA and PSA is completely out of whack, with the person spending as much as seven hours a day on these production-supporting activities and as little as an hour — sometimes less — on tasks that produce income!

Figure 16-1:
The three main divisions of a sales-person's job respon-sibilities.

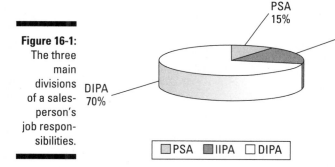

In this section, I discuss what each of these categories entails.

The money-makers: Direct income-producing activities (DIPA)

The job of a salesperson is to create and keep customers — after all, it's through these customers that you generate income. To keep customers, you have to understand their expectations of service and performance and then ultimately deliver on that while communicating at regular intervals, checking the customers' results, and gauging how satisfied they are with the service.

Any and all activities that lead to producing revenue for the company — and thus income for the salesperson — are considered *direct income-producing activities*, which I refer to as DIPA. What, exactly, can DIPA tasks consist of? Here are some of the biggies:

- Prospecting
- Cold calling
- Warm calling
- Calling on past clients to make more sales
- Seeking leads from your sphere of influence
- Networking
- Following up on leads
- Qualifying prospects
- Preparing and making sales presentations
- Overcoming objections
- Closing orders

The secret to success in sales is maximizing your DIPA time. The activities that comprise DIPA have a higher hourly value than anything else you do during the day. The most successful salespeople make a conscious decision to invest more time in DIPA as soon as they understand the value and power of actions directly linked to dollars.

How much time you can invest in DIPA depends on what you're selling and on the support system behind you to service your customers and clients. At a minimum, you want to invest 60 percent of your time in DIPA daily. Certainly, more is better and increases sales more quickly. Also, you want at least half of that time to be in the prospecting and lead follow-up categories of DIPA.

As a sales professional, speaker, and coach, I've discovered three actions that lead directly to leveraging your career and increasing your income: personal development, role-playing, and evaluating personal progress (I discuss all three in the "Planning your day around DIPA" section, later in this chapter). I've yet to meet a salesperson who didn't achieve top level when he or she consistently applied these three DIPA actions over time. The best news of all is that you can dive into these actions from day one of your sales career and never stop.

The prep work: Indirect income-producing activities (IIPA)

As a salesperson, you keep busy with a lot of actions that, although they don't directly bring in income the way prospecting, following up on leads, or making a sales presentation does, are essential because they support these activities. Indirect income-producing activities, which I call _IIPA,_ include the following:

- Developing programs to generate leads
- Creating marketing strategies
- Developing promotional pieces, such as brochures and mailings
- Encouraging brand-building and product awareness among the public
- Tracking, monitoring, and reviewing sales results

Although critical, IIPA shouldn't be time-consuming — keep these tasks to an hour or so (or 10 to 15 percent) of your day.

Many salespeople have a pretty easy time finding the right balance of IIPA time. Those who find it more challenging tend to lean toward the marketing side of sales: creating new marketing strategies or perfecting sales processes or sales systems.

In coaching thousands of salespeople, I've observed that the overload of IIPA usually comes in bunches. It's not a day-to-day problem but rather a weekly or monthly challenge. A salesperson devotes a few days straight to tracking, analysis, or marketing strategies, for example. But if you invest, say, even 80 percent of your time for four workdays in a month, that equates to 26 hours of time invested in IIPA, for a total of 15 percent of your time.

Although important to your overall results, marketing efforts can consume more of a bite in your schedule than is warranted. Overinvesting time in IIPA can throw off your DIPA attention and, as a result, lower your sales. If you see evidence of this, here's the solution: Pick up the phone now.

Administrative stuff: Production-supporting activities (PSA)

Numerous tasks support the direct and indirect income-producing activities (DIPA and IIPA). You know, all the administrative details (typing, processing, copying, mailing, stamping, faxing, and filing) that are an unavoidable part of the job. These tasks don't generate revenue or even indirectly lead to income, but you have to do them as part of the DIPA and IIPA process.

For example, calling on a prospect is clearly a DIPA action, and then developing a sales proposal for the prospect is an IIPA project. But the actual *typing* and *sending* of the proposal — and all this process entails — is a production-supporting activity, or *PSA*. The administrative staff often manages these tasks, but even among the most fully staffed sales departments, the sales folks themselves have to handle some of the PSA tasks.

Your goal is to reduce the time you invest in PSA to the smallest amount possible. Are you controlling your time so well that you're investing 10 to 15 percent — or less — in this area?

Although DIPA can be worth thousands of dollars an hour, PSA time is probably valued at $10 to $20 per hour, depending on the market rate for good administrative help. The time you devote to the big-money activities is diminished, and you earn much less than you could.

Tracking Your Time to See Where You Stand

It's hard to know exactly how much time you spend on DIPA, IIPA, and PSA functions unless you've tracked your activities over a period of time to determine an average. Taking stock is important, and it supports an undeniable truth in sales: When performance is measured, performance improves.

Recording your activities

By tracking your time usage, you're guaranteed to increase your time effectiveness. Figure 16-2 shows a form I use at Sales Champions to help our clients record and report how they use their time in half-hour increments. Most people have between 16 and 20 half-hour increments to invest at work daily. Here's how to use this form to help you make the most of those increments:

✔ Keep the form with you and fill it out as you go. Don't wait until the end of the day to complete it — you're bound to forget something.

✔ Track yourself for at least a week — longer is better. This allows for daily anomalies and helps create more of an average workflow.

Repeat the time-tracking process at least every six months. Over time, habits and behaviors may creep into your routine to diminish your effectiveness. A routine check-up keeps you on track.

The indirect income-producing activities are more subtle, and the definition of IIPA is more fluid than the definitions of DIPA and PSA. For your sales products or the services that you sell, what you consider to be IIPA may be different from what I do. There's no question that prospecting or lead follow-up is a DIPA action; and there's no question that faxing, mailing, licking, and sticking are PSA actions. However, the middle ground is more open to interpretation. The ambiguity can lead to a misrepresentation of your time.

Time	Activity	DIPA	IIPA	PSA
7:00-7:30		DIPA	IIPA	PSA
7:30-8:00		DIPA	IIPA	PSA
8:00-8:30		DIPA	IIPA	PSA
8:30-9:00		DIPA	IIPA	PSA
9:00-9:30		DIPA	IIPA	PSA
9:30-10:00		DIPA	IIPA	PSA
10:00-10:30		DIPA	IIPA	PSA
10:30-11:00		DIPA	IIPA	PSA
11:00-11:30		DIPA	IIPA	PSA
11:30-12:00		DIPA	IIPA	PSA
etc.				

Figure 16-2:
Tracking activity by the half hour.

DIPA Payoff Hours _____

IIPA Payoff Hours _____

PSA Payoff Hours _____

Total Hours _____

ANECDOTE

A DIPA success story

Kim, a one-on-one coaching client of mine, is an outstanding salesperson based in Eugene, Oregon. Every week, Kim gives me a report of her sales activity and time-investment breakdown into DIPA, IIPA, and PSA. I've worked with her for a handful of years and watched her income skyrocket from just over six figures to approaching seven figures this year. Her secret? She makes certain that her DIPA accounts for 75 percent or more of her time invested each week. She works an average of about 42 hours per week, with as much as 85 percent of those hours invested in DIPA. In addition, better than 50 percent of the DIPA hours invested are in the prospecting and lead follow-up segments of DIPA. She spends very little time in PSA. It's not a surprise that her income is higher than that of most heart surgeons in her town!

TIP

My best coaching advice is to free yourself to decide which sales-creating actions fit in each category. Really define your DIPA, IIPA, and PSA actions and create a list for each category so there's no guesswork and faking yourself out when your time allocation is off.

Evaluating your time-tracking sheets

The most successful salespeople are brutally honest with themselves and confront their strengths and weaknesses. They're able to look at their performance in an objective, real, honest, and constructive fashion. To get the most out of your personal evaluation, you should assess where you currently are with your time management before you plan how to allocate your time, noting where you're doing well and where you have room for improvement. Use your time-tracking sheets to identify how much time you spend in each category and when you perform tasks of a certain type. You can then use the review questions in this section during the self-evaluation sessions I talk about establishing in Chapter 4.

Looking back at your day

How often do you exclaim at the end of the day, "Where did the day go?" When you feel as though you've gotten nothing of significance done in the last eight hours on the job, go back and review the mix of PSA, IIPA, and DIPA. Then pinpoint the problems, plan for the next day, and nail down a schedule that ensures maximum productivity and keeps you on the path toward success. Ask yourself the following questions to identify what to change for tomorrow:

✔ When did you invest in DIPA in your day? Did you put off tackling your DIPA tasks until your day was derailed by interruptions?

✔ Were you so engrossed in IIPA tracking that you spent more time than you intended in analyzing the results?

- ✔ How did you break down DIPA time in terms of prospecting, lead follow-up, and sales presentations?

- ✔ Did you lose momentum by jumping back and forth between prospecting and lead follow-up?

Keep a level head as you evaluate your productivity by accepting that although today is gone, tomorrow is a new opportunity to get it right.

Reflecting on your week, month, quarter, and year

At the end of each week, wrap up with an evaluation of how you did, asking yourself the following questions. This needn't take any longer than 90 minutes.

- ✔ How much time did you spend in each category? Is your time investment a little off-balance?

- ✔ How many contacts, leads, appointments, and sales did you complete? Were those numbers better or less than your goals for the week?

When you're comfortable that you have a good handle on what happened this week, then evaluate what needs to happen *next* week:

- ✔ What needs to change next week to close any gaps?

- ✔ Which areas of DIPA do you need to focus on?

- ✔ How much DIPA time do you need to hit or exceed your sales goals?

- ✔ How can you increase the hours you invest in DIPA, and who or what can help you do so? What are the barriers to increasing DIPA time?

Repeat this process at the end of the month, quarter, and year, asking yourself how far behind you are for the month, quarter, or year to date. Your monthly reviews may take a couple of hours; a quarterly evaluation, perhaps a half-day. And at the end of the year, you may want to set aside a day or two to replay the whole year. Your yearly reviews differ in scope from your weekly and monthly recaps because you're looking for big-picture trends rather than daily or even hourly work routines.

Several years ago, my annual self-evaluation uncovered that if I don't take an extended break from work at about the ninth week, my effectiveness drops dramatically. I need at least a five-day break to recharge my batteries. If I don't put that break in my schedule, my intensity, focus, concentration, and results drop dramatically with each subsequent week.

Letting the numbers scare you straight

After asking hundreds of thousands of salespeople the normal amount of time they invest daily in DIPA and PSA actions, I've come to the universal numbers of two hours per day in DIPA and six hours per day in PSA. Does that sound like you? Here's a scenario that'll scare you straight. Say you earn $100,000 a year and work about 2,000 hours over that time. That means your value or worth is $50 per hour, or $400 a day.

Sounds pretty good, doesn't it? Even investing the majority of your time typing, filing, copying, and mailing, you're making decent pay for secretarial work. But consider this: Administrative skills have a market value of $15 per hour. So if you're spending six hours of your day on PSA, your earnings for that time are a total of $90 — which means in the two hours you spend on DIPA, you're earning $310, or $155 an hour. That's more than ten times the value of your PSA time!

Here's the time investment of a typical salesperson:

✔ **DIPA compensation:** 2 hours × $155 = $310

✔ **PSA compensation:** 6 hours × $15 = $90

See where this is going? Yep, if you invert those activities — working six hours on DIPA and two hours on PSA, your earnings would be $960 a day, or $240,000 a year. I know you may feel sick at this point, realizing how much money you may be leaving on the table. That's the normal reaction I get from salespeople when we look at the real numbers and costs of PSA. The good news is that now you're aware that you have a choice in where you channel your efforts, you can make a change.

Everyone knows about lawyers and their billable hours, the time they bill out to clients. I was recently having lunch with a friend, a long-time attorney, and asked him what his goal was for daily billable hours. "Seven hours," he replied without pause. He knew his number.

Think of your DIPA time as billable hours and your PSA time as nonbillable hours. A $100,000-per-year salesperson who reduces PSA time by one hour per day and invests that hour in DIPA can see at least a $38,750 increase in income. In practice, the increase is typically more than that because the salesperson creates more momentum, increases his or her sales skills, and increases confidence.

Planning Your Day around DIPA

Your first step in improving your time management is to decide to make DIPA a priority, to commit to it, to just do it! Stuff happens, and this is no greater a truth than in the world of sales. If you don't place your direct income-producing activities in your schedule, chances are that stuff will come along to commandeer your time — and the DIPA won't get done. If you fail to plan out the *where*, *when*, and *how* of your DIPA for the week or day, you can plan to fail.

Set out to increase your DIPA hours daily. Most salespeople invest less than 20 percent of their workday in DIPA when they should be investing in excess of 60 percent of their time in DIPA every day.

Picking time for DIPA and using that slot wisely

Because DIPA tasks are the most important, you want to put those actions in the part of your day when you have the most energy, intensity, and focus. When are you better, sharper, or thinking most clearly during your day? When do you have the most energy and greatest focus? For most people, this period of high productivity is typically in the morning.

Aligning your most productive time periods with your most important DIPA tasks is critical to your success on a daily basis. Whether you're an up-at-daybreak person like me or more like my wife, Joan — whose engine is misfiring until her second latte kicks in some time between 9:00 and 10:00 a.m. — you want to determine your personal prime time sooner rather than later.

The best way to arrive at your alignment is through personal observation. Monitor yourself for a few weeks. You may even journal through your day, finding the sweet spot where you're most productive. You can also seek out the opinion of those who know you well. Ask your spouse or significant other, your co-workers, or your sales manager. You can even ask a parent, someone who's followed your biorhythms from your birth.

If you discover that your best time of day is the afternoon or evening, be especially diligent in protecting that high-powered period. As your day progresses, you encounter more opportunities for stuff to happen and derail your plans for an afternoon of DIPA. I'm not saying you can't do it, but just be aware that if you book your direct income-producing activities later in the day, you have to be extra wary of distractions, glitches, interruptions, and other trip-ups. (For advice on handling interruptions, see Chapter 9.)

Giving priority to prospecting

Too many salespeople and even some sales trainers lump in lead follow-up with prospecting. Big mistake! These two actions are very different. *Prospecting* is the act of generating leads. *Lead follow-up* is keeping in contact with the leads in order to convert the leads into appointments or customers. During lead follow-up, you can dump some leads because their desire, need, ability, or authority isn't high enough or definable enough for you to serve them.

Getting off to a good start

I'm at my best first thing in the morning. I have a greater storehouse of energy to invest, better intensity, and laser-like focus at that time. One of my critical DIPA actions is writing (as in this book). So when I'm in the middle of a book, I devote my early-morning hours to writing. In fact, I often wake up extra early to squeeze more morning into my day. With a 6-year-old and a 2-year-old, most mornings at my house are like a fire drill (and about that noisy), so it's not unheard of for me to be at my desk writing as early as 3:00 a.m.

When selling was my primary job — as it was for decades — I blocked my prospecting and lead follow-up time first thing in the morning as well (although I assure you I wasn't calling prospects at 3:00 in the morning!). I wanted to be sure that I aligned the high-production time with high-production action.

Combining prospecting and lead follow-up in one category is a mistake because most salespeople then take action only on the lead follow-up portion. When you're not creating new leads, your production and sales are only as good as the leads you have already. What happens if the leads are really low quality? What happens to your sales and earnings? Everything in terms of production, sales, and personal income is negatively affected.

I recommend investing at least 25 percent of your day — or at least two hours — to prospecting. You should also work to make that time consistent each day, meaning no bingeing on prospecting. Schedule the two hours each day and sew them in the schedule. Don't get to the end of the week, find out you're behind, and try to do marathon sessions to catch up.

Part of your prospecting investment is in *qualifying* prospects — determining their motivation, time frame, expectations, and experience; and which other companies may be competing for their business. You also want to know how they're going to make the decision. The questions you ask, whether on the phone or in person, help you use your time in the most efficient manner by eliminating prospects who don't exhibit the characteristics of a customer. The process also helps you craft the most on-target proposals to the prospects who do qualify as customers. Here are the three core elements to qualifying a prospect:

- ✔ **How much?** What's the size of the potential order? What can you expect in orders for the future? Can this prospect buy other products and services from you? In the scope of your current clients, where does this prospect fit?

- ✔ **How soon?** What's the time frame to buy? If the prospect is six months away from the final decision, a lot can happen to derail the sale. You also have to invest six months of calls, e-mail, question answering, meetings, and presentations. However, if the prospect views you as a last-minute entry to the game, the prospect may perceive you as too risky because you haven't been part of the deliberations long enough. Some of selling is being there at the right time.

- ✔ **At what cost?** What's the cost in terms of your time, effort, energy, and emotion to create a sale? Some customers take large volumes of time for little return. You need to determine the costs and ask whether the sale is really worth it.

See Chapter 14 for more on qualifying prospects and holding appointments with them.

Leaving time for following up on leads

Lead follow-up is the process of converting your leads into customers — or at least into appointments. During lead follow-up, you can dump some leads when you determine they don't really meet the customer profile or it's clear that they're not in a position to buy at this time.

Continuing education: A lifelong journey

I remember attending my first professional sales seminar like it was yesterday. I was fascinated with the speaker's understanding of how to become more successful, how he broke success down to a simple series of actions. One of those actions was personal development. He asked the attendees how many books they'd read in the last year. I was relieved we didn't have to share our responses with the group. Reviewing the last few years out of college, I could count the number of books I'd read on the fingers of one hand. And it occurred to me at that moment that there was a direct connection between the low numbers in my bank account and the number of books read, seminars attended, and self-improvement CDs listened to.

That was 20 years ago. The amount of time and energy I've invested in continued learning and personal development is immeasurable. I couldn't count all the books I've read or experts I've listened to, but I can tell you they far exceed the number of fingers and toes I have — and probably the total fingers and toes of my family, employees, and professional colleagues combined. And undeniably, my bank account reflects the riches and wisdom I've collected.

Wherever you are in your journey of lifelong learning — whether you have a high school diploma or a doctorate degree; whether you're fresh out of school or many miles into your career — you can reap great rewards from continuing the process of learning. Don't feel limited to the confines of formal education; the knowledge you pick up from books, CDs, seminars, continuing education courses, and computer studies goes a long way in boosting your sales success.

You should be spending less time on lead follow-up than on prospecting. Shoot for a 2:1 ratio at a minimum, or an estimated one hour per day. If you invert this ratio, you may run out of leads sooner than you anticipate — and find yourself playing prospecting catch-up.

If you have an overabundance of leads, then swing the percentages to lead follow-up for a few days, a week at the most. Just don't remain there too long, or you'll find your new leads dwindling.

Blocking out time for sales presentations

Most sales are completed in the sales presentation, where you're pressing flesh. This is the most obvious component of the DIPA time you invest. It's also the segment of the sales process where you're closest to converting the order, getting contracts signed, and earning your commission check.

Preschedule sales presentations in your time-blocked schedule. (Turn to Chapter 4 for more on time blocking.) As a salesperson, I knew how long a sales presentation took to conduct, so I typically had preplanned slots to do them. When I was prospecting, I'd use alternate-choice closes to garner appointments, such as "Would Wednesday at 1:15 p.m. or Thursday at 3:15 p.m. work better for you?" It kept me focused on booking appointments, and it increased my effective use of time through better organization of my schedule. It also helped me avoid the poor technique that most salespeople employ, which is asking, "When do you want to get together?"

Planning for personal development

The books you read, seminars you attend, CDs you listen to, and videos you watch can all have a dramatic and positive influence your level of sales success. When you invest your time into these learning activities, you can count on a healthy return. Although formal classes and classroom study are good ways to continue your quest for knowledge, you can squeeze in lots of learning opportunities without giving up vast amounts of time. Here's how:

- ✔ **Sign up for seminars.** Sales and motivational experts make speaking tours to many cities throughout the country, and they frequently offer workshops or programs that may be no more than a day or a half-day in length.

- ✔ **Turn your car into an audio university.** Make the most of your commute. Turn off your favorite top 40 station or talk radio show and stick in a book-on-CD instead. Use the time to expand your knowledge about your industry, your career, or human psychology. With the amount of time you spend in your car over the course of a year, you can theoretically put in enough hours to earn a college degree.

- ✔ **Learn while you fly.** Turn business travel into an opportunity to bone up on a new topic. After you reach that comfortable flying altitude, you're free to turn on the laptop or pop on your earphones for CD study.

Role-playing: Getting ready for prime time

I put a great deal of emphasis on role-playing in preparing for appointments and sales presentations. These dress rehearsals are much more than a fun and frivolous exercise; they're a critical step in increasing a positive outcome from a direct income-producing experience. If you invest your time in role-playing, and perfect your scripts and delivery skills, you're bound to grow your sales results.

The time to practice isn't when your commission check is on the line! Here are some tips for working in some practice through role-playing:

- ✔ **Set a time and place to role-play and put it in your schedule.** Don't book appointments in your role-playing time — protect role-playing as if it were an appointment itself. Role-playing is usually the first thing salespeople cut when they get busy.

- ✔ **Start with your appointment-setting techniques.** These are the most important because if you can't get in front of the prospect to make a presentation, it doesn't matter how good your presentation is.

- ✔ **Enlist a partner.** To really role-play well, you need a partner. Why not practice on someone other than a prospect? You can find another salesperson in the office or you can ask someone who has a vested interest in your career.

    Early in my sales career, my wife, Joan, listened to literally thousands of my sales presentations, objection-handling scripts and dialogues, and trial and final closes. In fact, to this day she could probably outsell most of the salespeople in the field because she knows the scripts and can deliver them!

- ✔ **Have your partner offer various responses (without setting out to antagonize you).** The objective of role-playing is to develop good skills and gain confidence. You want to practice making the sale. You want stalls, objections, and problems brought forth from your role-playing partner. The other person just doesn't have permission to be a jerk.

To improve the quality of your message, you can rely on the two following theories:

- ✔ **The *X* Theory of Success:** Becoming proficient at anything always takes a certain amount of time, which I call *X*. *X* is different for each person because it's based on innate talents and previous experiences and skills. The more talents and previous experience you have, the less practice you need.

    For example, to deliver your presentation with power and conviction, handle objections, and persuade the prospect to sign the contract, you may need 100 practice sessions. I may have a tougher time and may need to practice 200 times before I get it down pat. However, the issue isn't that I take twice as long as you to achieve success but that I have an idea of where *X* is and that I'm working toward it regularly.

✔ **The *Y* Theory of Choice.** After you know how many times you have to practice your presentation, you can choose how long you'll take, which is the *Y Theory of Choice* in action. You can take ten years, five years, two years, one year, or perhaps even just six months. For example, if I conduct my presentation live only in front of prospects and don't practice, it'll take me a long time to reach my 200. If I'm in front of prospects three or four times a month, I may need more than five years to complete my 200 presentations.

Your success in improving the quality of your message is determined by crossing the finish line *(X)* and using the shortest amount of time *(Y)* to get there. A top salesperson uses a combination of presentations to prospects and a larger number of practice or role-playing sessions to advance further faster when striving to improver message quality.

Evaluating your sales presentation performance

The time you invest in evaluating your personal performance absolutely earns a DIPA rating. What you do with your time, how you invest it, how you make decisions, how you use your skills, how you work to improve — all these actions influence your personal productivity, and all warrant your most honest attention. (Although some people may feel that self-evaluation is IIPA, I really believe most salespeople don't invest enough time in evaluation, limiting their improvement.)

If you have aspirations to improve and increase your income, you have to be willing to critique your performance. Ask yourself the following questions:

✔ How is your opening statement? Does it create a high level of connection and interest?

✔ Do you harvest viable leads?

✔ How effective is your lead follow-up sequence?

✔ How well do you deliver your sales presentation?

✔ Do you give yourself high marks in confidence, conviction, enthusiasm, and assertiveness?

✔ Do you listen or speak more than your prospect?

✔ How well do you present benefits aligned with the needs of prospects?

✔ What's the conversion rate of leads to sales presentations? What's the conversion rate from leads to sales? What's the choke point to improvement in this area?

Also do sublevel evaluations for a sales presentation in the area of objections-handling and closing. These two areas really separate the top-level salespeople from the middle of the pack:

- ✔ How well do you know the objection scripts furnished by your company? Do you practice them weekly?
- ✔ Can you deliver them under pressure in a sales presentation with eloquence?
- ✔ At the end of an objection that a prospect raises, can you shift to closing?
- ✔ In closing, do you ask for the order in closing more than four times?

Honest personal evaluation takes guts. Focusing on your problems, mistakes, and faults isn't fun. Although many salespeople may rank prospecting as their least-favorite activity, I suspect that personal evaluation is really the most difficult task. But if you never look in the mirror, you may never glimpse those ugly truths and correct them so you can achieve the success you deserve.

Scheduling your DIPA time

To make sure you focus on the most essential direct income-producing activities, be sure to separate out the most important and devote a specific amount of time to each. Of the many DIPA functions that you regularly undertake, a handful are critical to perform regularly, if not on a daily basis. To stay focused, set aside time specifically for each function. Don't lump everything together in a single DIPA time slot.

As you schedule time for your direct income-producing activities, consider these tips (and see Chapter 4 for more-detailed guidance on scheduling your time):

- ✔ **Batch like activities together.** Don't make two prospecting calls, do a couple of lead follow-up calls, and then go back to more prospecting. This disintegrates into multitasking, which is inefficient.
- ✔ **Set aside at least one hour at a time.** Give yourself enough time to build momentum for greatest productivity.
- ✔ **Schedule a break between activities.** Giving yourself 15 minutes to stretch your legs, return some calls, or even get a cup of coffee enables you to clear your mind and transfer your thinking to a new prospect, lead follow-up call, or other action.

Incorporating IIPA into Your Day

After you've worked your schedule around your direct income-producing time, it's time to fit indirect income-producing activities (IIPA) into your day. Because they aren't linked as closely to bottom-line measures, IIPA tasks shouldn't take up as much of your energy, but in no way should you overlook them, either. Your goal is to budget time for them but keep them from eating into the most lucrative activities.

Using IIPA time to review sales results

By figuring out what works — and what doesn't — you can channel your efforts into activities that multiply your income. Examining how many leads a particular marketing piece generates, tracking the conversion rate of leads to sales, and plotting average order and average commission all fall under IIPA.

The time you spend gathering and analyzing data doesn't earn you money directly, but it does show you what works and which DIPA efforts you may need to tweak. For example, say your tracking reveals that from 20 leads, you convert only one of those to a sale. The barrier is likely between the leads and the sales presentation. I'm simplifying (you may have problems at the presentation level or at other stages, too), but the point is that by analyzing each step of the sales process, you can zero in on your strengths and areas of further work. Here's what you may discover from results tracking:

✔ **You're pursuing low-quality leads.** This may be true, but most of the time, it's not the case. Check with the other salespeople — if they're achieving low results from these leads, the problem probably *is* with the quality of the leads. However, if other salespeople are booking five appointments to your one appointment, look elsewhere for the problem.

✔ **Your lead follow-up strategy is off.** Take a look at your lead-qualifying tactics. You may not be doing an effective job of determining the time frame, motivation, and urgency of your prospects. You may not be assessing the level of competition or the level of commitment. The result is that you end up spending a lot of time pursuing individuals who should've been eliminated during your lead investigation. (Flip to Chapter 14 for info on qualifying prospects.)

✔ **You failed to grab the prospect's interest.** From the first moment of contact, you have seven seconds to hook a prospect. You need to hit that prospect between the eyes with your value proposition. What benefits you are offering with what you're selling?

Keeping IIPA in check

To keep IIPA in check while staying on top of everything, I suggest these three tactics:

✔ **Relegate IIPA to the afternoon.** Unless you don't fully engage in the day until noon, you want to set aside the morning for your most important income-producing activities. IIPA functions typically don't require the same level of energy as DIPA. And because they aren't as critical as DIPA, holding off on IIPA ensures that you wrestle the most important activities first, before something comes along to derail your day.

✔ **Keep IIPA to an hour per day.** Marketing, evaluating others' sales performance, analyzing your lead follow-up, scheduling the next day's setup, and reviewing call sheets are all effective uses of IIPA time, provided you don't spend hours daily doing them.

✔ **Use the end of the day to prepare for tomorrow.** One of the best uses of IIPA time is preparing your sales calls, sales strategy, opening statements, and call objectives for the next day. Investing a mere 30 minutes today means you're able to instantly click into DIPA tomorrow. You'll be less likely to stall, evade, and avoid the calls if your call sheets or call logs are on your desk.

Even if you do most of your prospecting and lead follow-up out of your computer customer relationship management (CRM) program (see Chapter 6), I still encourage you to at least print out a hard copy of your calls on paper during your IIPA time today before you leave. Engaging in creative avoidance is harder when you see all these names on a page rather than on a computer screen.

Decreasing Your PSA Time

The goal of any salesperson is to get those administrative production-support activities (PSA) down to well under two hours a day, freeing up more time for prospecting, calling, lead follow-up, and other direct income-producing activities (DIPA). Awareness is the first step toward the proper alignment of DIPA to PSA. For a good gauge of where your time is going, track your daily activities for a period of several weeks using the form in Figure 18-2, earlier in this chapter.

Armed with the understanding that spending time on PSA saps your DIPA energies, you may be tempted to set a zero-tolerance policy for PSA. The truth is you'll never be able to avoid PSA actions completely, even if you employ an army of administrative help. Here's the conundrum: The more you invest in DIPA, the more PSA actions you generate. The two are interconnected. You make prospecting calls (DIPA), and a prospect wants a brochure, marketing material about a product, a quote, or even a sales proposal (PSA). Or you make a sale to a prospect (DIPA), and you now have to write the order, turn it in, follow up on the order and administrative team, coordinate delivery, check back to make sure the customer is delighted and using your product, and possibly train the customer on the use (PSA). So frustrating though it may be, generating more PSA work because you're increasing your sales is a good thing. Your goal is simply to keep the PSA in check, making sure that you keep your DIPA-to-PSA ratio at a healthy 6:1.

PSA functions surrounding sales tend to be recurring, requiring weekly or even daily attention. Here are several ways to keep these supporting tasks on a firm leash:

- ✔ **Streamline the process.** Determine whether you can create a system to make a PSA process faster, possibly eliminating some unnecessary steps. It takes almost as much time to assemble one marketing material package and brochure as it does ten; invest the time to create the ten and have nine ready to go out the door.

- ✔ **Create templates.** Don't craft a sales or lead follow-up letter from scratch each time. The same goes for proposals. You can take a basic format and customize it for individual use.

- ✔ **Batch your work.** Make your PSA calls one after another. Bunch together the PSA actions as much as possible so you can move quickly from one similar call or action to another.

- ✔ **Eliminate the step.** Sometimes examining the process reveals that you don't need to do a particular task at all.

- ✔ **Delegate.** Is administrative help somewhere in your sales department? Can you find someone to lend a hand? Can internship programs provide some eager business students who want to learn the business from the ground up? A talk with your sales manger may help.

- ✔ **Hire help.** If you can't get support within your department, are you willing to pay a few bucks for it? Maybe you can hire a college or high school student, a stay-at-home parent, or a part-timer who just wants a low-pressure opportunity to earn a little money. For many of the PSA tasks that aren't proprietary, the work can be done off-site.

  Remember: If you don't have an assistant, you *are* one. What I mean is this: If you don't have someone you can delegate the mailing, faxing, research, typing, low-level customer service, and a host of other actions to, you become the administrative assistant — and you earn your income commensurately.

- ✔ **Turn PSA work into DIPA work by asking for a referral.** When you have to do PSA work, you can often take the opportunity to get in a little DIPA action at the same time. For instance, customer service follow-up calls are part of your PSA. Checking to confirm that the prospect or client has received expected materials or information is a routine task that doesn't relate directly to generating income. But don't stop there — get some extra mileage from this PSA effort by turning your customer service call into a prospecting call: Ask for a referral.

It's never too early in a sales relationship to begin building a referral base. A truly qualified referral request, however, takes a little time and attention. Be ready to invest at least five minutes in conversation to avoid appearing like a hit-and-run referral driver. You may use a great segue statement like this: "I have a very important question to ask you." This statement forces a pause, builds anticipation, and sets the tone for a meaningful conversation. And it requests permission to explore client or prospect contacts. You may even use a script like this to help you:

> *"I'm delighted that I've been able to serve you. I was wondering about others you might know who would also benefit from my service. Could we explore for a few minutes other individuals you believe I might be able to serve?"*

Questioning the way it's done

My friend Zig Ziglar tells a story about a 5-year-old boy watching his mother prepare a holiday meal. The boy asks her why she cuts off the end of the ham. "I don't know," she says. "My mother always did it this way." Now the boy says, "Let's call Grandma and find out why." So they call Grandma and ask her why she always cut the end of the ham off. Her reply? "The pan was too small."

People often continue to do their jobs a certain way because that's the way they've always done it. Sometimes the original reason for doing it is no longer relevant. Critically questioning your production-support activities can help identify and eliminate needless tasks, freeing up your energy for more-important activities.

Chapter 17

Time Management for Business Owners and Executives

Corporate executives and business owners are two of the most stressed-out and time-shorted categories of workers in the business world. A number of circumstances heighten the time pressures on these folks: Company leaders are charged with creating strategic plans and carrying them out. Entrepreneurs in the start-up stages are taxed with nurturing a fledgling business until it can fly on its own. And both feel the burden of bottom-line pressures: Is the company hitting the revenue goals? Are you making a profit? Are you growing the way you should? Are you in the black?

I've observed another interesting thing about these business leaders: Even after they've succeeded in launching and maintaining a viable and thriving enterprise, they can't seem to get off that fast track, gotta-do-everything-myself, 24/7 treadmill. Even when the business stabilizes and matures, these executives and owners struggle against pulling back, balancing their lives, and transitioning away from their insane work schedules. They seemingly become addicted to time deprivation.

If you suspect you're addicted to work stress, read on. In this chapter, I walk you through a successful withdrawal process to help you grow your business, empower your employees, and take a look at the big picture. It's painless, I promise. And I'm with you every step of the way.

Stepping Back and Observing Your Time Investment

Owners and executives may believe that a million things a day eat away their time. But in his book *The E-Myth* (HarperCollins), entrepreneur Michael E. Gerber claims that all the time spent falls into one of three big categories — and your business success depends on your ability to align these three realms in your schedule so you achieve the right balance:

- ✓ **Growth activities:** Expansion, increasing the customer base, adding to the product or service line, and other growth-oriented energies are what drive the long-term success of the business.

- ✓ **Work *in* the business:** This includes the administration, management, and internal operations of the company — in essence, what occurs within the company.

- ✓ **Work *on* the business:** These activities often involve stepping back and evaluating what's happening, assessing challenges, and looking for new opportunities.

To get your time under control, you have to be able to identify how you're spending it. The process is just like following a household budget: Before you can successfully manage your paycheck, you log your expenditures to determine where it's going.

Time-tracking is important for everyone, but executives and business owners can especially benefit from this self-knowledge. I use the chart in Figure 17-1 to help my clients monitor their time usage daily in each of the three time categories: growth, *in,* and *on* work.

What I've discovered over the years is that after tracking their time for a few weeks, most executives discover that they spend more than 80 percent of their time on working *in* the business. They typically spend less than 15 percent in growth activities and less than 5 percent working *on* the business. I've also found out that this is not the best time-mix formula for a successful business.

Owners and executives should invest 40 percent minimum in growth, no more than 25 percent in working *in* their business, and at least 15 percent of their time working *on* the business. I'm not a dilettante about the percentages — they vary upon your circumstances. You have some wiggle room to increase growth and *on* activities and even reduce the *in,* but this formula offers an excellent guideline. (And the best way to stick to the guideline is through the application of a time-blocked schedule. Turn to Chapter 4 for more on that.)

After tracking your time daily, use the T-chart in Figure 17-2 for an entire week, compartmentalizing your week in the three areas of *growth, in,* and *on.* It'll give you a road map so you can determine what to delegate and to whom you should delegate the lower-value *in* activities. You need only write an action or activity down once. At the end of the week, walk through the actions and determine how to delegate the low-value ones to another person or remove those activities. If you have to keep those activities, try to figure out where you may put these actions in the schedule so you can do them more efficiently or at a time when your energy is lower.

Time	Activity	Growth	In	On
7:00-7:30		Growth	In	On
7:30-8:00		Growth	In	On
8:00-8:30		Growth	In	On
8:30-9:00		Growth	In	On
9:00-9:30		Growth	In	On
9:30-10:00		Growth	In	On
10:00-10:30		Growth	In	On
10:30-11:00		Growth	In	On
11:00-11:30		Growth	In	On
11:30-12:00		Growth	In	On
etc.				

Figure 17-1:
Activity-tracking by the half hour.

Growth   Hours_____
"In"   Hours_____
"On"   Hours_____
Total   Hours_____

Activity Analysis T-chart

Growth	*In*

On

Figure 17-2:
A weekly T-chart helps identify tasks to delegate.

Total Growth Hours _____
Total "In" Hours _____
Total "On" Hours _____

Increasing Time on Growth Activities

When identifying growth activities, look for things that offer long-term returns on investment. In the world of sales, for instance, direct income-producing activities (DIPA) are always considered growth activities (turn to Chapter 16 for more on DIPA). Here are some examples of growth areas:

- ✔ Prospecting for new customers
- ✔ Following up on sales leads
- ✔ Developing customer service strategies to maintain and up-sell existing clients
- ✔ Coaching and training staff
- ✔ Developing yourself professionally
- ✔ Developing strategic alliances
- ✔ Launching new products or services

Such growth activities demand a higher focus and energy level than the *in* and *on* work categories. That's why it's wise to schedule these efforts first rather than last. Use a time-blocking system (see Chapter 4) to schedule your growth activities, and tackle them when your energy level is at its peak — before the day's troubles and surprises start sabotaging your schedule.

The amount of time you devote to growth depends on your work. If your business is sales, I recommend dedicating no less than 50 percent of your day to growth, whether you're actively selling or leading a sales team. If you're leading a team in an area other than sales, I recommend spending at least 40 percent of your time in growth. Whether you should set aside time on a daily or weekly basis depends on your job, but it's likely to be a daily activity.

Track the percentage of your overall time spent on growth: Do a back-end analysis to verify that you're putting in the necessary amount of effort. You may have a day spent putting out fires, but evaluating your growth activity regularly allows you to allot the needed catch-up time before the week is out.

Your success in allocating the proper amount of time to growth activities requires a commitment. Start by setting a goal to spend a specific number of hours on a daily or weekly basis. Write it down and post it where you can see it each day. Put a sticky note on your computer monitor or put an index card on your bulletin board or even on your mirror at home. This visual reminder reinforces your good intentions and helps you discipline yourself to stay focused on growth.

Sticking with activities that don't bring an immediate return takes discipline, and growth activities are definitely a long-term investment. If necessary, share your growth commitment goals with others: a colleague, your administrative assistant, or another executive.

Responsive Tasks: Decreasing Your "In" Time

Here's an astute observation from British scholar C. Northcote Parkinson that has become universally embraced as Parkinson's Law: "Work expands to fill the time available for its completion." It's no more apt than when describing the activities of the *in*-the-business category — you know, all the administration and management stuff.

Awareness is the first step toward reducing the *in* time investment in your business. Identify the *in* activities and how much time you're spending on them, and you're soon on your way to whittling them down. I have one simple measure for recognizing *in* activities: In most cases, they're *responsive* tasks: efforts generated by some external trigger. This trigger can be a staff person who has asked for direction or a customer who has a question about your product. These activities aren't necessarily one-time incidents; the same external triggers can create fixed routines that end up on your desk. Consumer inquiries, for example, lead to a standard response process that involves sending out an information packet. Or the need for your employees to keep you in the loop results in a weekly staff meeting. These triggers — all part of doing business — often turn into processes and procedures that demand your attention and keep you working *in* the business.

The reports, the ordering, the return phone calls, the administration and filling orders, and keeping order and all the routine details that must be done — it's easy to let them consume all your time because they all *need* to be done. And frequently, they're activities that take little thought or effort — or even time. Problem is, in total they derail all the effort and energy you ought to be putting into growth and working-*on*-the-business activities. This section tells you how to cut *in* activities down to size.

Solidifying your organizational chart

The hierarchical structure you follow can have an impact on the effective time management for you and all the employees within that structure. Unfortunately, especially with a young company, when a business grows too fast or changes too drastically, it's easy to end up with an organizational chart that's stunted or entangled with limbs that just get in the way. When this happens, you can count on more of the workload shifting to the executive and leadership branches of the company.

Businesses that rely on a build-as-you-go organizational chart typically end up with the same structure. And it looks something like Figure 17-3.

The owner or key executive is the hub of the wheel, and all the areas, departments, or segments of the business connect to the hub. All decisions, employees, customers, and problems end up on the center desk. Under this structure, the employees are rarely empowered to make decisions at a level that makes operations efficient. In fact, this type of structure results in constant involvement from the hub, which means regular interruptions, low productivity, high frustration levels, and more work hours. Hub leaders find themselves staying late and working weekends, not because business is booming but because they're too busy juggling all the hats to get three, four, or more jobs done by the end of the work day.

Business leaders, be warned! Without a clearly established hierarchy that distributes decision-making and empowers employees, you — the executive or owner — get stuck as the hub, impaled by a circle of spokes.

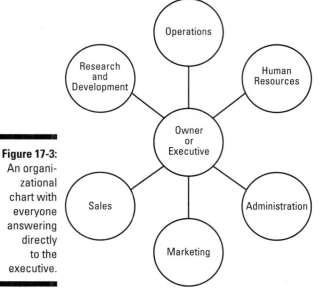

Figure 17-3:
An organizational chart with everyone answering directly to the executive.

What's most important for an effective organizational structure is a hierarchy with a solid foundation. And the traditional *pyramid* organizational chart, shown in Figure 17-4, is most widely used for good reason. It allows for the logical distribution of responsibility and decision-making — and level-appropriate weights — to a larger base. It relies on a chain of command in which the responsibility levels are clearly defined. This structure fosters a sense of ownership and responsibility at all levels. The upshot? Employees who have a clearly defined organizational chart to follow with a strong set of job tasks or job descriptions feel the highest sense of ownership, and what gets owned gets done!

Crafting clear job descriptions

Hiring capable people allows you to spend fewer hours *in* your business, and the first step to getting the right folks in the right seats is to have a clear set of job descriptions. You need to know precisely what you want the candidate to do.

However, good job descriptions are just as essential for your current employees. After all, the best way to keep yourself from hovering over the desks of your employees is to give everyone a clear idea of what's expected of them and then let them do their jobs. If all your employees are armed with a clear understanding of their responsibilities, you're bound to spend more time making progress and waste less time stepping on or over each other — and your pyramid organizational structure (see the preceding section) is much more likely to stand the test of time.

Figure 17-4: A pyramid structure empowers workers and reduces your burden.

Let my people delegate!

The challenges of building sound organizational structures are not just a 21st-century problem. In fact, this organizational overload has been around since Biblical times. Even Moses had his struggles with spreading the work. After leading the Israelites out of Egypt and into the wilderness, he found himself settling all the disputes for the whole nation of Israel. (Perhaps those run-ins with the Pharaoh made him particularly sensitive about "pyramid structure"?)

A typical day started first thing in the morning when Moses took his "seat of judgment" and ended at dark. It took his father-in-law, Jethro, the original productivity coach, essentially to say, "Wait a minute. Why are you the only one charged with this job?" Some translations indicate he said, "This is not good. You're going to wear yourself out and the people, too." Jethro then coached Moses through developing the first organizational chart and delegating some of the decision-making to others.

Be sure a detailed, clear job description exists for each person on your staff or in your company — including you. You should be as familiar with a job description as the employee in that position is. A good job description should

- ✔ So clearly describe the particular role in the company that it could be used as a want ad that would bring in the ideal candidate for the job

- ✔ Be so detailed that your employee can use it as a pretty good guide to follow — even in your absence

Think specifics: Sure, your sales reps are supposed to sell your product, but that's not enough for a job description. What, exactly, do they sell? How do they sell? What must they do in order to sell — make phone calls? Set face-to-face appointments. Go door-to-door? How often? Monthly? Weekly? Daily? Hourly? And there's more. Does their job require certain skills? What's their top priority? Second priority? Third? Do they have to know how to use a computer? Certain software programs? What decisions do they have authority to make? Who, within the company, must they interface with?

Putting together a solid job description is more science than art, and it often requires someone with a human resources sensibility. In an existing company, check with the HR department first — you may discover that job descriptions exist for the positions you need to define. Or maybe you can start with an existing description as a template to develop new descriptions.

Creating room for growth with supplemental task lists

A supplemental task list — to complement a job description — provides employees room for growth and advancement. It also strengthens the base of your organizational pyramid, allowing you to delegate more tasks and lighten your own load. The supplemental list includes the tasks you want to transfer to employees from either yourself or someone else in your department. For instance, a task list for an administrative assistant may look something like this:

- Answer all incoming calls, screen calls, and take care of any calls that you can handle, if not take complete messages.
- Return phone calls (within three hours or at least same day).
- Open and distribute all incoming mail, except anything marked *personal*.
- Schedule all appointments and make sure that they're reflected in the scheduling program or day planner.
- Review the daily appointments; send thank-you notes as necessary.
- Complete all correspondence in a timely manner.
- Order supplies. Keep enough on hand so you won't run out at any time.
- Handle all mailing functions — sending mailings, buying postage, and so on.
- Update and maintain current mailing lists.

And here's a sample task list for a salesperson:

- Make 105 outbound calls daily.
- Make contact with at least 25 people per day.
- Complete 125 contacts weekly.
- Schedule 15 sales presentations weekly.
- Conduct ten sales presentations weekly.
- Sell five water filtration systems weekly.
- Practice scripts, dialogues, and objection handling for 30 minutes every day.
- Complete daily tracking report.

Developing workers' talents: The secret of great leaders

Who's a great leader is always apparent when you look back to see how many of that leader's people advanced through the ranks to hold higher positions. You can find one of the best examples of this phenomenon in the field of athletics. Look at great football coaches, for example, and note that they often see their trusted assistant coaches get head coaching positions. It's almost as if there were a family tree that sprouts one head coach after another because of the immersion in values, excellence,

high expectation, training, and coaching. Head coaches such as Bill Walsh, Bill Parcells, and Tony Dungy have all developed numerous lieutenants who became head coaches themselves. That should be the goal of any executive or business owner: to develop the talent within and empower that talent to take on a greater role, increasing the overall success of the organization while reducing the exec's *in*-the-business time.

Devising a management plan

One step toward managing the *in* work is to develop and use an effective management plan. You don't need a manual the size of the New York City phone book; a *management plan* is simply a set of key guidelines and procedures that you and your staff can follow for greater productivity and focus on the goals. Here are some tips:

✔ **Base it on the core values.** A key component of your management plan is the core values and goals — the mission of your company (see "Balancing Your 'On' Time," later in this chapter). The mission serves as the umbrella under which everything else is sheltered.

✔ **Plug in the organization chart.** Establishing the who's-responsible-for-what flow helps keep everyone — including you — on the right track (see the earlier "Solidifying your organizational chart" section).

✔ **Add the job descriptions.** Include the detailed job descriptions of each person on your staff — and don't forget your own (check out the two preceding sections).

✔ **Gather activity-tracking charts on everyone in your company/department.** Have your staff fill out the activity-tracking chart in Figure 17-1 so you have a better idea of where everyone spends time currently.

As these components come together to form the management plan, you're bound to discover you still have some gaps in data. To gather that information, answer questions such as the following:

✔ How many people do you interact with regularly? How many people *should* you interact with?

> ✔ What are the top five time-wasters for you? Why?
>
> ✔ What are the top five time-wasters for the department/company?
>
> ✔ What are the daily or weekly time commitments that you can't change?
>
> ✔ What are the functions and work that only you can do?
>
> ✔ Are there any tasks or activities that only one or a few individuals can do?

With the answers to these questions, you're well-equipped to draw up a manifesto of the overall functioning of your area — establishing how much of the *in* work is to be performed and by whom. The goal of this process is to pinpoint the *in* work that can be removed from your plate and placed in the most appropriate spot.

Empowering your staff

When all decisions, both major and minor, need to be run through the executive, you end up with a tremendous waste of time. That setup does not motivate the employee and bogs down the executive. The solution is to *empower employees* to identify problems and come up with solutions — in other words, let them do their jobs.

In empowering others to make decisions, you have to accept that mistakes will happen. Give employees the freedom to make decisions and mistakes without fear of recrimination. If there are some areas so critical that you can't risk an error, then identify yourself as the final *okay* for those issues. (And hope that you aren't the one who makes the mistake!)

Some people claim they can do an activity faster than it'd take them to train someone, so it's not worth it. Sure, you may save time on this occasion if you just do the job yourself, but this outlook is only for the short term. I call this the *incandescent blind spot*: Compact fluorescent (CFL) light bulbs may cost twice as much as traditional incandescent bulbs today, but adding up the energy savings and a lifetime at least twice as long, there's no doubt that the CFL bulbs are the big cost-saver. Likewise, when you train your staff to take on some of the *in* activities that hijack your time, you save in the long run. Now that's a bright idea!

Encouragement can go a long way. Almost 20 years ago, I introduced a policy in my company that has dramatically reduced my *in* work. I call it the *No Problems, Only Solutions Policy,* and it works like this: Employees aren't permitted to come to me with a problem — unless they have at least two solutions. Everyone from the frontline administrative assistant to the senior executive is held to this rule. Prior to this, I realized that I employed smart people but didn't encourage them to use their problem-solving abilities. After I established the No Problems policy, I discovered it gave me more freedom, more time, and numerous teaching and coaching moments. I gained insight into how my employees thought. It also gave me a moment to encourage and further empower them.

Planning Ahead: Balancing Your "On" Time

On time is planning time — and it's the most often overlooked process in business. That planning should have its roots in your company's vision and values, which are at the core of your business success. Make sure you establish those visions and values with careful thought, communicate them to everyone on the staff, and continue to convey and instill them through ongoing coaching and accountability among all employees. Here are the major ideas you need to outline:

- **Core purpose:** Why does your company exist? And don't say "to turn a profit." Profit is the result of a well-run company that has a clearly defined mission. This core purpose should be easily summarized in one or two sentences.

  In my company, Sales Champions, our core purpose is "To teach and inspire people to use their God-given gifts to create excellence in life." One of my all-time favorite core purposes is from Mary Kay Cosmetics: "To provide unlimited opportunity to women." It has nothing to do with cosmetics — it's about people. I believe that if Mary Kay Ash had found another vehicle that would provide more opportunity to women, she would've changed businesses.

- **Core values:** These are the enduring tenets that guide your mission. Core values should be so simple and straightforward that you could explain them to your children. What are the values you'd hold onto even if they became a competitive disadvantage? For example, at Sale Champions, some of our core values are "hard work and continuous self improvement" and "exceptional execution of the fundamentals." Sony Corporation mentions "being a pioneer — not following others" and "doing the impossible," and Nordstrom values "service to the customer above all else." You save time by clearly knowing and living your core values — and having your staff know and live them as well.

Your core purpose and values serve as the foundation of your *on* responsibilities: your strategy, tactics, timing, people resources, and finances. They sit at the heart of every action, thought, hiring, firing, strategy, tactic, and expenditure. Aligning your big-picture view with your mission and values is a process that successful companies engage in regularly, investing at least 15 percent of their efforts in *on* activities.

Because planning time is so important to your success, you want to be sure that *on* time gets attention. The best way to identify your *on* duties and ensure they get the necessary attention is through weekly tracking (see Figure 17-1 for the activity tracking chart).

Take a look at your *on* tasks — study them to determine their frequency, asking yourself questions such as the following:

✔ Do these tasks happen or need to happen every day? Every week?

✔ Is this a periodic or even one-time activity?

✔ Have you neglected some planning activities that should be on the weekly or daily list?

✔ Are there easy opportunities to invest more time in *on* activities?

All staff members should be investing some time during their day in *on* time. Teaching the importance of *on* time is the first step. If you're leading other managers who get the standard of daily and weekly *on* time that's prescheduled, hold them accountable for it in your meetings. It'll be as hard for you to adhere to *on* time as it is for them, so ask them to hold you accountable to your *on* time as well.

Setting aside daily and monthly "on" time

On time has a tendency to be squeezed out more than the other two segments for a busy owner or executive. It gets the leftovers rather than the first fruits of your labor. But you need *on* time to evaluate your previous course so you can plot the adjustments you need to stay on track. Use this reflection time to set priorities, establish goals, and revise existing processes to further your efforts.

At a bare minimum, I recommend at least 30 minutes at the end of the day to review the day— you want to get insight from your day so you can improve tomorrow. Ask questions like the following:

✔ What went well today?

✔ What didn't go well today?

✔ What did you learn today?

✔ What would you have done differently?

✔ What are your priorities for tomorrow?

These questions and others like them will finish off today and set the table for tomorrow. I also advise that you schedule review time at the end of every week and month. An hour or two may be enough for an end-of-week wrap-up; for a month, you may need a half day.

Most people have fewer than 1,000 months in their whole lives, and you likely have more than a quarter of them gone as you're reading this book. So at the end of a month, you need to look at how the past month stacked up. Are you progressing toward your goals and objectives? What are the goals and objectives for the next months? What do you need your staff to focus on for the next 30 days? Take about a half day of *on* time to do a thorough evaluation of your month so you can invest it in the next month.

Performing a quarterly and yearly review of "on" time

You need to schedule quarterly and yearly reviews — wonderful predetermined *on* time breaks — with adequate amounts of time that correspond to their length. Owners and executives frequently omit the quarterly pause of *on* time — it really demands a day of uninterrupted focus — but that time is well worth it. Here's what to review:

- ✔ Where are your goals versus actual year-to-date results?
- ✔ What were the biggest challenges during the quarter?
- ✔ Has the competition changed in the quarter? Have the economic conditions changed?
- ✔ Do you need to make any adjustments in your strategy, tactics, lead sources, customers, products, presentation, marketing, or staffing?

This is the time to review business plan, staff, goals, and results. You have enough time and data to be able to make course corrections in your business or department, being confident that you're not being reactionary.

An off-site *on* day is the best strategy because it reduces distractions.

The end of the year is a time for the most thorough analysis and evaluation. Over the years, I've personally found the last week of the year to be my favorite. I take the whole week to replay the year and invest the whole week in the *on* business activities. The *on* time of this week can ensure that the new year is your most productive and fruitful ever.

Chapter 18

Coaching Others to Manage Time Effectively

*1*f you have employees who report to you, being a good time manager isn't enough. For maximum benefit, your staff members also need to improve their time-management skills. Coaching your employees is part of your job, and improved time management makes everyone's job, including yours, much easier.

Walking each of your staff members through this book may be the best solution, but most managers (even you, with your new and improved time management skills) probably can't devote a block of time to a mini-seminar for each of your employees on the whole book. However, you may want to walk your people through Chapters 3 and 4 and through the appropriate chapters in Part V — or simply provide this book as a reference. May I say I'd be pleased and proud to see a copy of *Successful Time Management For Dummies* on the desk of each person in your department?

But you can do more. This chapter offers a helping hand in getting your staff on board as to the value of time management and in helping them embrace strategies and techniques for lassoing that most important of resources: their time. In this chapter, I show you how to take a hard look at your employees' current time management practices and how to develop a growth plan that you all buy into. I walk you through ways to ensure that the plan sticks and help you support your staff's efforts. Then I offer some strategies for handling situations in which an employee fails to improve.

Finding Out Who'd Benefit from Training

What you accomplish is a direct result of how you use your time. Pretty simple, right? So how *are* your employees using their time? Your first step in getting your employees on board with time management is to find out how efficient they are currently and to assess their strengths and weaknesses in terms of time management.

You may begin by reviewing their past performance evaluations and spending time observing your staff and their work habits. Then, most importantly, talk to each employee, getting input about the challenges and goals in time management.

Using the four probabilities of success as a gauge

As you gather information about an employee's time management strengths and weakness, you may find it helpful to consider the four probabilities of success:

- Knowledge
- Skill
- Attitude
- Activities

When you improve employee performance in any one of these areas, your staff becomes more productive — and the individuals on your team become more successful.

Knowledge of time management principles

A strong knowledge of proven time management principles can increase the volume of work your staff can complete in an eight-hour day. Additionally, employees need to have a solid knowledge of their job and the responsibilities expected of them. When evaluating an individual's time management potential based on knowledge, answer the following questions — based on your observations:

- Does the employee have the knowledge necessary to do his or her job in an efficient manner?
- How well-defined are this employee's life and business goals?
- Is the individual aware that time management is an important priority?
- Are the business goals yours or the employee's?

✔ Does the employee know how to work effectively to meet time goals?

✔ Do you talk about goals frequently and specifically enough?

✔ Does the employee understand the 80/20 rule: that 20 percent of effort brings about 80 percent of results? (See Chapter 4 for more on the 80/20 rule.)

Skill in time management techniques

Skilled time managers usually acquire their expertise through practice, trial-and-error, and daily use of techniques (as well as a few failures). Your staff has to develop time management expertise in the same way.

Employees who have time-related skills — such as the ability to organize themselves and their work area and use tools such as day planners and organizers — are likely more efficient. Look at your staff and ask the following questions:

✔ Is the employee able to use organizational techniques and tools, including technology?

✔ Does the individual's work area seem organized and tidy?

✔ Do you notice that the person has difficulty diverting interruptions?

✔ Does the employee prioritize each day for the next before leaving for home?

✔ Have you noticed whether the employee regularly uses a planning system to track upcoming commitments or even the next day's work? Does he or she do this every evening or only once in a while?

✔ Is the staffer able to use a scheduling system to organize his or her day?

✔ Is the employee able to consistently keep commitments — including arriving at work and making it to meetings on time?

Attitude toward improving time management

Attitude is one of the most important factors in success. Maintaining a positive attitude is a choice, however, and it's one you have a right to expect your employees to make. A poor attitude leads to negative results and — you guessed it — more wasted time. Even if skills and knowledge are on the weaker side, a good attitude makes for faster and greater improvement in time management skills. As you study your employees, ask these questions to determine their attitude toward time management:

✔ Is the employee open to learning new techniques and skills to increase productivity?

✔ Has the individual proactively sought out advice or made efforts to improve time management practices?

> ✔ Has the staffer exhibited a positive attitude in other situations in which improvement was needed?
>
> ✔ Does the employee convey confidence that he or she is able to develop more time-efficient habits?

Activities

In the business world, action is king. The biggest increase in productivity comes from selecting the right activities on which to spend your time. In Chapters 15, 16, and 17, I outline areas in which administrative employees, salespeople, and executives have to spend their time to produce better results more efficiently. As you evaluate your employees' activities, you may include these questions:

> ✔ In which activities does the person spend his or her time?
>
> ✔ How does the employee's eight-hour day break down? What percentage of his or her time is spent on each of these activities?
>
> ✔ Does the staffer avoid or postpone activities he or she doesn't like?
>
> ✔ What activities is the individual most comfortable doing? Are those activities best for the department and the company?
>
> ✔ Does the employee accept direction in terms of prioritization of activities?

Tapping into an employee's motivation

One critical key to success in helping an employee manage time is to involve the individual, so be sure one of the first steps you take is to confirm employee buy-in. You want to put together a plan in which the employee has as much ownership as you do, and that means involving him or her at the outset.

You can't afford *not* to pass along time management tips to your employees. I liken true coaching to exercise: It may seem inconvenient and time-consuming, and sometimes it is, but the benefits so far outweigh the effort that it's impossible to justify skipping it.

If you're like most managers, you may find that training your employees in time management helps you improve your own time management skills further. Teaching others is the best way to reinforce your knowledge and discover even more about a topic.

Don't neglect the costs of employees who work excessively. Some people feel that how many hours they work in a week is a badge of honor. This warped thought process leads to excessive time at the job, which can lead to burnout, lower production, and lower levels of job satisfaction. If the employee isn't salaried, then overtime costs are significant to companies as well.

Discerning whether your employee is ready to change

My experience coaching hundreds of people worldwide has taught me that most people don't change their time management (or any other) strategy unless they're experiencing some type of pain: They've had enough, heard enough, or hurt enough:

✔ **Had enough:** They're frustrated and feel like they're always at work. They've missed enough dinners with family, T-ball games, swimming lessons, kindergarten graduations, and nights out to say, "I'm going to make a change." This one is the best of the three options because it's created internally, so it has greater odds of sticking. The employee may come to you for guidance.

✔ **Heard enough:** When a staffer reaches the "had enough" level but still presses on, ignoring repeated warnings in various forms, it may be time for the manager (that's you) to step in and have some serious discussions with him or her. Using this book, as well as stories of your victories and failures in time management, can bring the situation to light.

I'm not suggesting nagging as a strategy to improve an employee's time management; I *am* suggesting that repetition and consistency of message have their place.

✔ **Hurt enough:** As a manager, friend, and colleague, "hurt enough" is the learning experience you want employees to avoid. An employee comes home one day and the kids and spouse are gone because he or she was *never* home. Or employee health issues border on catastrophic because he or she never "had time" to attend to his or her physical well-being.

Spend some time talking to the employee and you're bound to discover whether he or she has reached — or is close to — one of these crossroads. Then you want to try to connect with the person on an emotional level.

Helping your employee want to change

Most human beings make decisions — even big decisions — largely based on emotions. Then they justify those decisions with logic, data, or facts. Achieving buy-in from employees isn't solely about goals, benefits, and time management skills. It's also about employees' emotions.

Tapping into your employees' feelings can help you persuade them to try your new time management strategies. Try these questions to explore their emotions regarding time management:

✔ *"How do you feel when you miss your quota for the month?"*

✔ *"How do you feel when you're interrupted regularly by others?"*

✔ *"What are your feelings when I delegate a few projects in a row?"*

Next, use follow-up questions to move from emotions to action:

> ✔ *"How can I help you reduce those feelings? How can you reduce them?"*
>
> ✔ *"What can I do to help you feel more positive and energized rather than drained and frustrated? What can you do?"*

The answers — or *emotions* — your questions elicit help prompt your employee to buy into a plan for improved time management. Tell your employees that based on their responses, you'd like to work with them to develop a time management plan with concrete steps they can take to improve their skills.

Establishing Goals

As soon as you understand a staff member's problem areas, the next step is to develop a plan to overcome these challenges and turn the employee into a productive, efficient dynamo. One of the first items on your agenda when you want to overhaul employees' time-management skills is to establish goals. As you craft the goals, you may want to turn back to Chapter 2 for more advice.

When establishing an employee's time management goals, keep these pointers in mind:

✔ **Cast the goals in a positive light.** Instead of "stop coming in late," try "work to consistently come in on time or earlier."

✔ **Make goals realistic.** Goals should be challenging but not so difficult that the employee may become discouraged. If an employee is always late for work, insisting on 100-percent on-time arrival starting on day one may be setting the bar too high.

✔ **Break goals into manageable steps when possible.** What steps does your employee need to take to accomplish the goals? For instance, you may have your employee identify his most important tasks before trying to put them in order.

✔ **Make goals measurable.** First, determine how you can measure the progress:

- By projects completed?
- By an increase in responsibility?
- By adherence to new time management strategies and systems?
- By a rating system you develop?

Then make sure you can measure the goals using numbers, whether percentages, totals, number of first-time responsibilities, or specific figures. With a measureable component, a goal such as "finish projects on time" becomes "strive to increase on-time completion of projects from 1 in 5 to 4 in 5" or "commit to completing all projects within 24 hours of the original deadline."

✓ **Give a target date for goals.** Without establishing a "by" date, your employees are less likely to be as motivated to do the hard work of change. To make sure the time line you attach to the goal is realistic, ask these questions:

- When do you want to see improvement? Next week? Next month? Next quarter?

- When is the employee's next performance review? Is it reasonable to expect X amount of improvement by that time?

- Are there company deadlines that have an impact on how quickly improvements need to be made?

With a target date, "reduce the number of interruptions to four times per morning" becomes "reduce the number of interruptions to four times per morning by month's end."

 Have your employees develop *skills time lines*, which determine which skills, tools, or systems they must learn and implement and by what dates. Help your employees create their time lines, but let them do the bulk of the work themselves: It builds employees' ownership of the goals, and it teaches them the skill so they can do it themselves the next time.

Incorporating Tools and Strategies

Chances are your employees could use some tools, technology, and resources to assist with the process of adopting new time management skills. As you put together your plan, select the tools you believe are most pertinent and work them into your overall strategy. Of course, all the content in this book is of great value, but here are some helpful tools and strategies your employees can use to address common time-management challenges:

✓ **Find where the time goes with time-tracking charts.** Plenty of people have difficulty identifying where their time goes. Your employees who struggle with productivity probably believe they're getting a lot done, when in all likelihood their days are peppered with disruption, drained from wasteful meetings, and dissolved by unimportant but time-consuming tasks.

A time-tracking chart commands users to look closely at their day, half-hour by half-hour. This tool is sure to unearth the worst time-stealing culprits, and the discovery of "where the time goes" is likely to liberate the employee into a more productive state of being.

✓ **Identify what comes first with the prioritization tool.** Some employees struggle with determining what's really important — which projects are most critical to address or which job to tackle first every day. What these folks need is a way to help them order their priorities. The prioritization tool spelled out in Chapter 4 helps individuals gather all their projects or tasks and go through a careful and deliberative process to put them in order. This is a process that you and the employee may want to work through together because work priorities are a combination of personal and business interests.

✔ **Get a grip on the day/week/month with time-blocking.** Who doesn't get so overwhelmed by a busy schedule that he or she misses an important meeting, forgets about a family event, or double-books appointments? The person who uses the time-blocking tool! By introducing your employees to time-blocking (see Chapter 4), you help them open the door to achieving so much more. Because time-blocking brings in all aspects of your life, from work to personal, those who use it often discover that they don't have to sacrifice family for work — or vice versa.

✔ **Head off drag time with the 11 a.m. rule.** As you direct your employees to block their time, arm them with the *11 a.m. rule,* scheduling the most important tasks of the day before 11 a.m. For most people, the hours before 11 a.m. are most productive. Workers tend to have more energy at the beginning of the day and, typically, there are fewer interruptions, problems, and "fires" to serve as distractions. When your employees tackle the most important tasks during their peak performance period, they're investing their best hours in the most critical activities before the day wears them down.

✔ **Combat interruptions with do-not-disturb policies.** All employees struggle with interruptions, but administrative staff are especially vulnerable. You may want to institute a time during the day when administrative employees are relieved of phone duties and other potential distractions (if you have more than one administrative assistant, rotate schedules so they're not all using their quiet time at once).

If a staff member has his or her own office, suggest that he or she shut the door, essentially hanging up a do-not-disturb sign. You can also have employees hang actual do-not-disturb signs if they work in a bullpen environment or cubicle. Help communicate their off-limits time to other staff members so they can be more productive.

Encourage employees to make the most of these time periods — somewhere between 60 to 90 minutes at a time — saving that time for the projects and tasks that require concentrated effort or intense focus, such as writing a report or doing research.

As you and your employee develop the plan for more effective time management, start small and then build on that. By starting small, you encounter less resistance. Employees won't roll their eyes when they see you coming, knowing you're on this "new time management kick." And they won't secretly hope it all blows over so they can return to status quo in a few weeks. Instead of pressing the employee to commit to doubling productivity, begin by getting the individual to incorporate time-blocking or reducing daily interruptions into his or her daily routine. Focus on one small tool, strategy, or routine for a few weeks.

Fostering Partnership and Encouraging Success

I'm a big productivity and efficiency nut. I want the best possible value out of every second in life. When I was younger and attended conferences or read books, I came away with 101 new ideas on how my companies could operate with higher returns. I wanted to implement them all by *yesterday*.

My staff members started wincing when I brought my new ideas to the office, and they especially dreaded my return from conferences because I could point to XYZ Company, which was doing business this way and was hugely successful. I had validated results! But I can tell you, I didn't generate buy-in when I came back.

Time management is an evolving process. Acquiring new skills, making noticeable improvements, and completing complex projects are big steps. That means they take time, which means greater potential for an employee to veer off-course. You can't meet with the employee, set up the plan, and walk away, expecting everything to work. The employee is accountable for achieving these benchmarks, but you, as manager, have accountability, too. You have to nurture the process along the way. In this section, I explain how to approach the time-management plan as a partnership between you and the employee.

Setting up benchmarks and check-ins to instill accountability

As for accountability and performance change, two universal truths stand out:

✔ When performance is measured, performance improves.

✔ When performance is measured and reported, performance improves *faster*.

So as you put together the improvement plan, define *benchmarks* — progress stops along the way to the time management goals (see the earlier "Establishing Goals" section) — and set check-in appointments in which you and the staffer meet to assess progress.

Check-ins with your employee may be frequent at first and become less frequent as time passes. You may schedule daily check-ins in the beginning, moving to weekly, biweekly, and monthly progress reports as the employee builds his or her time management skills and achieves greater confidence. As you schedule the progress report points, determine the following:

Taking a team-based approach to time management

If you feel uncomfortable engaging so personally in the lives of your team members, consider a group goal-setting session limited to business topics. Take your team off-site for an afternoon or, even better, a full day. Discuss departmental objectives, quotas, and benchmarks. Ask for input on goals, strategies to attain them, and bottlenecks where time is wasted or service doesn't meet the standard.

Set goals as a group and make sure everyone commits to them as a team. Then determine a

team reward that energizes employees. Make it clear the reward is available to everyone who works toward it. The reward needs to be their idea: their reward and their commitment to deliver with excellence.

You may establish weekly time management classes to raise awareness as well as skill levels, but make sure employees green-light the idea before you begin, or your results may be less than stellar.

 ✔ Whether employees need to hand in their measurement and tracking tools daily, weekly, or monthly; I have my employees hand in daily reports that track their activities by the half hour and show how they prioritize their tasks and projects

 ✔ Whether you'll meet face-to-face daily, weekly, or monthly to discuss employees' progress

If you can, schedule weekly or at least regular sessions with an employee, each session lasting at least a half hour. In addition to checking the benchmark status and getting an update from the staffer, you can introduce a new time management technique. These sessions can help you keep tabs on the individual's progress and inspire the employee to stick with the effort.

Employees want to see improvement fast, or they may begin to think this time management stuff is a bunch of bunk. So come up with some measurable and reasonable benchmarks that are certain to motivate the staffer to progress.

Being consistent

If you delve into successful time-management strategies, you find that consistency is the secret sauce of success. As a manager looking to groom your staff into better time managers, consistency is important both in terms of what you should expect from your employees and what they should expect from you.

Model the behaviors you'd like employees to exhibit. Establish routines and then help employees develop their own routines. As you keep tabs on an employee's progress toward better time management, be consistent with the following:

  ✔ Employees' schedules

  ✔ Strategies for minimizing interruptions

  ✔ Meetings and appointments

  ✔ Memos

  ✔ Time-block schedules

  ✔ Priorities

  ✔ Expectations

When your staff members are confident that the priorities you set for them yesterday won't turn on end today, and when they can look to you as a manager who consistently makes appointments and meetings on time and responds promptly, they're more likely to embrace their time management goals and improve their performance.

Fulfilling your role as a mirror

As your employees' manager and coach, you're in the mirror business. Ask employees to articulate their goals and then serve as a mirror to show them how what they do daily reflects what they claim they want. When you mirror an employee's vision — rather than your own expectations — you're more likely to motivate positively. Consider these two statements:

> *"You're not going to do a good job on this project if you're getting distracted by other things."*

> *"You shared with me that this project was extremely important to you. How do you see yourself completing it while directing most of your energy to these other tasks?"*

The first casts the goal as yours — not the employee's — and your feedback comes off as a reprimand. But when mirroring the employee's interests, as the second statement does, you come across as an ally in your employee's success.

Here are some effective mirroring phrases:

  ✔ *"You said you wanted to invest x hours a week in this activity. How are you doing so far? What do you need to do to improve that? What can I do to help you?"*

  ✔ *"What changes are in order to allow you to achieve those goals you told me about?"*

  ✔ *"Can I hold you accountable for meeting your goal?"*

> ## Waiting for the "Aha!"
>
> I once had a salesperson who struggled with a number of key issues but especially with investing too much time in unqualified prospects. He wanted to save these people, but he couldn't help them because his prospects hadn't arrived at a point where they wanted to change — and *not* changing didn't hurt them enough.
>
> The salesperson called me and asked what to do with a prospect he hadn't closed. After listening to his story, I knew the prospect wouldn't be converted to a customer because he didn't meet the criteria for Sales Champions'
>
> prospects. I asked the salesperson a few questions, and suddenly, the conversation changed. My salesperson took the lead, telling me why he should abandon this prospect and move on, even though he'd invested hours in moving the prospect toward a sale.
>
> I asked myself, "Has he finally gotten it? Did he just put the puzzle together?" Before he hung up, he said, "Dirk, I get it!" That was the moment I'd been waiting for: the got-it moment. All the sweat, worry, and frustration had been worth it.

The more clearly you see employees' goals, the more effectively you can remind them of their goals and reinforce that how they manage their time helps them achieve their goals.

Dealing with a Lack of Progress: Can This Employee Be Saved?

When you make a commitment to help an employee improve, you invest time of your own and you understandably don't want to give up, even if things don't appear to be progressing. Unfortunately, not everybody can be saved. Sometimes, even though you follow all the steps I outline to help your staff members attain time-management enlightenment, you can't get through. In these circumstances, you may have to take a good, hard look at the situation and make some tough decisions.

If you're committed to healing your problem employee no matter what, be careful. Early in my sales management career, I was determined to make a particular salesperson better. I vowed that I'd make him into a good salesperson, even if it killed me. It almost did! I worried more about this salesperson and lost more sleep over him than any other I've had in my career. It was a big waste of time and energy because I was really more determined to make him a success than he was.

Before you invest the time in trying to save an employee, determine whether this is a problem that *can't* be fixed. Look for these signs:

- The employee has consistently failed to meet time management benchmarks and goals established in your plan.

- The employee has failed to use the time management tools you identified in the plan.

- The employee is neglecting opportunities to acquire knowledge or skills that could help him or her attain time management goals.

- The employee has displayed a negative attitude despite your efforts to connect time management improvement to his or her goals.

- The employee's time management failures are having a measurable impact on your department or company goals. (Consider measurements such as revenue shortfall or missed deadlines.)

- The employee's limitations are having a detrimental effect on other staff.

If your employee meets even one of these criteria, you, as a manager, need to take action. Here are your options.

Accepting them, warts and all

If you're like most managers, you probably have at least one employee whose use of time makes you bite your lip (and your tongue). Despite your efforts and encouragement, you haven't seen any improvement. But because of other merits or strengths that the employee brings to the company, you may choose to let it go. Say, for example, the staffer is a prolific producer of business and meets all responsibilities, but simply can't manage her own time and often spends evenings and weekends in the office. Because her challenges don't affect her performance or disrupt anyone else in your department, you may be comfortable resigning yourself to this failing.

When evaluating this employee, address and document this shortcoming during the annual review. Your staff members need to be held accountable for their ability — or inability — to meet the goals you've set for them.

Giving it one more try

The original time-management improvement plan you mapped out with the employee should have had some give built into it. For example, the benchmarks you set may have allowed for extra time if the employee struggled a bit achieving that point. But if you want to give the employee one more chance, have at it: Be prepared to go through the discussion, review, and perhaps revision of the improvement plan, identifying tools and setting up a time line.

Maybe your problem employee only needs fine tuning. Answer these questions:

- ✔ What adjustment in the employee's time management process would improve his or her performance?

- ✔ What skill, if he or she mastered it, would make this employee more productive?

- ✔ How can you help this employee increase his or her earnings?

- ✔ What would have to happen to allow this employee to leave work at 5 p.m. rather than 6:30 p.m. each night? .

I suggest, at this juncture, that you tighten up the time frame for improvement. Suppose you originally had an overall time line of six months, with interim benchmarks every two weeks. This go-round, establish the expectation that the goals must be met within two or three months. After all, with all the time you've already invested in this employee, it's reasonable to expect results a lot earlier. In addition, be sure to clarify the consequences should the employee fail to improve at the end of this time.

Saying sayonara

One of my mentors, Dave Doeleman, taught me, "If you can't *change* people, you have to change *people*." Time management skills are critical to the success of an individual and to the team. If you have an employee whose failure to meet time management goals is affecting the success of your area, and if you've done everything you can (as outlined in this chapter) to help the employee attain time management skills, then you may find yourself obliged to let the individual go and replace him or her with someone who has his or her time under control — or who shows promise of developing the skills.

Part VI
The Part of Tens

The 5th Wave   By Rich Tennant

"So Frank, what's your secret for saving time?"

In this part . . .

Time is short, and this part — the famous For Dummies Part of Tens — provides short-but-complete answers to your most compelling time management issues. When you're hit with the need, say, to dump some time-wasting baggage, dive into Chapter 19. And when you're ready to adopt some positive habits, Chapter 20 does the job. Chapter 21 addresses time savers for your personal life, and Chapter 22 shows you how your favorite technologies can help you make the best use of your time at work or home. Finally, Chapter 23 tells you how to stay focused when you're on the job.

Chapter 19

Ten Time-Wasting Behaviors

In This Chapter

▶ Changing your approach to tasks

▶ Cutting out clutter

▶ Increasing your optimism

*W*ith all the things you have to accomplish in a given day, wouldn't it be nice if the day were just a bit longer? Before you start thinking of ways to slow the rotation of the Earth, try to cut out some serious time-wasters — or at least reduce the amount of time you devote to them; it'll seem like you're gaining one, two, three, or even more hours to your day to invest in activities and pursuits that are important to you. Here are some of the most voracious devourers of your precious time.

Failing to Stop and Think

When you spend too little time in preparation, you're forced to spend too much time in execution. The time you invest in collecting, compiling, and organizing your thoughts before you begin a project pays off in time savings and in the quality of the outcome.

Not only does planning ahead eliminate problems before you start, but it also helps you imagine how you'll perform the task. When you address the situation in advance, you feed your subconscious with the tools and information it needs to work on the problems, often without your awareness. That's kind of like sticking bread dough in a warm space and letting it rise overnight — just consider your planning efforts to be the yeast that brings your projects to rise to their full potential.

Preparation is valuable in efforts big and small. Even 10 minutes at the end of a day to review your schedule and set out the materials you'll need is sure to increase your productivity and effectiveness the next day.

Multitasking

The scientific evidence overwhelmingly suggests that *multitasking* — switching back and forth between two or more tasks — is an extremely ineffective way to get things done. Researchers say that when you multitask, you're making your brain take time to switch to a different skill set and a different memory experience.

One study shows that when people who speak two languages are asked to switch between languages when counting objects, they have to slow down for each switch — even the language they're most familiar with. Another study indicates that when people start-stop on several tasks in a given time period, they increase the time needed for completion by as much as 500 percent.

Sometimes multitasking can't be helped: You're cooking dinner, helping one child with her homework, and telling another where he can find his soccer shoes. And sometimes multitasking doesn't affect productivity: You're reading a book while listening to jazz and stopping occasionally to respond to your spouse who's reading next to you.

For those projects and tasks that require your best effort, you're better off to focus on one at a time. Here's how to keep yourself focused on the task at hand:

- **Turn off your cellphone or the ringer on your land line, or forward your phone to go directly to voice mail.** Even if you intend not to answer the call, the sound halts your attention and slows your progress.

- **If working on the computer, set your e-mail program so you're not notified every time you receive a new message.** You may check your e-mail at certain time intervals or even arrange to check and respond to e-mail in your time-block schedule. Turn to Chapter 4 for more about time-blocking.

- **If you're working on a report, article, or some project that demands a lot of concentration, set aside at least one hour of uninterrupted time.** You may not be able to finish it in that hour, but you'll get a good jump on it. An hour of focus is about all most people can do on an intense project without some type of break to get a cup of coffee or visit the restroom or just do a stretch.

See Chapter 9 for tips on handling interruptions.

Working without Breaks

There's a point of diminishing return where your focus and concentration start to fall dramatically. Too many people grind through, skip breaks, and cross that threshold. They sit and read the same paragraph over and over again because they're tired and out of focus. They review the same report again without realizing it until they're halfway through it.

 Everyone needs breaks from routine and the tasks at hand. You should take frequent breaks but for very short durations. If you're given two 15-minute breaks a day plus your lunch hour, I suggest trying to take three 10-minute breaks or two 5-minute breaks and two 10-minute breaks for the day. I'm not suggesting taking more time than you're allowed by your boss, but to use it in short spurts to regain your focus and energy.

Demanding Perfection

If you're expecting perfection out of yourself or others, you're wasting your time. Letting imperfection keep you from pursuing recreational interests or your career goals can end up limiting your fulfillment in life.

The amount of time, effort, energy, and emotion required to achieve perfection dramatically reduce production. You may invest as much time and energy to move from a 95 percent performance score to the 100 percent mark as you do to go from 0 to 95 percent. You're much better off investing your energy in starting something new than focusing on perfection.

And if you refuse to give it a go until you're perfect, how will you ever get to be perfect? One of history's most prolific inventors, Thomas Edison, made hundreds of failed prototypes before he perfected inventions such as the light bulb.

Worrying and Waiting

Hand-in-hand, *worry* and *waiting* are two time-wasters that can undermine your success and happiness in life. Worry usually comes from dwelling on factors that you can't control. It's scary to think about overpowering forces that can have a devastating impact: a downturn in the economy, a hurricane, global warming. But if you spend time worrying, you're not spending time on ways you can prepare or avoid such forces. Renowned self-help guru Dale Carnegie viewed it this way: "If you can't sleep, then get up and do something instead of lying there worrying. It's the worry that gets you, not the lack of sleep."

Another exercise to help you overcome worry is to ask yourself these four questions:

- What am I really worrying about?
- What can I do about it?
- What will I do about it?
- When will I take action?

A first cousin to *worry* is *waiting* — not the waiting for your spouse to meet you for dinner. Or the waiting to hear back from a client about your proposal. Or the waiting for the price on HDTV to go down. I'm talking about the waiting that often accompanies worry, the waiting that keeps you from taking a productive course of action.

Why not know now rather than later? If that client hasn't called you back, call her. You're going to find out the answer, anyway. If she gives you the bad news that you lost the competition for the business, find out now so you can do something about it or replace the business by prospecting. If you're waiting for the price of a TV to go down, how much do you really expect it to fall? Is enjoying it for a few months in your home worth a couple hundred dollars?

Hooking Up to the Tube

According to the Nielsen Company, the average person in the United States watches more than 28 hours of TV a week. Think about it: If you could eliminate that much viewing time, it'd be like having an eight-day week. Just think of all you could do with 28 extra hours: read a good book, spend time with your family, take a class, start working out — and even get a good night's sleep!

If you're a committed TV watcher, kicking the habit cold turkey probably isn't realistic. The withdrawal pains would be too severe. And truth is, television isn't all bad. Just like coffee, a little bit can do you some good. But to me, 28 hours of TV a week is the equivalent of a four-cup-a-day espresso habit.

Here are some ways to wean yourself off evenings and weekends glued to the couch:

- **Leave the TV off if you're not watching it.** Some folks like to have the tube on for company, but it's too tempting to wander over and plop yourself down if Oprah is hosting a controversial guest or the tribe is about to cast another member off the island.

✔ **Preplan your TV schedule.** Decide what's really important for you to watch. On Tuesday evening, if it's the 9 p.m. crime investigation series, so be it. But don't turn on the TV until it starts, and turn it off immediately upon seeing the closing credits.

✔ **Schedule no-watch zones throughout your week.** Maybe set aside a specific weeknight or weekend day when all household TVs remain off.

✔ **Reduce the number of TVs in your home.** Keep the TV out of the kitchen and bedroom, especially. Just as diet experts advise weight watchers to eat only in certain places in their houses, limiting the number of TVs helps keep the habit under control.

✔ **Prerecord what you want to watch and view it on your own schedule.** The added bonus? You get to skip over all the commercials, which reduces your viewing time by about one-third!

Surfing the Web

Nothing is wrong with hanging ten on the Internet — as long as the *ten* isn't ten hours. I'm not exaggerating when I report that although studies indicate the average per-day time online is one or two hours, a measurable percentage spend seven or more hours a day glued to their monitors! Studies also show that Internet time is increasing — and usurping other activities, including watching TV and reading.

The Internet is incredibly valuable as a time-saving tool. Just think how much faster pulling data and tracking down information is than in the past. But the Web is a storehouse of *useless* information as well. You can spend hours sifting through waves of data in search of what you really want to know, and before you know it, more than half the day has passed. Your original intentions suffer a wipeout as you get pulled off-course by information undertow.

When using the Internet for research or information-gathering, it pays to stay focused on your mission: What are you in search of? The annual report from a company you're pursuing as a client? The best bed-and-breakfasts available in St. Thomas in May? Don't get sidetracked by related information that steers you off-course. Put specific phrases in quotation marks to get exact matches or use the advanced search features to avoid certain words or limit your search to `.org`, `.com`, `.gov`, or `.edu` sites as needed. Bookmark sites you find especially useful, or copy and paste important info into a separate document, along with the URL where you found it, for later reference.

A big use of the Internet is for recreational pursuits: music, shopping, computer games, blogs, virtual worlds, porn. My advice: In some cases, you're best to cut off this activity completely. Many of these online behaviors can lead to serious problems, addictions, financial risk, and even personal safety issues. In other more benign situations, it's still a good idea to keep the online activity to a minimum and find your kicks in the real world instead.

Getting Caught in Junk Mail Undertow

As if it weren't enough to be inundated with credit card offers, catalogs, and direct marketing materials in your mailboxes, now your e-mail in-boxes are slammed with unsolicited tidings, commonly known as *spam*. At least e-mail offerings don't waste the thousands and thousands of tons of paper that gets tossed in the recycling bin. But everyone wastes too much time sifting through both paper and electronic mail to make sure they don't miss critical correspondence.

Recently at our house, I collected a month's worth of junk mail, which included 30 catalogs addressed to Joan. Interesting thing: She had only ever ordered from two of the catalogs. Apparently, these catalog companies sold her name to the other merchants.

Selling or exchanging mailing lists is a common practice among catalog companies. I bet if you check in the stack of offers you receive, you'll find a few different companies that misspell your name in exactly the same way. Coincidence? I don't think so.

Getting off all these lists is more of a challenge than it ought to be. Calling the company and asking to be taken off its list doesn't always work. And after you do get off a list, the same company may purchase a new list with your name on it, and the mail starts up again. Although many companies commit to purging your name from future purchased lists, this just doesn't always happen.

You can take some steps to reduce the deluge of paper and electronic mail that comes your way. However, it does take a little bit of a time investment to stop this time-waster:

- ✔ Register with www.dmachoice.org to be removed from direct-mail lists for up to three years.

- ✔ Go to www.optoutprescreen.com to get off mailing lists for prescreened credit and insurance offers.

> ✔ To reduce your catalog load, sign up with www.catalogchoice.org. You can manage your mail by selecting which catalogs you'd like to continue to receive and which you don't.
>
> ✔ Online, install a good spam manager program. Most capture the spam mail and offer you the opportunity to view it if you like.

Be prepared: It can take as long as ten weeks to see a reduction in your junk snail mail. Also, be sure to enter the names of all the people in your household — as well as variations of your name and address. Joan was actually receiving two catalogs from one fashion company: one to Joan Zeller and one to Joan Seller.

Killing Time in Transit

I used to envy those folks living in major metropolitan areas who could take advantage of efficient mass transportation. With the idea of hopping on a train and spending the commute reading, catching up on reports, and scheduling business commitments while leaving the driving to others, I wouldn't care if the commute were an hour!

That was an unrealistic fantasy, of course — my job required lots of driving to places not well-served by public transportation. That meant long, unproductive hours behind the wheel. Unproductive, that is, until I discovered that my automobile provided me with one of the most valuable opportunities I could've imagined. My vehicle became my very own *auto-university*.

At the time I turned to the cassette player — now it's a CD player — and turned my vehicle into a classroom for skills development and self-improvement. Instead of listening to commercial radio, switching stations as I drove out of signal, I put my ears to work listening to motivational speakers and how-to books on everything from personal finance to personal relationships.

I recommend some of my favorite audio programs from over the years: Jim Rohn's *The Art of Exceptional Living*, Earl Nightingale's *Lead the Field*, Brian Tracy's *The Psychology of Achievement,* and *Goals,* by my good friend Zig Ziglar. I also recommend some of my own CD programs, which you can find at www.saleschampions.com or www.dirkzeller.com.

Although there's nothing wrong with listening to music or radio talk shows (one of my very best friends owns a number of radio stations), when you spend a lot of time in your car, you're better served by putting some of that time to good use.

Spending Time with Negative People

One way to bring down your energy level, reduce your enthusiasm, darken your outlook, slow your productivity, and drain your glass from half-full to almost-empty is to invest your time in negative people. The more you reduce the influence they have on your life, the happier and more productive you can be.

Easier said than done, I know. Chances are you have at least one foul-weather friend in your close circle. And you're likely related to someone who likes to remind you that you're not living up to your potential or that everyone is out to trip you up. Your negative associates don't necessarily focus their malcontent mojo toward *you*. They may, in fact, look at you as a shining success while they cast themselves as a poor victim of the world's injustices. But their pessimism is bound to rub off on you.

I don't suggest that you abandon friends and relatives who are suffering through hard times, whether due to illness, financial problems, or personal troubles. I'm talking about avoiding those people who are prone to see the negative side of life, no matter how much good fortune they have.

Do your best to minimize the time you spend in the company of curmudgeons and contrarians. Not only do you take back valuable time to direct toward positive endeavors, but their absence also breaks the dark spell over your optimistic outlook.

Chapter 20

Ten Time-Efficient Habits

Time management isn't a talent you have to be born with. You may need an amazing set of DNA to sing opera, win a triathlon, or get signed by the New York Giants, but with time management, you can work your way up to champion level without having the efficiency gene. Successful time management is a matter of habit. And in this chapter, I present you with the ten best habits to adopt for winning at time efficiency.

Start Your Day Early

Most people are more productive in the morning. That's logical: After sleep, you have more energy, you're more alert, and you've had less "day," when everything that could go wrong does. No doubt, a half-hour first thing in the morning is easily worth two hours at the end of the day.

When I have deadlines to hit and projects to complete, I set my alarm clock for a couple of hours earlier than normal. That's much more effective for me than trying to squeeze in the time in the evening. I'm generally too tired to focus well. I may go to bed as early as 8:00 p.m. in order to get up at 3:00 a.m. to put in some dedicated time. The house is quiet. I'm refreshed. My mind is alert. And my productivity is at its peak.

You don't have to set your alarm for the crack of dawn. An extra hour can buy you plenty of bonus time to take a big bite off your to-do list. Even just a half-hour earlier a day adds 182.5 hours to your year — 23 additional workdays:

365 days × ½ hour ÷ 8-hour workday   22.8 workdays

It really is the closest thing to buying more time.

Plan for the Next Day

Set aside time every day, at the end of the workday or before you wind down in the evening, to set up for the next day. Investing a half-hour, even as little as 10 or 15 minutes, can guarantee a higher return on productivity in as little as 24 hours.

As you confirm tomorrow's schedule and add to your to-do list, take your entire day into account — not just your work hours but your personal obligations, too. Think through all that you hope to accomplish, from the time the alarm clock goes off (need to take the cat to the vet or pick up dry cleaning?) through your workday (what meetings and presentations are scheduled?) and through the hours you have before your day concludes (time to return some phone calls to family and friends?). Then adjust your schedule accordingly.

As you set aside some uninterrupted planning time, do the following:

- Review tomorrow's work commitments and be sure your schedule is up-to-date.
- Integrate any personal appointments into your schedule, too.
- Make sure you have no scheduling conflicts. (Does your morning meeting allow you to get to your noon dentist appointment on time?)
- Add any items you didn't get to today.
- Anticipate and work in any plans or arrangements necessary for accomplishing tomorrow's to-dos.
- Identify your top priorities — if everything that could go wrong does, what do you absolutely have to accomplish?

See Chapter 4 for advice on planning your days using time-blocking.

Take Care of Your Health

Taking steps to stay well is one of the best time investments you can make. After all, if you lose work time because of frequent illness or you just don't have the stamina to put in a full day of activity, you lose productivity and get behind at work and at home.

Eating for optimal performance

You don't have to fuel up like a mountain climber or marathon runner, but eating healthy is as important for desk jockeys as it is for anyone who requires his or her body to be in top shape. A proper diet ensures the physical and mental energy required for a productive day. Here are some eating tips:

- **Schedule your meals.** If you have a tendency to skip meals, work them into your daily schedule, along with your business meetings and personal appointments.

  - **Breakfast:** Don't skip breakfast. Starting the day on an empty tank means you'll run out of steam before you get everything done.

  - **Lunch:** The break in the middle of the day works to rejuvenate you as much as the food you consume.

- **Pass on the empty calories.** A bag of chips and a soda may stop your stomach from growling, but it doesn't provide the slow-burning fuel you need to make it through the day.

- **Choose small frequent meals throughout the course of the day.** Eating just one big meal or two big meals may leave you full and lethargic.

- **Eat a balanced diet.** Learn the basics of nutrition and let science, not the latest diet fads, guide your food choices. (For more on basic nutrition, visit www.mypyramid.gov or check out *Nutrition For Dummies,* by Carol Ann Rinzler [Wiley].)

Exercising for energy and stamina

I can't count how often I hear people say that physical activity helps their mental outlook as much as their physical well-being. Scientific evidence supports that exercise stimulates chemicals that send positive thoughts and increased energy to the brain, all sensations important for peak productivity. So if you often talk yourself out of going to the gym because you don't have time, consider that you don't have time *not* to.

Carrying extra pounds is hard on your body, and it definitely slows you down — not the best condition for maximum time efficiency. But even folks who don't have a weight problem benefit from regular physical activity. To up your productivity, follow this advice:

✔ Work some physical exercise — as little as 20 minutes — into your schedule every day.

If scheduling exercise time is difficult, work it into your day in small increments: Park farther from your office to get in a brisk walk; take the stairs instead of the elevator; use your lunch hour to get in some walking, stretching, or even a half-hour in the gym. Lift hand weights, do squats, and/or do crunches in your living room. Don't refuse to work out simply because you can't do a full hour — you're missing out on valuable opportunities to work your body. A little bit does go a long way.

✔ Find an activity that gets your heart rate up — walking or running, bicycling, swimming, or an aerobics class — and participate two or three hours a week.

✔ Find an activity you enjoy instead of forcing yourself to follow some unappealing regimen.

Sleeping for rejuvenation

Getting enough rest to recharge is paramount. Going to bed early enough so you're well rested can improve your time management and energy level the next day. Know your amount of needed rest that your body craves. Establish your schedule to coincide with that amount.

One of the best techniques for helping yourself recharge with sleep is napping. I'm especially fond of afternoon naps on weekends. They help me to catch up on my rest and wake up really refreshed.

Set Aside Downtime

An issue that's gotten a lot of press in the world of parenting is overscheduling children. Child development experts point out that kids' schedules are so packed with school, music lessons, sports activities, play dates, and other commitments that they have virtually no downtime in which to develop their creativity and imagination.

Whether you call it prayer, meditation, clearing your mind, quiet time, or goofing off, adults need these unstructured blocks of time, too. Extremely busy people may find it hard to justify doing nothing when so much work awaits them, but these periods of reflection stretch your thinking muscles, release built-up stress, and lead you to new insights and greater understanding. And that's hardly "nothing."

I notice a significant improvement in my effectiveness, energy, and outlook when I adhere to a morning routine that starts with prayer and reading the Bible each day at 5 a.m. Here are some ways to find a quiet time that works best for you:

- Sit outside, in your backyard or a public garden, and let your mind wander.
- Take a walk with no destination in mind.
- Listen to wordless music.
- Meditate.
- Read spiritual, inspirational, or thought-provoking material.
- Pray — most religions have some tradition of daily prayer.

Plan Meals for the Week

My mother, one of the most efficient people I've ever known, demonstrated her proficiency at organization in the very deliberate way she planned our meals. She sat down each week with paper and pencil and mapped out our meals for the next seven days, considering our schedules, special occasions (birthdays, for example), and what items were on special at the grocery that week. She reviewed the cupboards and pantry to make sure she had all the ingredients she needed, and then she made her grocery list. When she hit the supermarket, she shopped with a plan: Not a superfluous minute was wasted on impulse. She was a mom on a mission — she knew what she wanted and where to find it. And she only had to do it once a week — no quick stops for a forgotten ingredient. My mom's extreme efficiency in meal planning paid off in time freed up to enjoy dinner and conversation with her husband and sons.

Make a habit of making a once-a-week meal plan so you don't have to waste time contemplating what to eat — no more frantic sweeps through a fast-food drive-through because you don't have anything in the house.

You can apply a weekly-plan habit to aspects of your life other than meals as well. For instance, plan what you're going to wear each day so you can be sure everything is washed, returned from the dry cleaner, shined, and repaired.

Delegate Almost Everything

Figure out what's most important to you, and delegate everything else. In Chapter 4, I walk you through the process of identifying your priorities. As soon as you have that list (and I suggest you write them down and keep them in front of you), you can better determine which activities support those priorities and which, though necessary to complete, can be handled by someone else.

 Sometimes, what seems like an activity to be delegated is, in reality, one that's close to the heart of your most cherished values. I can't say that I'm big on playing tea party. But the joy I see in my daughter Annabelle's face when I join her on the floor with her dolls brings me joy and deep fulfillment. I wouldn't delegate doll-playing to anyone. On the other hand, I detest yard work. Of course, it's important to me — and my neighbors — to keep up with cutting the grass. But in my grand list of top priorities, spending time in my yard doesn't even make the top 100. So I delegate it, along with other manly responsibilities such as changing the oil in my car, repairing a leak in the sink, and other choice tasks. Faced with one of these activities, I say, "Pass me the imaginary cream, please."

Say No More Often

You've heard it said that if you want something done, then ask a busy person to do it. It's true that the most productive people seem to be able to juggle more responsibilities and activities. But what a too-busy person achieves in quantity often comes at the cost of quality. To get the most satisfaction out of the work you do and the pastimes you engage in, you need to protect them from getting swallowed up by other commitments.

 The demands on your time are limitless. Time is a finite resource. Figure out how to recognize when the hourglass is almost out of sand, and protect your time by saying *no*. Return to your list of priorities and evaluate whether your plate is filled with unrelated commitments. If so, scrape them off as possible to make room for the things that really matter to you. And when the next wave of people serves up more requests for your time, politely put your hand over the plate and say, "No, thank you. I'm full."

Always Use a Time Management System

To best retain your time management skills, adopt a system for managing your time. And stick to it. With regular use, such a system gets easier to use and brings a greater return with time. In Chapter 4, I show you how to use time-blocking, a system I stand by because I've seen how it yields success time and again.

Simplify Your Life

Just as material possessions take up space in your home and office, they also clutter up your time. I have a client who lived in Manhattan for several years and decided he needed to buy a car. He kept it for less than a year before he realized it was costing him money and time: filling it up, maintaining it, parking it, insuring it. He initially bought the car because he thought it'd simplify his life, but he quickly realized it added complexity that he hadn't imagined. Life was much simpler when he relied on taxis and subways.

Having and caring for possessions takes a lot of time. The fewer you have, the simpler life becomes. I'm not suggesting you return to Walden Pond or join a commune. Nothing's wrong with having things that bring you happiness and pleasure. If you love getting in your daily laps and spending time sunning yourself by your in-ground swimming pool, savor the joy it brings you whenever you can. But the more you can divest yourself of your other leisure toys, the more you're able to focus on your time enjoying the pool.

Return to your priorities list and take stock of how your material wealth aligns with your goals. Identify what relates, and get rid of as much of the rest as you can. Having fewer material burdens is one of the most liberating feelings you can experience.

Begin Every Day at Zero

Leave all your baggage from the day before where it belongs: in the past. Whatever mistakes, disappointments, losses, embarrassments, and failures you suffered yesterday don't have to affect the outcome of today.

As the saying goes, the past is history. The future is a mystery. Today is a gift; that's why they call it the *present.* Unwrap each day with the anticipation and expectation of unfolding a wonderful day of production, success, fulfillment, service to others, results, and relationship-building. Use your time to create the largest, best, most significant return on your time as possible.

Chapter 21

Ten Time Savers for Your Personal Life

Time management isn't just for business. Just as smart use of your time at work brings you professional success, adopting time-wise tactics when you're off the clock means more freedom to do the activities you really enjoy with the people you most love to be with. Today's service-oriented economy means that finding someone to take on the tasks you don't have time for is easier than ever. Even the most expensive service providers earn far less than highly paid professionals. What's the worth of a few hours a week with your family and children? Priceless!

Hire Out Your Yard Work

Some people find mowing the lawn, raking leaves, and planting flowers relaxing, even therapeutic. I'm not one of them. Whichever side of the fence you're on, lawn work can add hours to your weekly home maintenance responsibilities, and it's the type of task your neighbors won't be too happy about if you neglect it for long. Why torture yourself when you can hire someone else to do it? You can have a well-manicured lawn that all the neighbors will envy — and the time to enjoy its dandelion-free beauty.

The sophistication of services ranges from the neighbor kid eager to make some summer money to the landscaper maneuvering a machine that looks like it could compete in a monster truck show. Ask your friends who they use for yard work, elicit high school or college age kids, or even look in the nickel ads or on Craigslist (www.craigslist.com) to find someone who can fill this role.

Invite a Personal Chef for Dinner

I love to cook, but when Joan and I both were running our businesses, neither of us had the time to put together so much as a quick dinner of mac and cheese! The services of a personal chef can be a lifesaver for a family that values healthy, tasty meals.

Our chef came into our home two days a week and prepared fresh meals that we kept in the fridge or freezer until we were ready to heat and serve. He brought in all his own cookware and ingredients and within a couple of hours, he put together a month's worth of dinners based on a menu that we selected in advance. In addition to the entrees, he whipped up snacks, salads, and other dishes we could pull out for lunches or to-go meals.

The personal chef movement has found a strong following in cities of all sizes throughout the United States. Most services provide a broad menu of options that meet any dietary preference or restriction: from low-fat to low-carb, from vegetarian to dairy-free. Heck, you can even tailor it to your taste for spicy foods or forbid a stalk of broccoli from entering your kitchen.

The cost for personal chef services varies depending on circumstances, but in my experience, you spend significantly less money — and time — than you would taking the family out to dinner.

If your budget doesn't allow the luxury of hiring a chef, you may consider two alternatives:

- ✔ **Meal-preparation businesses:** For a reasonable fee, these businesses help you prepare a number of meals for your family in advance. Places like Dream Dinners (www.dreamdinners.com) or Dinners Ready (www.dinnersready.com) do all the work of menu planning, shopping, and chopping. You just add a few hours of your time a month to combine all the ingredients in the provided bakeware and take it home.

- ✔ **Cooking in bulk:** You can set aside a single day to prepare all your dinners for a month (or week), freezing or vacuum-sealing the food and pulling it out as needed. You make fewer grocery trips, save yourself the time of deciding what to fix each night, cut down on cleanup time, and reduce the number of nights you have to eat out because you don't feel like cooking. Look for cookbooks or Web sites devoted to once-a-month-cooking (OAMC) or freezer cooking.

Hire a House Cleaner

The growth of the home cleaning industry exploded after women began entering the workforce in greater numbers, and many discovered that they couldn't and didn't want to clean the house at all. Fact is, after spending 40 hours or more every week bringing home the bacon, few women or men care to sacrifice two, three, four, or more hours each week to dusting, sweeping, washing, and polishing.

Busy people can turn to cleaning professionals to take care of many of these thankless tasks. You can choose from self-employed individuals, who may work on a more unstructured and informal basis, to home cleaning franchises that send out teams that fulfill a precise list of tasks. These businesses typically provide an estimate based on an hourly rate for a regularly weekly, biweekly, or monthly appointment. You agree on exactly what jobs you want done (Change the sheets? Make the beds?), and a team of workers sweeps into your home and puts it in order in as little as an hour — a job that may have taken hours of your time. And the fringe benefit? After a frenzied and frustrating day at work, what a joy it is to walk into a gleaming-clean home!

In hiring a house cleaner, a referral from a friend might be the best approach. A word of caution: Make sure that your friend's standard of cleanliness is similar to yours. You may want to check out how your friend's home looks right after the cleaner leaves before you consider hiring him or her.

If a referral isn't an option, you may want to consider a service like Merry Maids or some other national brand for cleaners. The advantage is that most national brands require their franchisees and employees to be licensed, bonded, or insured (for liability purposes), which gives you a measure of confidence in their work.

Enlist Childcare for Errand-Running

I'm blessed to be a father and keenly value all the time that I get to spend with my children. That said, taking care of errands such as shopping with two kids in tow is not my idea of quality family bonding time. In fact, I consider that family *bondage* time because it takes me twice as long to get everything done when they're along for the ride!

When you need to run errands, you're likely to get a lot more done in a much shorter time and with much less pain when you hire a sitter and leave the kids at home. Get a referral from a friend, hire a teenager you know well, or even trade childcare with a friend who'd appreciate an unencumbered errand-run, too.

Use Pick-up and Delivery Services

In terms of pick-up and delivery, businesses today are light years past pizza and diaper service. The list of personal business you can take care of without getting in your car gets longer every day. I have my dry cleaning picked up and delivered for just a few dollars extra. It's worth the cost to me because the time I'd spend driving it to and from the cleaners (when I remember) is worth far more to me than a few bucks. I schedule the pickups so I don't have to do anything but hand over my dirty shirts and wait for them to be returned, clean and pressed.

Even as more businesses add pickup and delivery services, courier companies are popping up in communities nationwide to transport merchandise to and from your door. Whether you need to get a contract to a client across town today or simply can't swing by the jewelers to pick up that anniversary gift before meeting your spouse for dinner in two hours, call on a courier service to come to the rescue.

Explore Shopping Alternatives

With all the options for acquiring the merchandise you need or want, you may never have to shop at the mall again — unless, of course, you crave the slow crawl of parking lot traffic, the challenge of finding a parking space, and the thrill of dodging the crowds as you search from store to store for the item you're seeking.

Online shopping makes it easy to find and buy almost anything. Whether you head for eBay or click on the Web site of your favorite designer boutique, chances are you can order and pay for whatever you want — and have it delivered the next day — all in the time it'd take to get your car out of the driveway.

Even many grocery stores offer scheduled ordering and delivery services, which means you can skip all the steps between making out your list and putting the items in the pantry. Order your groceries online, and they're delivered to your door on the day you choose.

Another possibility is to leave the shopping to the pros — the personal shoppers, that is. Yes, some people are experts in these matters: They know where, when, and how to find just what you need. They can sniff out a sale before it's advertised, and they also offer a valued second opinion on matters of style and taste. Although you can hire personal shoppers to help you hunt for just about any item (from the perfect wedding gift to office furniture), they tend to specialize in wardrobe issues. Some come to your home and provide image consultation, review the contents of your closet, take your measurements, and itemize your needs. Then, based on the budget you agree on, they go to work. Many department and clothing stores also offer in-house shopping services.

Check out your local Yellow Pages listings for the "Personal Shopping Services" category.

Let the Detailers Come to Your Car

Especially if your job demands that you spend a lot of time in your automobile, a clean car may be a high priority for you. But taking it to the detailer is just one more trip that you'd rather not make time for — and you don't have to. In almost every community, numerous auto detailers offer on-site services. While you're in your office making business appointments, the detailer tracks down your car in the parking lot and transforms it into a gleaming chariot to whisk you away on your next road trip.

Have a Travel Agent Book Your Trip

Here's a paradox: As the number of travel Web sites continues to soar, planning your own travel can consume more time than ever before. It can take hours to find the best flight deal, and then you have to coordinate accommodations, car rentals, and other trip details. Getting all the pieces of the puzzle to fit can be challenging. Despite all this, it looks like the do-it-yourself movement is here to stay; however, using a travel professional can be a time-saving alternative.

Travel agents have at their disposal some sophisticated tools that others don't. They can take all your trip requirements and limitations and quickly come up with an itinerary that meets your demands ("We can travel only between the fifth and the twenty-first, we prefer afternoon flights, and our flight miles are on Transatlantic Airlines. We need no-smoking rooms in hotels that have a fitness center."). And frequently, they can find deals on flights and hotels that your hours online won't ever unearth.

Most travel agents now charge a service fee, but it's a small price to pay to ensure a stress-free family vacation, second honeymoon, or dream getaway.

Let Someone Else Do the Wrapping

Whenever you have a gift-giving occasion, do your best to look for a two-for-one deal — by that, I mean buying the gift and having it wrapped in one effort. Many stores offer a complimentary gift-wrapping service. Your sales attendant takes just a couple of minutes to expertly wrap and add a bow to your purchase. At the very least, most shops provide attractive boxes and a gift card — sometimes you just have to ask for them. And most department stores and shopping malls offer gift-wrapping kiosks in a customer service area.

Don't give up on the idea if you're shopping by catalog or online — ask whether they'll gift wrap and include a card. This often costs, but it's never more than a few dollars. Better yet, save yourself even more time and ask whether they can ship or deliver it to the recipient if you have to mail it, anyway.

Write Off Greeting Cards

Recently, a friend introduced me to a fabulous service. It's called Send Out Cards (www.DirkZeller.com/SOC), and it does exactly that: You create an account and input your list of card recipients and addresses, the occasions you want to send cards for, select your cards from a broad selection or create your own custom cards, and even the way you'd like to sign the card. Then, for about $1 per mailing, the company does the rest. Every year. On time.

If you're one of those people who never gets around to sending out birthday cards out until a week late — or forgets the occasion entirely — this service can be a godsend. And just think about how much time it can save for those massive mailings around the holidays.

Many may feel that it's somehow cheating to pay somebody else to remember these things, but preparing to send the card in advance is getting it done well. This type of service can be a boon for busy professionals who know the importance of remembering clients' special occasions.

Chapter 22

Ten Great Time-Saving Technologies

*E*very day, people introduce more and more technology to save you time. This technology, whether created for the home or office or even for use on the road, can put minutes and even hours back into each day. Here's my list of personal favorites.

Handheld Digital Voice Recorders

You generate new ideas daily to improve your department, increase your service or sales, or help your subordinates. You may even need to remember to send flowers or bring a gallon of milk home. With a handheld digital voice recorder, you can record numerous messages and save them in folders for use now or later. These units are very versatile and cost less than $100 for a good version with a number of features.

They're also effective for dictating letters and other business correspondence. After you have your voice in this digital format, the options are endless: e-mail the file, upload it, post it, and edit it.

Many recorders come with additional accessories, such as docking stations so you're always charged and ready to go. Another great feature is a lapel microphone. This add-on can really improve the quality and cut out unwanted background noise.

Customer Relationship Management (CRM) Software

Too many businesses — especially small businesses — are archaic in keeping data on customers, clients, and prospects. These businesses have written files, forms, notes, custom lists, call sheets, and past work orders that double as their database. They also use standard software such as Outlook to perform database management functions that it was never designed to do.

I consult, coach, and speak to successful companies regularly, and I'm always amazed when I ask about what CRM they use and get a blank look from the senior management team. *Customer relationship management* (CRM) is specialized software that you use to keep clients, prospects, customers, and suspects in a database. The database of a business is the lifeblood of a successful business, and being able to know what you've done, sent, marketed to, sold to, add-on sold to, or upsold to a client, customer, or prospect is good business.

For instance, if you run a heating and air conditioning company, you may be able to triple your business with a good CRM program and a solid follow-up strategy. You can contact people regularly through the CRM via e-mail, mail, and phone — all in bulk with a few keystrokes. You can market your services systematically, telling customers to have their air conditioning units serviced before the weather gets hot so your service team isn't overworked when the first heat wave hits for the summer. Your customers may also receive better service and be more loyal to you because you care enough to remind them.

Numerous quality CRM products are in the marketplace, including ACT! (www.act.com) and GoldMine (www.goldmine.com). This software allows you to establish multiple users and have everyone working in concert in your company or department. Most programs also have scheduling features, so you can put your time-block schedule right in your CRM. Most are also compatible with PDAs, so you can always have your CRM data and schedule wherever you go.

Finance Software or Internet Banking

With the electronic technology age, bill paying is easier than ever before. You can enter your bills once in a finance program such as Quicken (quicken.intuit.com), and every time you start to enter the first few letters, it automatically fills in the categories, the expense, and even the last amount from a month ago. You'll never have to enter more than a few characters to pay your mortgage again.

You can also print the checks in your printer if you're more old-fashioned (like me) and still like to use checks. I personally like the record-keeping and evidence of a check in case I ever get audited.

Most banks offer electronic checking in which you get features similar to those of financial software with one more benefit: For a few dollars, you can have them mail the checks for you or send the funds electronically if you have that set up with your bills, increasing the time savings.

Phone and Web Conferencing Solutions

One exciting category in the telephone communication world is *conference* or *bridge lines*. These allow you to put hundreds of people on a single call at once. On a small scale, you can use a bridge line to have a family call with all six of your children who are away from home. In business, you can use a bridge line to conduct educational teleseminars, sales presentations, meetings, strategy sessions, and more. Everyone invited on the call has a specific phone number to dial and then a multi-digit code so he or she enters the right conference line. At Sales Champions, we use these conference lines daily with our small-group coaching programs.

Some phone conference services even offer you the feature of recording the calls. This allows you to upload the call to your intranet site and allow all the people in your organization to hear the training or strategy session. It's really a big value for less than $100 per month.

Beyond the telephone bridge line level, an explosion of technology in Web conferencing solutions can enhance your presentations, sales, and meetings. A few years ago, your only option was WebEx (www.webex.com). It's certainly a good resource, but you can now opt for GoToMeeting (www.gotomeeting.com) or even PresentationPro (www.presentationpro.com). Web presentations are designed to be more interactive. You can take polling questions, break off in chat rooms, or allow participants to ask instant questions. The participants can also see a PowerPoint presentation just as if they were in a seminar or live program. The advantage is that both the presenters and listeners can do all this from the comfort of their own homes in their slippers and bathrobes (provided, of course, that they aren't using videoconferencing features at the time).

Wireless Headsets

If you're on the phone a lot, wireless headsets are a phenomenal advancement in technology that can save you hours a day. You don't even have to hold the receiver — your hands are free to flip through documents, take notes, or do whatever else helps you get your work done. You also don't have to be tied to your desk. You can walk around your office to clear your thinking and increase your focus. You can go down the hall to get a drink of water, all the while negotiating your big deal. At home, you can be cooking dinner, doing the laundry, or dusting while you're catching up with an old friend.

Don't buy an inexpensive wireless headset, or you'll be disappointed in the sound quality. A high-quality headset runs you about $300, but the freedom you feel and the increase in your productivity are well worth it. Besides, you may have always wanted to look like Janet Jackson on stage.

Mobile Phones and Text Messaging

Although the telephone isn't a brand new technology, you can always find improvements in speed, cost, and expansion options with the telephone. With the advancement of mobile technology, people are rarely out of touch. You can effectively reach anyone in the world at any time with a few punches of the buttons. (Unfortunately, the reverse is also true: You can be interrupted more easily. Turn to Chapter 9 for advice on handling interruptions.)

Mobile phones also give you the ability to text a quick message to get through to someone, which can save time or simply give you another avenue to communicate. If someone isn't returning your call, try texting a message to save you the time of making more calls.

Instant Messaging

I have to admit I love instant messaging in the office environment. I'm sure it works between friends as well, but my use is solely business. To be able to send a quick note or delegate a quick, easy item instantly is tremendous.

Instant messaging is really effective when you have colleagues who work in different locations. At my companies, I have multiple offices and employees in four time zones. Being able to instant message instead of picking up the phone and incurring long-distance charges is invaluable.

As handy as instant messaging can be, it can also be a huge source of distraction, leaving you with less time on your hands and less productivity if you don't keep it under wraps. Be sure to turn off your instant message when you really need to focus. The sound of a new message can drive you to distraction. That flashing toolbar compels most people to stop what they're doing and see what the sender wants.

E-book Readers

I love electronic book readers. In my Sony Reader (www.sonystyle.com), I can carry 160 books in something the size of a gift book. It saves me time deciding which book to take with me on the road — I can take them all. When I feel like reading something light, I can. When I want to read the Bible, a business book, a relationship book, or a self-help book, I can do it with ease.

GPS Navigation Systems

One of the best new technologies for people who travel around town or even long distances is global positioning system (GPS) navigation. It can save you hours in trying to find that pesky address that doesn't appear on the old map. It also saves you the time and cost of looking up and printing out pages of directions from an Internet site.

You can even make midcourse corrections when you take a wrong turn. The soft computer voice tells you something like, "Recalculating route. Make a U-turn in 0.5 miles." It beats pulling into the nearest gas station and trying to get directions from someone who may be as confused as you are.

Digital Video Recorders

Although television is a waste of time in many cases, most people have at least a few shows that they enjoy. If you have a digital video recorder (DVR), you'll never miss the shows you really want to watch. Better yet, by approaching your TV watching with intention and by setting beginning and ending times, you aren't as likely to get trapped in the mindless approach to watching TV, where you're tempted to channel surf or continue watching after your show has ended.

The other advantage is that you can skip every commercial in the program and dramatically reduce the time to view a show. An hour-long show often cuts down to less than 40 minutes. That's a time savings of 33 percent just for commercial zapping.

Chapter 23

Ten Ways to Fine-Tune Your Focus on the Job

• •

In This Chapter

▶ Minimizing distractions

▶ Motivating yourself to work

• •

Making the best use of your time is closely connected to your ability to concentrate. That hour you set aside to finish your report should be plenty of time. But if you drift away from your effort — perhaps lured away by the you've-got-mail flag at the bottom of your computer screen — an hour doesn't cut it, and you may end up spending two hours, even more.

Maintaining your focus on those most critical tasks — the ones that bring you 80 percent of your achievement — is one of the most perplexing challenges you face as you strive to effectively manage your time. I've identified ten habits that anchor your focus where your attention needs to be, rather than on the unimportant distractions that so often demand it.

Start Small

Concentration is a skill you can learn. I liken the process to weight training. Flexing your concentration muscles requires commitment, regular workout, and a willingness to push yourself a little further, bit by bit.

Just as you wouldn't try to lift a 200-pound barbell on the first day of your weight-training program, you don't want to put an unrealistic strain on your concentration efforts as you're building up your skills. Forcing yourself to spend the entire day trying to make sense of all your receipts and files to complete your tax return may be more than you can handle in the beginning.

Start with lighter weights — the smaller tasks, the less complex projects. And build up your time, perhaps starting with segments as short as a half-hour; then give yourself a break. Step away from the task to make sure you release the tension and give your mind the recess it needs. Get something to drink or take a short 5- to 10-minute walk outside. Then go back to your project. As you build your endurance, you can increase the work periods, working up to a few hours of uninterrupted focus.

Seek Out a Quiet Place

The ambient noise of the world around you — humming computers and copiers, ringing phones, the drone of conversation — can distract you, reducing your focus and thereby diminishing the effectiveness of your time management. When you need to concentrate, seek out a quiet place or a quiet time of day. I often get up at 3 a.m. to write: no kids playing or TVs chattering, no traffic noise. My ability to focus is far greater in the dead of the night merely because of the quiet.

You may not want to change your work hours to the graveyard shift, but to maximize your focus and time, look for opportunities to reduce distracting noise. Shut your door if you have an office. Seek out an unused conference room.

Despite your best efforts, you may not be able to eliminate the sound distractions that interrupt your focus. So when you can't beat 'em, join 'em. Seriously. Create your own noise. I'm talking about white noise — you know, that smooth, even drone that seems to level out the sound challenges. Think ocean waves, a gentle rainstorm, the wind rustling through leaves. Look for CDs of soothing music or use a small fan to create a constant low-level noise. These types of sounds don't affect your focus, but they do block out other noise.

Some people swear by classical music. Some studies indicate that classical music helps concentration and creativity. I've used classical music to help me through all types of projects. My preference is music with a greater emphasis on strings. (I tend to avoid works like the "1812 Overture" and other compositions with lots of cymbals.) But each person responds differently to music. Find what works for you — whatever drowns out other sounds and is easiest for you to tune out.

Get an Early Start (or Stay Late)

Some people claim to be early birds; others insist they're more productive later in the day or even at night. But even if you consider yourself a night owl,

I maintain that everyone benefits from getting an early start. You're always freshest first thing, when your day hasn't had a chance to throw any upsets your way. For most professionals, the distractions, problems, and challenges increase as the day progresses. The earlier you begin, the less likely you are to encounter interruptions. You also have fewer issues to consider and a higher level of focus.

Heading into work a little earlier than the official start time is a tactic that gives you a jumpstart on your progress. Fewer people are at their desks or phones to disrupt your concentration. Plus, a productive start works to bolster your outlook and energy level for the rest of the day.

Of course, when you can't work in an early start, another tactic is to stay late. You may be a bit more worn down after a long day, but you can still take advantage of the more peaceful atmosphere after most of your co-workers have left for the day. Stay at your desk and squeeze in an hour or more of uninterrupted work — and skip all the rush-hour traffic.

You're better served in increasing your schedule to stay a little late daily or for a number of days each week. Staying 3 hours late once or twice a week may defeat the purpose: It can cause you to be tired and late the next day. A better strategy is to stay an hour late 3 to 4 days a week and make sure you leave at that time from work.

Adjust Your Lunch Hour

Move your lunch break *away* from the noon hour — when everyone else is taking lunch — as much as possible. If you get an early start on the day, you may want to break by 11 a.m. If you find yourself on a roll, you may prefer to hold off until 1 or 2 p.m.

The point is that by steering clear of the busy lunch rush, you increase your odds of enjoying a leisurely break (fewer restaurant crowds, a less-congested break room), which means you return to your work refreshed and ready to focus. And you capitalize on the quiet time, when most of your co-workers and business colleagues have clocked out for their midday break. Stay in at noon (or the stretch between 11:30 a.m. and 1:30 p.m.) and discover a slower-paced environment more conducive to concentration.

You also may consider eating small meals more frequently, which can help you avoid the blood sugar crash that many peoples experience. When their bodies are craving fuel, they just feel like they're stick in low gear. By eating the small meals, you can take quick breaks and become energized.

Take Shorter, More Frequent Breaks

You can't stay focused at high levels for 8 to 10 hours a day if you work in a production-oriented job environment. You can save time at work and increase productivity by working at intense levels and then taking a short break. For most people, 90 to 120 minutes is all their brains can do without some relief. Even by taking a 5 to 10 minute break, you raise your energy, intensity, and focus.

What are the toughest actions you have to do in your job? What can drain you fast? What do you know you need to do but struggle to make yourself do consistently? That's the activity you have to do for shorter durations with quick breaks in between. The hardest job for salespeople is prospecting, looking for new business, so I always tell salespeople to make 60 minutes of prospecting calls and then take a 10 to 15 minute break.

Control Personal Interaction

The coffee machine. The water cooler. The copy room. The workplace can be a minefield for the committed employee who wants to be productive. Social encounters are waiting around every corner, threatening to blow up your well-intentioned plans to get something done.

Personal interaction with others is hard to discourage without coming off as antisocial or being labeled the office recluse, but one surefire way to counter this result is to plan for social time. You've heard of the leadership strategy *management by walking around?* This tactic is an offshoot of that scheme.

Schedule your daily social time and seek out your co-workers on a personal level. You may want to do this first thing in the morning as employees get settled into their day. Or take a break between projects and spend no more than a half-hour making the rounds. Catch up on your assistant's weekend ski trip. Find out how your boss's son did in his soccer game. Check in with your office mate who's recuperating from the flu. Wish the receptionist a happy birthday. Then return to your work. It's a win-win strategy: You remain productive, and your co-workers know you as a caring colleague.

If you need to minimize visits from others at inopportune times, put up a sign outside your cubicle that says something like "Please do not disturb — hard at work. Contact me via e-mail or voice mail from [start time] to [end time]; I'll check e-mail every hour on the hour."

Acknowledge and Dismiss Distracting Thoughts

Inevitably, when I sit down to slog through a project that demands intense concentration, a random thought zips into my consciousness like the annoying whine of a mosquito, and I'm off chasing it down. "Did I forget to turn off the coffee maker?" "I wonder how Wesley's field trip went." "What was the name of that book I wanted to read?"

Whenever this happens, I follow a tip from my friends who do yoga. They tell me that in order to reach a true state of meditation, they focus on their breathing and allow those stray thoughts to flit past their consciousness; they don't fight those thoughts, but they don't let them settle in, either. It's as though a round of tug-o-war has just ended, and I drop the rope at my side; though it's still there, I'm not fighting with it. I figure out how to be present with it. Well, my breathing is my project, and I can let go of those random thoughts by making a note so I can follow up and dwell on them later, when I'm done with my project.

The best strategy is to accept that those distracting thoughts are going to hit you. Keep a notepad handy, and when something bubbles up to your consciousness, write it down and then forget about it. Because you've recorded it, you're more likely to feel comfortable in letting it go.

Reward Yourself for Success

You probably already use the carrot approach to encourage yourself toward bigger goals: Get that promotion, and you'll take the family on a cruise; make an important sale, and you'll buy that pricey designer suit. But rewards work just as well for reaching the interim steps that help you get to your goal, even on a day-to-day basis. If you love golf and want a new set of clubs, give yourself the clubs, one at a time for each day of focus. If you're struggling to complete a report that's taxing your concentration skills, promise yourself that if you wrap it up this afternoon, you'll reward yourself with a dinner out or even a bubble bath, to be redeemed that day.

Break down the activities you plan to reward into even the smallest incre-ments. I know a woman who treats herself to a square of dark chocolate for every productive hour she finishes. A med student allows himself to listen to one side of a favorite CD after two hours of study. As for me, I induced myself with a massage for getting this chapter done today!

Tackle the Big Opportunities

Have you ever noticed that the best athletes, such as Tiger Woods and Michael Jordan, raise their level of play for the playoffs or a major championship? Champion performers increase their focus and play better in the big game because they know more is expected of them.

A challenge can motivate you to perform at a higher, more efficient level. In life, success is in stretching yourself to be better and then testing yourself to see how you did. When attacking a big opportunity, you're forced to invest time to improve your skills, and you have to invest the attitude to improve your future results. Because the big challenges are harder, you also get to test your skills.

The other advantage of big opportunities is that they certainly align with the 80/20 rule (see Chapter 4). It takes the same amount of time and effort to land a whale type of account as a minnow type. In sales, you can focus on fishing for whales while catching a few minnows in your nets along the way to keep your cash flow solid.

Maintain a Steady Pace

Persistence and consistency are traits of successful people. The ability to focus, to stay on track, or even to be plodding with your efforts can help you work through failure and frustration and eventually achieve your goals. If you don't see the results right away, recognize that you may need more time, so invest more time with patience. If you're seeing progress but the results are short, don't quit — keep on going.

Index

• *E* •

• I •

SINESS, CAREERS & PERSONAL FINANCE

ounting For Dummies, 4th Edition*
0-470-24600-9

kkeeping Workbook For Dummies†
0-470-16983-4

modities For Dummies
0-470-04928-0

ng Business in China For Dummies
0-470-04929-7

E-Mail Marketing For Dummies
978-0-470-19087-6

Job Interviews For Dummies, 3rd Edition*†
978-0-470-17748-8

Personal Finance Workbook For Dummies*†
978-0-470-09933-9

Real Estate License Exams For Dummies
978-0-7645-7623-2

Six Sigma For Dummies
978-0-7645-6798-8

Small Business Kit For Dummies, 2nd Edition*†
978-0-7645-5984-6

Telephone Sales For Dummies
978-0-470-16836-3

SINESS PRODUCTIVITY & MICROSOFT OFFICE

ess 2007 For Dummies
0-470-03649-5

el 2007 For Dummies
0-470-03737-9

ce 2007 For Dummies
0-470-00923-9

look 2007 For Dummies
0-470-03830-7

PowerPoint 2007 For Dummies
978-0-470-04059-1

Project 2007 For Dummies
978-0-470-03651-8

QuickBooks 2008 For Dummies
978-0-470-18470-7

Quicken 2008 For Dummies
978-0-470-17473-9

Salesforce.com For Dummies, 2nd Edition
978-0-470-04893-1

Word 2007 For Dummies
978-0-470-03658-7

UCATION, HISTORY, REFERENCE & TEST PREPARATION

can American History For Dummies
0-7645-5469-8

ebra For Dummies
0-7645-5325-7

ebra Workbook For Dummies
0-7645-8467-1

History For Dummies
0-470-09910-0

ASVAB For Dummies, 2nd Edition
978-0-470-10671-6

British Military History For Dummies
978-0-470-03213-8

Calculus For Dummies
978-0-7645-2498-1

Canadian History For Dummies, 2nd Edition
978-0-470-83656-9

Geometry Workbook For Dummies
978-0-471-79940-5

The SAT I For Dummies, 6th Edition
978-0-7645-7193-0

Series 7 Exam For Dummies
978-0-470-09932-2

World History For Dummies
978-0-7645-5242-7

OD, GARDEN, HOBBIES & HOME

ge For Dummies, 2nd Edition
0-471-92426-5

Collecting For Dummies, 2nd Edition
0-470-22275-1

king Basics For Dummies, 3rd Edition
0-7645-7206-7

Drawing For Dummies
978-0-7645-5476-6

Etiquette For Dummies, 2nd Edition
978-0-470-10672-3

Gardening Basics For Dummies*†
978-0-470-03749-2

Knitting Patterns For Dummies
978-0-470-04556-5

Living Gluten-Free For Dummies†
978-0-471-77383-2

Painting Do-It-Yourself For Dummies
978-0-470-17533-0

ALTH, SELF HELP, PARENTING & PETS

er Management For Dummies
0-470-03715-7

iety & Depression Workbook Dummies
0-7645-9793-0

ing For Dummies, 2nd Edition
0-7645-4149-0

Training For Dummies, 2nd Edition
0-7645-8418-3

Horseback Riding For Dummies
978-0-470-09719-9

Infertility For Dummies†
978-0-470-11518-3

Meditation For Dummies with CD-ROM, 2nd Edition
978-0-471-77774-8

Post-Traumatic Stress Disorder For Dummies
978-0-470-04922-8

Puppies For Dummies, 2nd Edition
978-0-470-03717-1

Thyroid For Dummies, 2nd Edition†
978-0-471-78755-6

Type 1 Diabetes For Dummies*†
978-0-470-17811-9

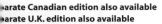
arate Canadian edition also available
arate U.K. edition also available

able wherever books are sold. For more information or to order direct: U.S. customers visit www.dummies.com or call 1-877-762-2974.
ustomers visit www.wileyeurope.com or call (0)1243 843291. Canadian customers visit www.wiley.ca or call 1-800-567-4797.

INTERNET & DIGITAL MEDIA

AdWords For Dummies
978-0-470-15252-2

Blogging For Dummies, 2nd Edition
978-0-470-23017-6

**Digital Photography All-in-One
Desk Reference For Dummies, 3rd Edition**
978-0-470-03743-0

Digital Photography For Dummies, 5th Edition
978-0-7645-9802-9

**Digital SLR Cameras & Photography
For Dummies, 2nd Edition**
978-0-470-14927-0

**eBay Business All-in-One Desk Reference
For Dummies**
978-0-7645-8438-1

eBay For Dummies, 5th Edition*
978-0-470-04529-9

eBay Listings That Sell For Dummies
978-0-471-78912-3

Facebook For Dummies
978-0-470-26273-3

The Internet For Dummies, 11th Edition
978-0-470-12174-0

Investing Online For Dummies, 5th Edition
978-0-7645-8456-5

iPod & iTunes For Dummies, 5th Edit
978-0-470-17474-6

MySpace For Dummies
978-0-470-09529-4

Podcasting For Dummies
978-0-471-74898-4

**Search Engine Optimization
For Dummies, 2nd Edition**
978-0-471-97998-2

Second Life For Dummies
978-0-470-18025-9

**Starting an eBay Business For Dumm
3rd Edition†**
978-0-470-14924-9

GRAPHICS, DESIGN & WEB DEVELOPMENT

**Adobe Creative Suite 3 Design Premium
All-in-One Desk Reference For Dummies**
978-0-470-11724-8

**Adobe Web Suite CS3 All-in-One Desk
Reference For Dummies**
978-0-470-12099-6

AutoCAD 2008 For Dummies
978-0-470-11650-0

**Building a Web Site For Dummies,
3rd Edition**
978-0-470-14928-7

**Creating Web Pages All-in-One Desk
Reference For Dummies, 3rd Edition**
978-0-470-09629-1

**Creating Web Pages For Dummies,
8th Edition**
978-0-470-08030-6

Dreamweaver CS3 For Dummies
978-0-470-11490-2

Flash CS3 For Dummies
978-0-470-12100-9

Google SketchUp For Dummies
978-0-470-13744-4

InDesign CS3 For Dummies
978-0-470-11865-8

**Photoshop CS3 All-in-One
Desk Reference For Dummies**
978-0-470-11195-6

Photoshop CS3 For Dummies
978-0-470-11193-2

Photoshop Elements 5 For Dummi
978-0-470-09810-3

SolidWorks For Dummies
978-0-7645-9555-4

Visio 2007 For Dummies
978-0-470-08983-5

Web Design For Dummies, 2nd Edi
978-0-471-78117-2

Web Sites Do-It-Yourself For Dumm
978-0-470-16903-2

Web Stores Do-It-Yourself For Dumm
978-0-470-17443-2

LANGUAGES, RELIGION & SPIRITUALITY

Arabic For Dummies
978-0-471-77270-5

Chinese For Dummies, Audio Set
978-0-470-12766-7

French For Dummies
978-0-7645-5193-2

German For Dummies
978-0-7645-5195-6

Hebrew For Dummies
978-0-7645-5489-6

Ingles Para Dummies
978-0-7645-5427-8

Italian For Dummies, Audio Set
978-0-470-09586-7

Italian Verbs For Dummies
978-0-471-77389-4

Japanese For Dummies
978-0-7645-5429-2

Latin For Dummies
978-0-7645-5431-5

Portuguese For Dummies
978-0-471-78738-9

Russian For Dummies
978-0-471-78001-4

Spanish Phrases For Dummies
978-0-7645-7204-3

Spanish For Dummies
978-0-7645-5194-9

Spanish For Dummies, Audio Set
978-0-470-09585-0

The Bible For Dummies
978-0-7645-5296-0

Catholicism For Dummies
978-0-7645-5391-2

The Historical Jesus For Dummies
978-0-470-16785-4

Islam For Dummies
978-0-7645-5503-9

**Spirituality For Dummies,
2nd Edition**
978-0-470-19142-2

NETWORKING AND PROGRAMMING

ASP.NET 3.5 For Dummies
978-0-470-19592-5

C# 2008 For Dummies
978-0-470-19109-5

Hacking For Dummies, 2nd Edition
978-0-470-05235-8

Home Networking For Dummies, 4th Edition
978-0-470-11806-1

Java For Dummies, 4th Edition
978-0-470-08716-9

**Microsoft® SQL Server™ 2008 All-in-One
Desk Reference For Dummies**
978-0-470-17954-3

**Networking All-in-One Desk Reference
For Dummies, 2nd Edition**
978-0-7645-9939-2

**Networking For Dummies,
8th Edition**
978-0-470-05620-2

SharePoint 2007 For Dummies
978-0-470-09941-4

**Wireless Home Networking
For Dummies, 2nd Edition**
978-0-471-74940-0